REFORM JUDAISM TODAY

BOOK ONE
Reform in the Process of Change

BOOK TWO
What We Believe

BOOK THREE
How We Live

EUGENE B. BOROWITZ

Behrman House, Inc. New York

ISBN 0-87441-364-8

REFORM
JUDAISM TODAY

Book One
REFORM IN THE
PROCESS OF CHANGE

Book One

REFORM IN THE PROCESS OF CHANGE

REFORM JUDAISM TODAY

Eugene B. Borowitz

BEHRMAN HOUSE, INC. New York

Library of Congress Cataloging in Publication Data

Borowitz, Eugene B.
    Reform Judaism Today.

    CONTENTS: Book 1. Reform in the process of change. Book 2. What we believe. Book 3. How we live.
    1. Central Conference of American Rabbis. Reform Judaism, a centenary perspective. 2. Reform Judaism—United States. I. Title.
BM197.B67   296.8'346   78-24676

To
Alicia Seeger
whose competence has kept Sh'ma *operating*
smoothly and whose grace has made
our friendship a joy.

ACKNOWLEDGMENTS

My thanks to Dr. Paul M. Steinberg, Dean, and Miss Frayda Ingber, Registrar of the New York School of Hebrew Union College-Jewish Institute of Religion for their special efforts in getting much of this manuscript typed by the limited secretarial services available to them.

I am also indebted to Seymour Rossel for his sensitive editing of this book.

נְדָרַי לַיָי אֲשַׁלֵּם, נֶגְדָה־נָּא לְכָל עַמּוֹ.

מָה אָשִׁיב לַיָי כָּל תַּגְמוּלוֹהִי עָלָי.

How might I repay the Lord for all the goodness God has done to me? Let me, in the presence of God's people, fulfill my vows to the Lord.

E.B.B.

CONTENTS

INTRODUCTION

When the Central Conference of American Rabbis at its June 1976 meeting overwhelmingly voted to adopt *Reform Judaism: A Centenary Perspective*, there was a momentary sense of high excitement in the assembly hall. It was the first time since 1937 that the CCAR had approved a statement describing "the spiritual state of Reform Judaism." While from time to time it had made statements on individual issues—for example, on the meaning of the State of Israel to Reform Jews—it had not broadly tried to define where the movement now found itself. But the forty years since the Columbus Platform had been momentous: in Europe, Hitler and the Holocaust; in the land of Israel, the founding of a Jewish state, the ingathering of refugees, and the building of a vital Jewish society despite incredible international hostility; in North America, the economic rise of our community and its suburbanization. Moreover, in recent years there had been such a division among Reform Jews that few believed a genuine unity could be found in the movement, much less that any serious statement could be written about it, or be accepted by so contentious a body as the Conference. It will help, then, to give some sense of the situation to which *Reform Judaism: A Centenary Perspective* responded and how, in my opinion, it did so.

As Reform Judaism entered the 1970s there was a general feeling that the movement needed to rethink its directions. The tremendous enthusiasm generated by the rapid expansion of the number of Reform congregations in the 1950s and '60s had passed. The integration of American Jewry into the society had largely been accomplished, but the style of synagogue life that resulted, which seemed so fresh a few years previous, in the '70s, seemed somewhat stale and in need of invigoration. The crisis in American society, the peril to the State of Israel, the new American appreciation of ethnicity, all seemed to call for a reexamination of Reform Jewish principles. Since the hundredth anniversary of the founding of the Union of American Hebrew Congregations (UAHC) was shortly to be celebrated in 1973, and two years later that of the rabbinical school which it had founded, the Hebrew Union College-Jewish Institute of Religion (HUC-JIR), it seemed "an appropriate time for another such effort"—to take a comprehensive look at Reform Judaism.

The original hope had been to prepare a full-scale "platform." This term was not officially used by either of the previous classic comprehensive statements, that of Pittsburgh in 1885 or that of Columbus in 1937, but usage had attached it to both of them, thereby conferring on them some special if unofficial status. The centenary of the UAHC now became the target date for the issuance of a new platform, a document or series of documents which would speak to the grievous Jewish and human challenges of our time with the full resources of Reform Jewish thought and belief. This turned out to be so great a task that despite the lay and rabbinic expertise brought to bear on it for several years, the project had to be suspended. The *Centenary Perspective*, by contrast, sought to perform a far smaller task, retaining only the historical orientation of the previous effort.

The immediate origins of the CCAR's document, then, lie in the suggestion of its president, Robert Kahn, made to the meeting of 1975, that the painful split in its midst might be healed by the rabbis trying to write a statement "of the unity of our movement today." It was a daring proposal. Less than two years before the CCAR, long troubled by arguments over freedom versus discipline, individualism versus group loyalty, universal human betterment versus immediate Jewish interests, had almost torn itself apart voting its disapproval of the performance of intermarriages by Reform rabbis. By 1975 the factions in the CCAR had become so aggressive that it was not clear whether that rabbinic body would long be able to function as a unit. At the 1975 meeting itself a major debate on discipline in Reform Judaism was to be held, and no one knew what would happen after this clash of factions.

The CCAR accepted President Kahn's suggestion eagerly. Perhaps the members were so desperate for a respite from the strains of recent years that the unlikely therapy of writing a unifying statement of principle was worth a try. What happened in the intervening year until the *Centenary Perspective* was formally approved by the CCAR is a fascinating story. As chairman of the committee that drafted this document and led it through the process of revision and deliberation by the CCAR, I have set that history down in some detail, and it is to be found as a supplement to *Reform Judaism Today: What We Believe.* By way of introduction, however, I think it necessary to point out the critical decision our committee made which set much of the tone and content of the document. We were determined not to seek unity at the cost of blandness. We felt it better to have no statement than to have one which effectively said nothing. We felt we should try to face, as directly as possible, the major difficulties confronting the Reform movement now. We wanted as strong and as positive a response to them as the overwhelming majority of the CCAR members would accept.

The more we worked at our task, the more it became our conviction that, despite the factionalism of the previous years, there was far greater spiritual unity in the Reform rabbinate than had been apparent. The drafting committee sought to make itself the voice of unarticulated common commitments, and in the strikingly large vote for our document we found the happy confirmation of our optimism.

Though we were not conscious of it as we worked on the separate sections of the *Centenary Perspective*, the need to face our historical situation helped us speak strongly to what was troubling Reform Judaism. Once we had something of a historical perspective on our movement, the roots of our present difficulties—specifically over the issues of diversity, religious duty, the State of Israel, and our duties to humanity—were exposed. The first three sections of the document which we will analyze in this book, make this plain. Consider their rubrics: "What We Have Taught," "What We Have Learned," and "Diversity Within Unity." When considering what we have taught all the Jews over the years, and then what we ourselves have had to learn in that time, it is possible to understand why we have so great a problem with diversity. Our history sets the thesis from which the whole document proceeds.

From "a centenary perspective" it is clear that many of the things Reform Judaism was struggling for in 1873 are by now accepted by many Jews. Having won these major successes over the past century, the Reform movement has become uncertain in recent years of what it should be doing. There is little sense of excitement in continuing to fight battles by now as good as won. Reform Jews must now seek new frontiers to conquer. Some of these may also emerge from history. A major Reform Jewish triumph came in pioneering our adjustment to Western culture. In the last generation or so we have had to relearn our duties to our particular people. We thought the betterment of all humanity would solve all problems, including our Jewish ones. What has happened to the Jews and general culture has taught us a new realism. Our duties to the Jewish people must now become "of highest priority." Having been expert in the universal we now need to give major attention to the particular.

To a great degree this explains the unusual tension developing in our movement. One large segment of Reform Jews is calling upon us to be primarily concerned with our Jewishness. Reform Jews of an earlier day could not have imagined such devotion to the particular, and many Reform Jews today, while acknowledging that we must be more concerned with our Jewish responsibilities, do not want to see our old priorities so radically changed. They want us to continue to subordinate our Jewish concerns to broad-scale humanitarian interests. That is where our struggle of recent years is being fought.

The *Centenary Perspective* seeks to explore the shape of a Reform Judaism in which our particularism is given higher priority than it once had. There is no way of specifying what such a Reform Judaism must be like. Differing in the balance we assign to the two central values, we will certainly also differ on specific issues. What we need most, then, is to gain some sense of the new balance with which we approach living as Jews today—and that is what the *Centenary Perspective* tries to give us. Thus what is opened up, in the subsequent paragraphs of the document, is the dialectical quality of a Reform Judaism which tries to keep our love for our people and our devotion to humanity a dynamic, mutually reinforcing tension. Perhaps that is what we thought we had been doing all along in our movement. Now it is clear that a fresh statement of our commitments was badly needed. It is not taken very far in the few pages of this document, but as a new time produced new priorities, the acceptance of the *Centenary Perspective* signaled that the Reform movement had responded to the command of this hour.

Reform Judaism:
A CENTENARY PERSPECTIVE

The Central Conference of American Rabbis has on special occasions described the spiritual state of Reform Judaism. The centenaries of the founding of the Union of American Hebrew Congregations and the Hebrew Union College-Jewish Institute of Religion seem an appropriate time for another such effort. We therefore record our sense of the unity of our movement today.

We celebrate the role of Reform Judaism in North America, the growth of our movement on this free ground, the great contributions of our membership to the dreams and achievements of this society. We also feel great satisfaction at how much of our pioneering conception of Judaism has been accepted by the Household of Israel. It now seems self-evident to most Jews: that our tradition should interact with modern culture; that its forms ought to reflect a contemporary esthetic; that its scholarship needs to be conducted by modern, critical methods; and that change has been and must continue to be a fundamental reality in Jewish life. Moreover, though

One Hundred Years: What We Have Taught

some still disagree, substantial numbers have also accepted our teachings: that the ethics of universalism implicit in traditional Judaism must be an explicit part of our Jewish duty; that women should have full rights to practice Judaism; and that Jewish obligation begins with the informed will of every individual. Most modern Jews, within their various religious movements, are embracing Reform Jewish perspectives. We see this past century as having confirmed the essential wisdom of our movement.

Obviously, much else has changed in the past century. We continue to probe the extraordinary events of the

One Hundred Years: What We Have Learned

past generation, seeking to understand their meaning and to incorporate their significance in our lives. The Holocaust shattered our easy optimism about humanity and its inevitable progress. The State of Israel, through its many accomplishments, raised our sense of the Jews as a people to new heights of aspiration and devotion. The widespread threats to freedom, the problems inherent in the explosion of new knowledge and of ever more powerful technologies, and the spiritual emptiness of much of Western culture have taught us to be less dependent on the values of our society and to reassert what remains perennially valid in Judaism's teaching. We have learned again that the survival of the Jewish people is of highest priority and that in carrying out our Jewish responsibilities we help move humanity toward its messianic fulfillment.

Reform Jews respond to change in various ways according to the Reform principle of the autonomy of the
Diversity Within Unity, the Hallmark of Reform individual. However, Reform Judaism does more than tolerate diversity; it engenders it. In our uncertain historical situation we must expect to have far greater diversity than previous generations knew. How we shall live with diversity without stifling dissent and without paralyzing our ability to take positive action will test our character and our principles. We stand open to any position thoughtfully and conscientiously advocated in the spirit of Reform Jewish belief. While we may differ in our interpretation and application of the ideas enunciated here, we accept such differences as precious and see in them Judaism's best hope for confronting whatever the future holds for us. Yet in all our diversity we perceive a certain unity and we shall not allow our differences in some particulars to obscure what binds us together.

The affirmation of God has always been essential to our people's will to survive. In our struggle through the
I. **God** centuries to preserve our faith we have experienced and conceived of God in many ways. The trials of our own time and the challenges of modern culture have made steady belief and clear understanding difficult for some. Nevertheless, we ground our lives, personally and communally, on God's reality and remain open to new experiences and conceptions of the Divine. Amid the mystery we call life, we affirm that human beings, created in God's image, share in God's eternality despite the mystery we call death.

The Jewish people and Judaism defy precise definition because both are in the process of becoming. Jews, by

II. The People Israel

birth or conversion, constitute an uncommon union of faith and peoplehood. Born as Hebrews in the ancient Near East, we are bound together like all ethnic groups by language, land, history, culture, and institutions. But the people of Israel is unique because of its involvement with God and its resulting perception of the human condition. Throughout our long history our people has been inseparable from its religion with its messianic hope that humanity will be redeemed.

Torah results from the relationship between God and the Jewish people. The records of our earliest confrontations

III. Torah

are uniquely important to us. Lawgivers and prophets, historians and poets gave us a heritage whose study is a religious imperative and whose practice is our chief means to holiness. Rabbis and teachers, philosophers and mystics, gifted Jews in every age amplified the Torah tradition. For millennia, the creation of Torah has not ceased and Jewish creativity in our time is adding to the chain of tradition.

Judaism emphasizes action rather than creed as the primary expression of a religious life, the means by

IV. Our Obligations: Religious Practice

which we strive to achieve universal justice and peace. Reform Judaism shares this emphasis on duty and obligation. Our founders stressed that the Jew's ethical responsibilities, personal and social, are enjoined by God. The past century has taught us that the claims made upon us may begin with our ethical obligations but they extend to many other aspects of Jewish living, including: creating a Jewish home centered on family devotion; lifelong study; private prayer and public worship; daily religious observance; keeping the Sabbath and the holy days; celebrating the major events of life; involvement with the synagogues and community; and other activities which promote the survival of the Jewish people and enhance its existence. Within each area of Jewish observance Reform Jews are called upon to confront the claims of Jewish tradition, however differently perceived, and to exercise their individual autonomy, choosing and creating on the basis of commitment and knowledge.

V. Our Obligations: The State of Israel and the Diaspora

We are privileged to live in an extraordinary time, one in which a third Jewish commonwealth has been established in our people's ancient homeland. We are bound to that land and to the newly reborn State of Israel by innumerable religious and ethnic ties. We have been enriched by its culture and ennobled by its indomitable spirit. We see it providing unique opportunities for Jewish self-expression. We have both a stake and a responsibility in building the State of Israel, assuring its security, and defining its Jewish character. We encourage *aliyah* for those who wish to find maximum personal fulfillment in the cause of Zion. We demand that Reform Judaism be unconditionally legitimized in the State of Israel.

At the same time that we consider the State of Israel vital to the welfare of Judaism everywhere, we reaffirm the mandate of our tradition to create strong Jewish communities wherever we live. A genuine Jewish life is possible in any land, each community developing its own particular character and determining its Jewish responsibilities. The foundation of Jewish community life is the synagogue. It leads us beyond itself to cooperate with other Jews, to share their concerns, and to assume leadership in communal affairs. We are therefore committed to the full democratization of the Jewish community and to its hallowing in terms of Jewish values.

The State of Israel and the Diaspora, in fruitful dialogue, can show how a people transcends nationalism even as it affirms it, thereby setting an example for humanity which remains largely concerned with dangerously parochial goals.

Early Reform Jews, newly admitted to general society and seeing in this the evidence of a growing universalism,

VI. Our Obligations: Survival and Service

regularly spoke of Jewish purpose in terms of Jewry's service to humanity. In recent years we have become freshly conscious of the virtues of pluralism and the values of particularism. The Jewish people in its unique way of life validates its own worth while working toward the fulfillment of its messianic expectations.

Until the recent past our obligations to the Jewish people and to all humanity seemed congruent. At times now these two imperatives appear to conflict. We know of no simple way to resolve such tensions. We must, however, confront them without abandoning either of our commitments. A universal concern for humanity unaccompanied by a devotion to our particular people is self-destructive; a passion for our people without involvement in humankind contradicts what the prophets have meant to us. Judaism calls us simultaneously to universal and particular obligations.

Previous generations of Reform Jews had unbounded confidence in humanity's potential for good. We have

Hope: Our Jewish Obligation lived through terrible tragedy and been compelled to reappropriate our tradition's realism about the human capacity for evil. Yet our people has always refused to despair. The survivors of the Holocaust, on being granted life, seized it, nurtured it, and, rising above catastrophe, showed humankind that the human spirit is indomitable. The State of Israel, established and maintained by the Jewish will to live, demonstrates what a united people can accomplish in history. The existence of the Jew is an argument against despair; Jewish survival is warrant for human hope.

We remain God's witness that history is not meaningless. We affirm that with God's help people are not powerless to affect their destiny. We dedicate ourselves, as did the generations of Jews who went before us, to work and wait for that day when "They shall not hurt or destroy in all My holy mountain for the earth shall be full of the knowledge of the Lord as the waters cover the sea."

REFORM
JUDAISM TODAY

Book One
REFORM IN THE
PROCESS OF CHANGE

PART I

What Reform Judaism Has Taught Jewry

	We celebrate the role of Reform Judaism in North America, the growth of our movement on this free

We celebrate the role of Reform Judaism in North America, the growth of our movement on this free ground, the great contributions of our membership to the dreams and achievements of this society. We also feel great satisfaction at how much of our pioneering conception of Judaism has been accepted by the Household of Israel. It now seems self-evident to most Jews: that our tradition should interact with modern culture; that its forms ought to reflect a contemporary esthetic; that its scholarship needs to be conducted by modern, critical methods; and that change has been and must continue to be a fundamental reality in Jewish life. Moreover, though some still disagree, substantial numbers have also accepted our teachings: that the ethics of universalism implicit in traditional Judaism must be an explicit part of our Jewish duty; that women should have full rights to practice Judaism; and that Jewish obligation begins with the informed will of every individual. Most modern Jews, within their various religious movements, are embracing Reform Jewish perspectives. We see this past century as having confirmed the essential wisdom of our movement.

From the Centenary Perspective

1

CHAPTER ONE

Freedom and the Growth of Reform Judaism

In Europe, Reform Judaism grew with great difficulty. While the ideas of the Reformers quickly gained currency few communities acted on them. In Germany, where the movement began, there were only two "Reform" Jewish temples, Hamburg and Berlin, and the impulse to modernize had its effect largely through what was called Liberal Judaism, whose practice tended to the traditional even while the theology of its adherents could be quite radical. In England only after World War II was there a substantial expansion of the number of Liberal (here the less traditional) and Reform (the more traditional) synagogues. By contrast, in the United States, Reform Judaism grew quickly and by the end of the nineteenth century it was providing leadership to the entire American community, and continued to do so until relatively recently. The *Centenary Perspective* suggests that this unique development has resulted from our being "in North America . . . on this free ground." Much is hidden in these few words.

3

REFORM JUDAISM IN CANADA

Canadian Reform Jewry merits some special treatment in any discussion of Reform Judaism in the New World. There are long traditions of liberal Jewish practice and involvement with the Hebrew Union College-Jewish Institute of Religion and the Union of American Hebrew Congregations in Toronto, Montreal, and Hamilton, to mention the oldest and largest congregations. Since these communities have been closely tied up with the development of Canada as a country, they have, for all the small size of their early Reform Jewish constituencies, had a special national role to play. Like the Reform congregations in the United States, they stood between an immigrant community and the general society and they pioneered the development of Canadian-Jewish relationships.

There are some intriguing special features of their story—a somewhat later migration than that to the United States; a rather tighter British- or French-dominated society to break into; a slower economic development; the decided advantage of a record of the errors and successes of United States Jewry from which to learn. These and other factors make Canadian Reform Jews somewhat different from their southern neighbors. Yet in the new Jewish experience of freedom, the Canadian story is not unique. What made Reform more acceptable in the New World than in the Old was that Jews found themselves living in a democratic, relatively open society. With some differences, this holds true of Canadian as well as United States Jews.[1]

Since those of us in "the States" so easily overlook Canadian Jewry, the *Centenary Perspective* refers to "the role of Reform Judaism in North America." Had it said only "America" one might have thought it referred only to the United States. The addition of "North" reminds us that the Jewish involvement with freedom in the Western Hemisphere has international dimensions. I shall henceforth use the words *America* and *American* in this binational sense.

SPECIAL CONDITIONS IN THE UNITED STATES

The United States seems unique in human history. It is the first great country consciously brought into being by settlers from elsewhere. All the usual economic, political, and social considerations which shape states played their part. But the citizens of this new country did not simply carry on age-old customs but set out purposely to create new social patterns which would remedy the evils of Europe. This effort

---

[1]There has been no Reform movement in Mexico. This surely is largely due to the problems attendant on the growth of Mexico as a nation, particularly its pervasive Spanish-Catholic atmosphere, the slow growth of its democracy and its difficulties in absorbing non-Spanish European immigrants. The contrast with Mexico highlights the special circumstances which made Reform Judaism prosper so in America.

was often made possible by the extraordinary resources of the new land, not the least its immense size and the relative sparseness of its population. A passion for the new and the better became a major component of the country's ethos and thus made the United States a particularly hospitable place for Reform Judaism to find a home. Consider, for example, the effect of the constitutional provision of the United States that there shall be a rather strict separation between "church and state." In many European countries the government collected a religion tax. One registered with whichever religious community one wished to be affiliated and one's religion tax was then allotted to that community. Under such an arrangement the community leadership wields a good deal of control over religious institutions. (And the government becomes easily involved in religious disputes.) For a group to try to get financial backing to establish some new institution or to experiment with changes in long-established institutions can be quite difficult. Needless to say, liberal Jews often had to battle just such an unsympathetic establishment in many parts of Europe. Occasionally, since governments tended to use religion as a force for maintaining the status quo, they could be encouraged to stop any movement toward reform for fear that it might set a precedent for political as well as religious change.

Nothing of the sort was possible in the United States. The Constitution prohibited religion taxes and kept government authorized bodies from either supporting or discriminating against given religious communities. This lack of a legalized religious community structure has given rise to the constant paradoxical complaints that American Jewry is anarchic and over-organized. It has also meant that Jewish activities, like those of other religions, are voluntary. Thus if Jews here wanted a Reform synagogue, no community structure stood in their way, refusing to let them use their "religion tax" in ways they thought desirable; they only had to find people of like mind in order to proceed.

Moreover, there were few old bodies to replace. Much else had to be created anew in this country, including Jewish institutions. Particularly as the frontier pushed westward, Jews had to reach out to one another to provide for a cemetery or a minyan, generally the first two communal needs. While they were free to draw on European precedents, they were not constrained by the overwhelming weight of centuries of local custom if they wanted to do things differently. They had already differed with their forebears by immigrating to the United States. Here they found themselves part of a society creating a new way of life. Innovation was a positive value.

And this nation was remarkably open to its Jewish citizens. There was no long history of anti-Semitism, no memories of crusade, inquisition, or pogrom. The barriers Jews found were hardly significant compared to what they had known in Europe. Jews could move ahead economically with few religious restraints. Educational and cultural opportunity seemed boundless. The values of the new land seemed to parallel closely the traditional concerns of Judaism. The emphases on justice rather than class, education rather than family, equality rather than title, were quite like the teachings of Judaism. Indeed, the Jews had for so long carried on their affairs without a hierarchy or a creed that democracy itself seemed somehow "Jewish." Many Jews therefore felt that by fully identifying themselves with this country they would benefit in unprecedented ways. So Reform Judaism, which advocated actively embracing freedom and adapting Judaism to it, was especially appealing to Jews in the United States.

Some scholars argue that the slow growth of Orthodoxy in the United States and the relatively lengthy preeminence of Reform Judaism were due to the late migration of strongly observant Jews to this country. Some had termed the United States religiously unclean because it had so many temptations for giving up Jewish practice. They were also fearful because there were few cities where Orthodoxy was an established Jewish way of life—and even in these cities, it was more a clinging to old-country patterns than an acculturated post-immigrant style. This thesis, which seeks to explain the relatively late establishment of the major Orthodox Jewish institutions in the United States, gives indirect testimony to the special openness of this country to Reform Judaism.

DEMOCRACY AND THE GROWTH OF REFORM

It seems no exaggeration to see a special connection between the practice of democracy and the Jewish immigrants' acceptance of Reform Judaism. The more a country is open to all its citizens, the more freedom and equality it grants to everyone, the more its Jews will want to ground a substantial part of their lives in the general society. And so the more will Reform Judaism appeal to them. I think this equation largely explains the unique Reform Jewish experience in the United States. As perhaps the freest of all countries, it provided the most positive environment for the growth of Reform Judaism, thus providing special satisfaction that the centennials of the founding of the UAHC and the HUC-JIR so closely coincide with the bicentennial celebration of the founding of the United States.

The *Centenary Perspective* adds another thought in this regard. Not only did this continent provide a uniquely congenial setting for Reform Judaism, but the movement, in turn, made constructive participation in the society a major Jewish responsibility. Responding to the moral opportunity democracy opened, it taught its members the universal ethic of Judaism, which, because of the strained social circumstances of most of Jewish history, had largely been repressed in Jewish teaching. By stressing the general ethical obligations which devolve upon the Jew, the Reform movement enjoined its members, as a matter of Jewish duty, to work in every positive civic cause. The result is part of the nascent folklore of American Jewry. There is hardly a city into which one can go without hearing of the Jews who were active in establishing or developing its cultural and social welfare institutions. For a group so tiny in size, its effect for the common good has been utterly disproportionate. We Reform Jews are proud of that record and happy that our modern evocation of Jewish ethics has made possible "the great contributions of our membership to the dreams and achievements of this society."

CHAPTER TWO

Reform As a Revolutionary Movement

Having paid tribute to the unique social circumstances which made the gains of the previous hundred years possible, the *Centenary Perspective* now turns to three historical considerations. First, it analyzes what Reform Judaism has contributed to the Jewish people over the last century, then what it has learned during this period, and finally it looks at the special nature of contemporary Reform Jewish diversity. The rest of the document speaks to the present; these introductory paragraphs assess the meaning of the past. Literally, they present a "centenary perspective." Yet already here one sees the particular concern of this statement. Its focus is primarily on Reform Judaism as part of the Jewish people rather than a particular society or of humanity as a whole. Why not, instead of a sentence, include a paragraph or more discussing the special compatability of Reform Judaism and the American ethos, or, perhaps, the unique synthesis between Judaism and American ideals which resulted from it? Not so long ago—the celebration of the American Jewish Tercentenary in 1954 comes to mind—these themes

11

would have been given pride of place in such a document. Yet we stand in a different place and therefore have a somewhat different perspective. We do not fail to appreciate what America has meant to the Jews. Yet, for reasons specified in the second of these historical paragraphs—the Holocaust, the State of Israel, the emptiness of Western culture—we feel we must give primary attention to our people and its survival. Thus, instead of speaking at length of what Reform Jews have gained from and given to America, the document focuses on Reform Judaism primarily in its relationship to the Jewish people as a whole. This concern and its effect on Reform Judaism dominate the *Centenary Perspective* and will therefore be a major theme in this commentary.

"ONE HUNDRED YEARS" OF REFORM

The first historical paragraph speaks of "what we have taught" in these hundred years or so. Here, I think, lies the wisdom of taking a historical approach in these opening paragraphs. On the surface most American Jews today seem to act out their Judaism in much the same way and Reform Judaism appears only vaguely distinguishable from other varieties of Judaism, or they from it. Why, then, specifically celebrate the Reform movement? Because as soon as one thinks from the perspective of a hundred years of Jewish history, one can perceive the many major changes Reform pioneered for all modern Jews.

It will be somewhat easier for me to make my point if I may take some liberty with the term "one hundred years," perhaps justifying this with the observation that central institutions normally come into being only after some years of a movement's existence. Let us consider four specific practices which were termed heretical when Reform first introduced them early in the nineteenth century: the use of the vernacular for some prayers; music sung with voices in harmony; mixed seating at services; and preaching. All these practices were denounced as violations of Judaism. Some were said to have partial justification in Jewish law; others were denounced merely on the basis that they were not Jewish custom. Thus though preaching was introduced so as to educate modern Jews in a modern way, it was considered such a breach of Jewish practice that, in Berlin, the Jewish religious establishment appealed to the Prussian police and the Beer temple was closed for a time in 1823.

THE CO-OPTED REVOLUTION

"A hundred years" ago Reform Judaism was a revolutionary movement. It proposed major changes in Jewish life, and particularly in the location of the power to make such changes. It had to fight long and often bitter battles in order to legitimate its interpretation of Judaism within the Jewish community. As a matter of religious faith and vested interest, the established community resisted Reform innovations. The large masses of the Jewish community were more ambivalent. While they may have found the Reform Jews too daring, they too were committed to coming into the modern world; they too needed to find ways to adapt the old, segregated Jewish style to their new, participatory social situation. Hence while they may not have formally become Reform or, in Germany, Liberal Jews, they eventually adapted such new Reform patterns as they felt were desirable. This is but another example of the revolution being co-opted by the establishment—which then says that the new ways were always part of what had been. It is also the case that, some time after the first, radical phase of a revolution, it becomes evident that the original, utopian vision was unrealistic. The revolution went too far, we say, and, accepting many of its lessons, we blunt its radical thrust. All this is true of Reform Judaism. If there is some difficulty today in perceiving its special contours that is because of its success, co-optation, and deradicalization. What follows in the *Centenary Perspective* details this general acceptance of Reform without neglecting to note what the movement itself has learned and how it has changed internally.

CHAPTER THREE

Four Major Battles Reform Has Won

MODERN CULTURE — MODERN JUDAISM

The *Centenary Perspective* specifies four general principles—not merely individual practices—which Reform has taught all modern Jews. The first of these is "that our tradition should interact with modern culture." One might consider this statement a truism. Such interaction is so central to our view of life that we cannot conceive of many normal human situations in which it is not present. Reform Judaism, however, makes such involvement with culture a positive Jewish duty. Loyal Jews should become acquainted with contemporary science, philosophy, and the arts to see what they might add to our Jewish understanding of reality. As we today look back at even the most segregated Jewish communities in our history we can detect the outside social influences which affected them. We are fascinated by the Alexandrian and the Spanish epochs of Jewish history, for they seem to parallel our own conscious involvement in the general society. But this openness to gentile culture has been the exception rather than the norm of Jewish experience. In the immediate premodern period a strong sense of resistance had been built up to anything that seemed external. Wearing short jackets, shaving, speaking in the vernacular—anything that smacked of *hukkat hagoy,* non-Jewish practice, was deemed sinful.

It was daring indeed for Isaac Mayer Wise, when he founded the Hebrew Union College in 1875, to insist that his rabbinical students also earn high school and college diplomas. No traditional rabbinical school had any such requirement. To this day, those schools run according to the old European model—as in the State of Israel—require no secular proficiency from their rabbis at all. For traditional ordination a Jew needs to know Jewish law and that alone qualifies him. A hundred years ago Isaac Mayer Wise realized that a modern rabbi must be at home in modern culture in order to mediate properly between the demands of Torah and those of the general society. Wise saw secular education as a positive good for he thought there was much we could learn from it. He could no longer say that everything humanly good was already contained in the Jewish tradition and that all we had to do was be expert in our sacred texts. In due course all the major American rabbinical seminaries followed Wise's model. Today we consider it self-evident that our rabbis will be learned in general as well as Jewish affairs, and we expect them to set an example of living in both cultures.

How much the more so does this positive concern with the general culture hold true for those of us who are not rabbis. For all our desire to be serious Jews, we do not wish to live a ghetto existence. We expect our homes and our activities to reflect a well-rounded participation in America even as they show that we are Jews. Someone who read only Jewish books, thought only about Jewish ideas, was interested only in Jewish art and literature, and was concerned only about Jewish politics would seem to us unbearably narrow, if not a spiritually displaced person. Following the way blazed by Reform Jews, most American Jews now are committed as part of their Jewishness to "interact with modern culture."

A NEW ESTHETIC BALANCE

Much of the early struggle of Reform Judaism was to make it possible for Jews to express themselves in contemporary esthetic forms. One is hard put to give Jewish legal reasons for insisting on the use of only certain tunes in the synagogue or ruling out certain patterns of architecture as "not Jewish." Clearly matters of taste and the weight of accustomed usage have an important role to play in religion. Yet, although there was ample room within the tradition for esthetic development, particularly as it relates to Jewish worship, the notion that one could be authentically Jewish in modern artistic idioms was strongly resisted. One need not go back a century to the Reform fight for the organ or modern music to illustrate this point. Only a generation back our community was agitated by the proposal that synagogue ritual objects be crafted in a contemporary style. Many insisted that Torah mantles, Torah ornaments, Ark covers, and Eternal Lights follow the stereotypes that had arisen and quickly degenerated in a time of mass production, little interest, and almost no money. It was Reform Judaism, under the leadership of the UAHC, which gave major stimulus to the creation of ceremonial objects with a modern look and raised American Jewish taste to the level of our growing general sense for beauty and design. So too it was our Union which pioneered the education of congregations to the possibilities of using contemporary architectural styles for the design of synagogues and our College which first established a School of Sacred Music.

I do not want to leave the impression that in esthetics only the new is desirable. During much of the past century our problem was how to break out of the encrusted forms which seemed to have become artistic law in our community. Thus progress meant receptivity to modes of expression which varied widely from the past. Now that we have attained some openness to the new we recognize that we must also reassert the value of the familiar. The problem is most manifest in our music. If it must always be fresh to be acceptable, then we shall never have the pleasure of recognizing a familiar chant, or of being able to join in its familiarity with other times and other Jews. The same must be said of our art-work. We cannot insist on having new Ark and Torah covers for each service or even each year, and it is certainly a major problem in our community that due to shifting population some new synagogue buildings hardly last three or four decades. The point is a simple one: "contemporary" need not mean "disposable." We can use a certain measure of input into our esthetic life to keep it fresh even as we need to develop an American Jewish tradition. Though we now wish to balance innovation with continuity, we shall still want, as Reform Judaism has taught us, to reflect in our Jewish life that which modernity suggests is good art.

THE INTRODUCTION OF CRITICAL SCHOLARSHIP

Modern scholarship is another area where Reform Jewish innovation has become commonly accepted. The intense Jewish devotion to study can easily be documented for the past two thousand years. However, through humanism and the university a new general scholarship was created whose hallmarks are criticism and the notion of change. Reserving the discussion of the latter for a moment, let us note that study from a critical perspective was quite different from anything Jews had done with their tradition in the past. In part this is because the critical method takes a largely but not entirely negative stance toward the text under consideration. The modern scholar continually asks: What claims is this document making? On what basis? Might the author(s) have reason for wanting us to believe this even if it were not true? Is there any external evidence which corroborates this document? Can one reconcile it with contrary evidence? and so forth, in obsessive skepticism. Traditionally Jews approached their major text, with reverence, for "God gave the Torah to Moses and Moses to Joshua and Joshua to the Elders. . . ." As one accepted the written Torah as God's own work, so one accepted all the books which followed from it—those of the Bible and, in turn, those of rabbinic literature. Traditionally inclined Jewish scholars often see problems in utilizing modern methods to study the great classics of Jewish faith. Some even consider the two methods irreconcilable.

Reform Jewish scholars adopted the modern way of studying Judaism because it seemed the most powerful method for getting at the truth. Its negative overtones did not deter them, for they did not any longer believe that the Talmud, or even the Bible, should have unquestioned sway over their lives. They were willing to be critical because this also enabled them to see Jewish books within the framework of human spiritual development generally. Studying their people's books in the way all great human works were to be studied enabled them to celebrate, in fully modern fashion, the greatness of the

Hebrew spirit in its continual upward striving. Abraham Geiger in the first half of the nineteenth century, in the early years of Reform Jewish scholarship, already took an analytic approach to the records of the past and thereby sought to expose their enduring truth.

The first great book of modern Jewish scholarship, Leopold Zunz's study of the history of Jewish preaching, shows the relation of modern study to Reform (though Zunz was not in the radical Reform camp). As noted above, the Beer temple in Berlin had been closed by the state when the traditionalists asserted that preaching was not a Jewish practice. In response, Zunz studied this thesis but did so on the basis of his university training. He proceeded in a way no Jew had ever utilized before him. First he located the relevant Jewish sources, mostly the midrash books. He then analyzed these volumes to determine the time and place of their likely authorship—the books themselves being unconcerned with such questions. By studying their language, their allusions and their relations to other books, he was finally able to arrive at a chronological order and geographical situation for these works. Only then was he ready to ask what these sources said about the history of Jewish preaching. Read out of their time and place the Jewish texts clearly indicated that whenever the authorities had not forbidden it, the Jews had in fact preached and that only as a result of governmental pressure did preaching cease for a given period. Thus, although contemporary authorities might insist that preaching was not a Jewish practice, an independent, critical attitude toward the relevant documents showed the opposite to be the case. (Incidentally, Zunz's method and results were so accurate that it was decided some years ago not to try to do the work afresh but to translate Zunz into Hebrew and add some notes to bring his research up to date.)

Reform Jews have not been afraid to ask the most searching questions of any Jewish book, as long as they were not so phrased as to prove the books foolish or our religion false. Sometimes prejudice masquerades as critical scholarship. But insofar as religious truth involves a continuing search, it is necessary for us to be as open to what we see in our classics as to what they claim to reveal. Isaac Mayer Wise wanted his College to exemplify the best of modern Jewish scholarship, though he insisted that the Torah text be exempt from critical analysis. With that odd exception, the century of the Hebrew Union College has been one of thoroughgoing devotion to the modern study of Judaism. Its faculty has numbered many of the leaders of modern Jewish scholarship. In the thirty-five years I have been a student and faculty member at HUC-JIR, I have been deeply moved by the open spirit of investigation our rabbinical school fosters. Had our school not pioneered the application of this method to our tradition—one since largely adopted by Conservative and some Orthodox institutions—how would the American rabbinate ever have been able to speak adequately of Judaism to the increasing number of Jews who have been college-trained? We face no danger of schism in the Jewish community because teachers of Jewish studies in secular universities today will operate by radically different procedures from our Reform and Conservative seminary professors. If anything, we may now say that, because HUC-JIR made the modern, critical study of Jewish texts the accepted standard in our community, the universities are only now catching up to the level of instruction our community reached long ago.

CHANGE AS A "FUNDAMENTAL REALITY"

The fourth Reform conception the *Centenary Perspective* which most Jews have accepted asserts "that change has been and must continue to be a fundamental reality in Jewish life." For anyone who had been conscious of historical events in the past decade or so that seems, if anything, an understatement. Early in the nineteenth century, when Reform Jews introduced the idea to the Jewish community, it was only the opinion of a minority of sophisticates. Ensuing events made their view irresistible. Hegel's philosophy taught a new, dynamic notion of history, and Darwin theorized that living species evolve, while the changes the

Industrial Revolution introduced brought the idea of continual adaptation home to most people and made progress the great human ideal. Yet traditional Jewish authorities resisted the idea. The idea that change is a fundamental quality of all human life conflicted with their sense of Jewish history. Asserting that it is a positive good challenged their sense of Jewish law and their authority. Judaism had taken the same sort of static view of things most pre-moderns had, believing that all significant truth had been given by God to the Jews in the Torah, Written and Oral. While this view allowed for some development, the ideal of radical change seemed foreign to the system; continuity, not innovation, was its hallmark. Thus, though there seems some measure of playfulness in the midrash, it often tries to show that Adam and the Patriarchs, who lived before the giving of the law at Sinai, nonetheless already fulfilled its yet-to-be-known precepts, including the rabbinic elaborations unknown to the Bible.

One can easily imagine the dismay, therefore, which overcame naive traditionalists when modern scholarship convincingly demonstrated that much of what had been held to be unchanging tradition was only some centuries old. We cannot trace the *Bar Mitzvah* ceremony or the Star of David as a Jewish symbol or the insistence on Jews worshiping with covered heads, much farther than the thirteenth century. Jews once did things differently, and not so long ago as Jewish history goes. This leads to the idea that since things have changed once they can rightly change again—a notion so permissive it had to be resisted by the traditionalists. Yet the intellectual power of the idea of historical adaptation and development is so great it had to be accepted no matter how grudging and slow the concessions.

All modern study takes this dynamic, historical tack. We are as much interested in what thinkers took from the past or the environment as in their genius. We are fascinated by the way the economic or technological shifts ended old social patterns and brought new ones into existence. Studying the records of old Jewish communities this way overwhelmingly discloses that Jewish beliefs and practices have been alive and adaptive. The Hellenic world, Babylonia, Rome, Spain all brought forth new and creative forms of Jewishness. No period of our history to our day is immune from this pattern, and no document of extensive Jewish experience fails to reflect it. Thus, for all the hostility the Reform notion of change once evoked, most Jews now consider it fundamental to their understanding of Judaism. More, they agree that it is the chief instrument of our survival, that "change . . . must continue to be a fundamental reality in Jewish life." Conservative Judaism is formally committed to this view, and modern Orthodoxy, which may set limits upon its application, is unthinkable without it.

To summarize, in the century during which organized Reform Jewish life has gone on in

America, four "pioneering conceptions of Judaism" advanced by Reform Jews have been "accepted by the Household of Israel": the interaction with modern culture; the acceptance of contemporary esthetics; the utilization of modern scholarship; and the acceptance of and commitment to change in Jewish life.

CHAPTER FOUR

Three Battles Largely Won

Three further claims are now set forth in the *Centenary Perspective*. In these instances, while it is acknowledged that "some still disagree," the assertion is nonetheless made that "substantial numbers have also accepted our teachings." The doctrines involved concern ethics, the role of women, and individualism.

AN IDENTIFICATION WITH ETHICS

Reform Judaism, for many reasons, early identified itself with an emphasis on ethics. The concept had strong intellectual appeal in the nineteenth century, particularly because of Immanuel Kant's teaching that ethics is as much a constituent of the rational life as is science. This made deed more important than faith and explained to Jews why becoming modern did not mean converting to Christianity. At the same time the accent on ethics rendered the rest of Jewish law, now valued mainly as strengthening one's ethical impulses, of secondary significance, a valuable distinction for people eager to be at home in the modern world. Finally, ethics now were understood to mean the duties all people owed all other people, universally, without distinction. If so, it was rationally unethical for others to discriminate against Jews, and Jews, in turn, now showed that their religion involved them in obligations not only to other Jews but to all human beings. This modern, rational sense of ethics not only seemed true, but fit the social needs of emancipated Jewry spectacularly well. As a result, Reform Judaism, and through it all modern Judaism, became committed to speaking of Judaism primarily as a religion of ethics.

This understanding still has extraordinary appeal. Any suggestion that Judaism is not intimately concerned with human ethics seems repulsive, perhaps anti-Semitic. Yet this idea raises two problems which deserve consideration here. (In Part 2 of *Reform Judaism Today: What We Believe,* I will analyze the problems this creates with regard to Jewish ritual observance.) The first of these is scholarly in nature. The teachers of a previous generation so closely identified Judaism with a universal ethical teaching that one got the impression that this was explicitly stated in the major Jewish sources. A critical examination of their proof-texts, however, shows that many refer only to duties to one's fellow Jews. Thus the commandment to love one's neighbor as oneself found in Leviticus almost certainly means one's Jewish neighbor, for its parallels there are "one who is of your people," "your brother," and "the son of your people." So too the appealing prophetic appeal

"Have we not all one Father? Hath not one God created us? Why do we deal treacherously brother against brother?" continues "profaning the covenant of our fathers."

This is not to suggest that there are no statements in the Jewish tradition about our involvement with or duties to humanity. The Talmud prescribes specific duties which Jews have to the gentile poor and wretched as part of "the ways of peace." And the first eleven chapters of the Torah are concerned with all humanity. Yet such directly universal material is relatively rare in Jewish writing—and for a simple reason: the Jews were not a proper part of the general world. In biblical times Jews were radically estranged by a humanity devoted to idolatry; and concentrated on preserving the Jewish community, which alone was faithful to the one God. In later times, when belief in God spread through much of the Western world, Christians and Muslims segregated and oppressed the Jews.

Living without effective involvement in the destiny of humanity at large, Jews largely ignored the hypothetical question of their duties to non-Jews. Not until the nineteenth century, when European Jews were given equality but questions continually arose whether Judaism had a full-scale sense of duty to gentiles, was the previous relatively undeveloped teaching of Judaism in this regard given full exposure. And in the new social circumstances, where this doctrine spoke to the realities of life, it was made central to modern Judaism. The *Centenary Perspective* expresses this development in its succinct statement "the ethics of universalism implicit in traditional Judaism must be an explicit part of our sense of duty."

The second problem in this regard has to do with the importance Jews should attach to their general social responsibilities. This will be discussed in some detail in Part 4 of *How We Live.* Here it must be noted that some Jews, deeply concerned about the survival of the Jewish people, have suggested that Jewish duty today should be largely confined to their folk. They do not see that working for general human goals "must be an explicit part of our Jewish duty," at least not anything more than common decency in face-to-face encounter. The overwhelming majority of us I believe, still consider the common good a major concern of our Jewish responsibility. But since a minority today derogates or denies the "ethics of universalism" which Reform Judaism extricated from the tradition and heavily emphasized, this teaching, though widely accepted, must be noted as one with which "some still disagree."

THE ROLE OF WOMEN

The second disputed Reform Jewish idea, that women should have equality in Judaism, has been much in the news recently. With the rise of the feminist movement many Jewish groups, heretofore able to avoid this issue, have had to face the problems of the Jewish tradition's discriminatory treatment of women. In theory, Reform Judaism has been a clear-cut supporter of women's rights in Judaism. Here many of the Reform concerns mentioned above intersect. When ethics are universal, they apply to women as well as to men. If ethics are central to Judaism, then law and custom must bow to them. If change is basic to a living Judaism, then we must change Jewish practice so that it no longer reflects Middle Eastern civilization in which women were customarily considered legal inferiors. Living in a democratic time, we thus have added reason not to hold on to the invidious distinctions between men and women in Jewish law. For all these reasons and more, Reform Judaism has since early in the nineteenth century called for the equality of women in modern Jewish life.

By contrast, Orthodoxy insists there is no good reason to change this fundamental thrust in Jewish law, the *halachah*. Perhaps the authorities could theoretically find a way, despite the heavy precedent against it, to change the law. Yet they have done almost nothing in this area and in all likelihood will not allow any significant changes in established Jewish practice. The Torah, as interpreted by the authoritative sages of our age, is superior to any modern sense of the ethical. Orthodox feminists are therefore limited to defending the special role assigned them by

Jewish law as a sexually appropriate form of equality and to pointing out how much fulfillment women can find within its limits.

Conservative Jews have been put to a difficult choice by this question. For years they have argued that while Reform Jews were right in saying that Judaism can change, they were wrong in not recognizing that change must come by accepted Jewish legal procedures. Against the Orthodox they have argued that Jewish law has more flexibility than its Orthodox interpreters have utilized in modern times, and that if this flexibility were made the basis for its modernization then Jewish law could once again give leadership to Jewish life. The feminist movement now confronts the Conservative movement with making good on this claim that halachah is capable of meeting our modern needs. To its credit, the Conservative legal leadership has voted to authorize counting women in a minyan and permitting them an *aliyah*. But that is all. It has not moved to lessen their disabilities under the law (for example, not being able to grant, but only being able to receive, a Jewish divorce) or to give them privileges now barred to them (for example, the right to be a rabbi or cantor). If the Conservative movement wished to find a halachic basis for innovating many of the things women are now demanding, I am certain they could find one. They hesitate to do so, apparently because they feel the Jewish community is not yet ready for so daring a step. In this case, they believe, the need to innovate with caution takes precedence over the ethical consideration.

From a Reform perspective this is an improper choice; the primary commitment to ethics makes the Reform Jews willing to take radical action. This different attitude to altering our tradition thus distinguishes Reform from Conservative Judaism. It must immediately be added that until recent years Reform Jews had not done much to practice women's equality except to have synagogues with mixed seating and choirs. Only since the 1960s have women regularly served on congregational boards (other than as sisterhood representatives) or been temple presidents. In that period, too, the tempo of giving women equal opportunity with men has increased, most dramatically as women have been ordained as rabbis and invested as cantors. Much of the language of the latest Reform prayerbook nicely avoids sexist references. Some Reform Jews are resisting this effort to make women's rights in Judaism a reality, but most of our adherents know it is our duty to do so and a sign of our willfulness or immaturity when we balk at it.

Something similar seems to be felt in the Jewish community as a whole. No other ethnic or religious group in the world is nearly equally committed to fuller general rights for its women. We take their college education as a natural right and are delighted at their entry into professional and graduate schools. No group of women in the

world is as well educated and socially productive. Caring about marriage and the family as we
do, we cannot tell how far this Jewish commitment to women's equality can go or how it can
be harmonized with a rich family life. A new
Jewish life-style now needs to be created, for the
heavy Jewish emphasis on women's education
and self-fulfillment has unleashed a dynamic
that will not soon come to a halt. "Some still
disagree, [yet] substantial numbers have also
accepted our teaching[s] . . . that women should
have full rights to practice Judaism."

JUDAISM AND THE INDIVIDUAL

The third claim made of a widespread adoption
of Reform teaching is the idea that "Jewish
obligation begins with the informed will of every
individual." Tradition allowed for some personal
initiative in determining one's duty, but by contemporary standards of free choice this latitude
seems quite restricted. One of the central implications of modernity is that individuals have the
right and obligation to think for themselves
rather than passively accept what society or one
of its institutions says. Thinkers of the eighteenth century were already teaching that much
of what people thought it necessary to do or to
believe made little sense once one rejected the
idea that what had always been done and
believed was by definition good or true. In politics this led to replacing monarchy with democ-

racy, where each individual has some control over who should rule. In religion the radicals turned to free thought and atheism, while the less rebellious made ethics rather than worship or ceremony the criterion of worthwhile belief. Immanuel Kant gave individualism special power when he argued that the key notion of this movement, the Enlightenment, was personal autonomy, that is, being true to ourselves ethically cannot be equated with conforming to society's expectations or efficiently executing certain rules but only the proper exercise of one's moral will. People have minds—including what we loosely call conscience—and if they do not use them they are no more than beasts. So, too, Kant pointed out, if people surrender their freedom to others—priests, the upper class, trend-setters, defenders of custom—they have given up their humanity. Likewise, to live in uncritical acceptance of old practices is to deny one's rationality and thus one's very self.

Kant argued that the essence of modernity is that people ought to use their minds and person-ally decide what they should do. Choosing for oneself, being an active moral agent, thus became the touchstone of modern existence. Kant was particularly influential because his philosophy showed the rational structure in which morality operated and thus educated people so that they might judge when they were making rational judgments. Factors other than Kant's philosophy made this new understanding

of the individual widely accepted, but because of
his great influence on later Jewish thinkers, his
contribution deserves special emphasis.

Kant wrote at the turn into the nineteenth
century, just before the earliest moves toward
Reform Judaism. When the movement clearly
emerged some decades later, it was fully involved
with the ideas of the Enlightenment, to the point
that, intellectually, it seems almost a creation of
the older cultural development. Politically, too,
it took the Enlightenment emphasis on mind,
not church affiliation or class status, to make
possible the Emancipation, the grant of social
equality to the Jews. Yet if the rights now came
because Jews could be seen as individuals (and
not as members of an Asiatic, Christ-denying,
inner-directed, peculiar faith-community), then
individualism must be the fundamental premise
of Jewish modernity.

Reform Judaism accepted the new freedom
and the principle on which it was based, the
ultimate dignity of the individual as a self-
determining, responsible being. And Reform
now hoped to create a form of Judaism acceptable to such individuals and true to Jewish tradition. Historically, I must confess, I exaggerate.
This was not what the earliest Reform Jews
said—they were too busy with practical questions—and even when it came to conscience they
embraced individualism in their belief that all
minds operate by the same rational patterns,
hence, by thinking properly, everyone knows

what people should do. Nonetheless, from a centenary perspective, one can see Reform as a slow but steady affirmation of the rights of individual Jews against the tradition and for what they believe is good and Jewish.

Since Judaism is primarily a religion of action, this stress on individual decision could easily become dangerous, for people might use their freedom to do little or nothing. This has always been the great risk of Reform Judaism. It treats people with full personal dignity, and they may then act irresponsibly. Many Jews have taken Reform's teaching about the right of individual choice as a sanction to do only what is personally convenient. For Reform Judaism that is the primal sin, for making one's basic choices frivolously is using one's unique human power in a way that demeans it and thus lessens oneself. Reform, in placing the dignity of the self on an equal or superior level to the Torah tradition, expected the individual to answer every significant call to duty with full human power. Reform Jews have therefore argued that their standard of proper Jewish behavior is more demanding than Orthodoxy, where one generally knows what one must do. For Reform Jews must decide for themselves and thus bear responsibility for their standards as well as their actions. This insistence on personal freedom is too much for many people, who prefer having others think for them or otherwise refuse to think seriously for themselves. Being self-determining is a burden, but we give it up only at the cost of much of our uniqueness as human beings.

Reform may be faulted for having had too high an estimate of people, but when religion relieves them of their freedom, ostensibly for their own good, it relegates them permanently to an infantile status. Reform Jews have preferred taking the risks which make mature humanity possible. It has often been disappointed in some of its adherents, but it has never found a good reason to deny them the right to exercise their minds and conscience. We should, therefore, see much of Reform Jewish innovation as an effort to reach and strengthen the will of the individual Jew. Thus the use of the vernacular in prayer helps Jews to know what they are praying. The sermon was introduced to make a direct appeal to the mind and heart of each congregant. The heavy emphasis on esthetics came from the recognition that what each person feels as we practice our Judaism will be critical to what we decide we need to do to be good Jews. The Reform creation of a new style of Jewish education for children, largely still insufficiently appreciated, which substitutes for rote study of the Torah (traditionally beginning with Leviticus!) vernacular instruction according to the child's ability to deal with the material, is designed to produce an appreciative, informed Jewish will. Future historians may say Reform Judaism failed in its effort to devise a mode of being Jewish which was as individually appealing as it was traditional. But I do not see how they can say it did not exercise great effort and ingenuity in trying to keep the individualism it fostered from being trivialized.

The *Centenary Perspective* asserts that, though some Jews still disagree with the Reform teaching on individualism, many have come to agree "that Jewish obligation begins with the informed will of every individual." More bluntly, although modern Jews respect the Bible and Talmud, they feel they themselves should make the decision as to what they ought to do as Jews—and that this is the right way to be Jewish today. In my experience there are many Jews who would contest this untraditional thesis but who, in practice, live by it, themselves choosing what will and what will not constitute their Jewish duties. For tactical purposes, at least, this principle has been accepted by certain spokesmen for Orthodoxy. Their appeals for this or that commandment no longer are presented essentially on the grounds that God gave us the Torah, but in terms of what the practice does for the individual as a person or as a Jew. Similarly, the Lubavitcher Chasidim have appeal because we are delighted that people so devoted to the tradition will not try to force it all on us but only ask us to try one of the *mitzvot*. The claims of the Torah for our full allegiance have, for the moment, been moved into the background. They have had to be, for it is reasonably clear to almost everyone that modern Jews will not give up their autonomy, their right to make up their own minds, even to what impressively pious rabbis say God wants and Torah teaches. People may not always acknowledge it, but in practice very many modern Jews have adopted the Reform principle that Jewish obligation begins with the individual Jewish will.

CHAPTER FIVE

The Century's Experience As Validation of the Reform Revolution

By now seven ideas initiated by the Reform movement have been adopted by most or much of American Jewry. They do not deal with insignificant matters. Rather, they have been the bases for dramatically changing ghetto-oriented Judaism into our modern Jewish way of life. Had Reform Jews not had the daring to rebuild Judaism along these lines, it is difficult to imagine what would have happened to our community. Without such bold innovation or something very much like it, there might well have been no modern Judaism at all, and we might exist in the modern world in some anticultural form as do the Amish or Mennonites. Though the validity of these seven principles is essentially an intellectual matter, since Judaism is a religion of history, we are particularly interested to know how the Jewish people has responded to them. At this centenary, then, we take special pride in noting that most modern Jews have come to accept our basic approach to Judaism. The bitter battles we had to fight in previous generations have largely ended in rather complete, if not often acknowledged, Reform

victory. Our founders' vision of a modern
Judaism attuned to its culture and changing with
the times has become the perspective even of
movements which once passionately denounced
it. Hindsight makes it possible to say, "We see
this past century as having confirmed the essential wisdom of our movement." We do not claim
that Reform Jews were always or altogether
right, only that our "essential wisdom," epito-
mized here in seven theses, has commended itself
to the Jewish mind and heart over these years.
There are not many bold truths which are so
heartily affirmed one century later.

REFORM JUDAISM AND MODERN JEWRY

The *Centenary Perspective* summarizes this
history in a somewhat provocative statement:
"Most modern Jews, within their various religious movements, are embracing Reform Jewish
perspectives." It declares that there is a sense in
which all modern Jews, regardless of what labels
they apply to themselves, are Reform Jews.
Many people, I am sure, will find this somewhat
shocking, particularly those to whom Reform is
a lesser form of Judaism than their own. Thus
much negative comment—a lot of it on the wording—was forthcoming when the working draft
was circulated to the CCAR (Central Conference
of American Rabbis). Most of the rabbis who
raised objections wondered if it was proper for
us to be so self-congratulatory. Others felt that

Conservative and Orthodox Jews would find this claim false and offensive. The committee which drafted the document examined these charges in some detail. It agreed that its earlier wording was faulty and that what it had intended to say required more precise formulation. Thus while the resulting sentence still talks about "most" Jews and their relation to Reform, it qualifies its assertion about them in several ways. It limits itself to those who are "modern," that is, those who have accepted the general society as the context of their lives and acculturated to it. This includes the modern Orthodox but omits the Chasidim and those European-oriented Orthodox communities who remain basically antagonistic to American culture. The sentence speaks in the historical present—"are embracing"—for what it describes as going on over a century has not been completed, but is still widely under way. Finally, it does not say that they "are" Reform Jews or that they "believe in" Reform Judaism, but only that they are embracing "Reform Jewish perspectives," a vague term loosely filled in by the seven concepts of the preceding material. Yet despite these qualifications, the committee felt that its position is historically valid and contextually appropriate.

THE EFFECT OF REFORM

If all this is even nearly correct, then Reform Judaism has powerfully shaped modern Judaism and the self-understanding of most modern Jews. This is not to deny that other movements have modified or added to these Reform Jewish notions so as to produce their own variety of Judaism. It is only to declare that Reform Judaism deserves to be acknowledged not merely as the creator of a new understanding of Judaism for its adherents but as a major influence in the shaping of all modern versions of Judaism. If there is a note of triumph in this statement—even though the committee sought to avoid it—it should be attributed to the context within which the statement was made: the celebration of the oldest form of nationally organized Jewish life in America, one hundred years of Reform Judaism. That is a proper time to take pride in one's accomplishments, and the milestone makes it possible to see what everyday routine obscures— that the movement has not only endured but contributed very much to all American Jews.

It is also true that much of our community remains antagonistic to Reform Judaism. One still runs into vulgarians who attack Reform Jews in the hope of making their own movement more acceptable. Some, I suppose, still carry resentment from the days when Reform Jews were rich and German and felt superior to the immigrant Eastern European Jews flooding into this country. Others, needing a scapegoat for the ills of modern Jewish life, find Reform Judaism a reasonably acceptable target in many circles. There are also some Jewish idealists—though few who claim such purity of motive actually have it—who are sincerely disturbed by Reform's authentication of the neglect of classic Jewish observances—*kashrut,* for example. For all these reasons and others it is rare to hear anyone outside the Reform Jewish community say anything positive about us. Even the general impression that Reform Jews are coming back to tradition is treated as proof that they are finally admitting their mistakes. No statement by the CCAR could hope to correct the skewed views Jews have about Reform Judaism. But it can set straight the record of modern Jewish history as Reform Jews see it. Looking at the attitudes most Jews today have toward their Judaism, one discerns their profound indebtedness to Reform Judaism. They may prefer repressing it. We, observing American Jewish life from a centenary perspective, cannot avoid saying it as a matter of simple self-respect. And if that should lead to some greater respect for Reform Judaism among other Jews, it will only add to the joy of the centennial celebration.

PART II

The Lessons Reform Judaism
Has Learned

Obviously, much else has changed in the past century.
We continue to probe the extraordinary events of the

**One
Hundred
Years:
What We
Have
Learned**

past generation, seeking to understand
their meaning and to incorporate their
significance in our lives. The Holocaust
shattered our easy optimism about humanity and its inevitable progress. The
State of Israel, through its many accomplishments, raised our sense of the Jews as a people to
new heights of aspiration and devotion. The widespread threats to freedom, the problems inherent in the
explosion of new knowledge and of ever more powerful technologies, and the spiritual emptiness of much
of Western culture have taught us to be less dependent
on the values of our society and to reassert what
remains perennially valid in Judaism's teaching. We
have learned again that the survival of the Jewish
people is of highest priority and that in carrying out
our Jewish responsibilities we help move humanity
toward its messianic fulfillment.

From the Centenary Perspective

CHAPTER SIX

Reform As a Process Rather Than a Doctrine

If the *Centenary Perspective* seems somewhat immodest in its opening claims for Reform Judaism, that mood must be understood as balanced by the humility of the following paragraph. From the perspective of a century one quickly sees that Reform Jews have had to rethink some of their initial assumptions about humanity and the Jewish people. Had Reform Judaism presented itself to the Jewish community as a doctrine which, once and for all time, answered the problems posed by Jewish modernity, it would have been devastating to admit in recent years that some major early Reform ideas needed to be changed as a result of our experience. Fortunately, it has been reasonably clear all along that to say Judaism must adapt to altered circumstances means that Reform itself is included in that rule. It has been a commonplace in discussions of our movement to point out that it calls itself Reform Judaism, not Reform*ed* Judaism. The latter term would have implied that all the changes needed for a modern Judaism had already been made. We are far more conscious of the inner dynamic of Reform Judaism than that.

Reform is more a process than a program, more a way of approaching Jewish life than a creed or a set of practices. I do not know just how early this activist sense of Reform Judaism was first articulated, but I can recall it when I studied the debates of the 1920s in the Union and Conference over the place of ritual in our movement.

SOME REFORM JEWS ARE "ORTHODOX"

Characterizing Reform as an ongoing process has a paradoxical consequence. It now becomes possible to see that some Reform Jews are really "Orthodox." That is, they identify Reform with one or another practice or idea—say, playing the organ during the silent meditation, or the mission of Israel. To them, the suggestion that the congregation meditate in silence or that Jews exist essentially for their own sake, seems Reform Jewish heresy. They like the changes of another generation and do not want them modified, so they now comprise a Reform "orthodoxy." Changing one's religious practice the way one changes one's fashion in clothes is folly. Yet we now see that our religious life is largely determined by emotional ties to familiar symbols, and to deny that old Reform patterns can be altered is a contradiction of what our founders said about history and human growth. The content of what is defended may be different from that of Orthodox Judaism; the insistence on its fixity is strikingly similar.

A COMMITMENT TO
PURPOSEFUL CHANGE

The fortunate consequence of viewing Reform as process is that unlike most institutions we need not be embarrassed and defensive at having made mistakes and gained a more adequate understanding. The *Centenary Perspective* is thus matter of fact, perhaps even proud, with regard to the changes which have taken place within Reform itself over this past century, that as Reform has taught so it has learned in this period. Only three, especially significant phenomena are mentioned: the Holocaust, the State of Israel, and the emptiness of much of Western culture. Perhaps a judgment is implicity being rendered here on previous generations of Reform Jews. If so, it is not evident from the wording just what that judgment is. To take the most obvious case, some people would say flatly that early Reform Jews were wrong in opposing Zionism despite their good reasons for doing so. They passionately desired full membership in their new societies. They feared Zionism would deflect Jewish energies toward separatism when people were largely uncertain that Jews had any significant commitment to working for the general welfare. Still, they were badly mistaken. I do not see why one cannot believe that they showed poor judgment of Jews and non-Jews and still feel oneself part of the movement they founded. They are not the first rebels who made mistakes in a worthwhile cause. A more charitable estimate sees them as making a response to Zionism which was appropriate to their day but which hindsight shows to have had grievous Jewish consequences. One might make similarly harsh or lenient judgments of their high sense of humanity's goodness and society's continuing progress. Shall we say they were wrong in thinking that liberal democracy had changed what Judaism had taught and history so often shown about the human propensity for evil? Or shall we say that their experience of Emancipation and social progress in a pre-Holocaust era lulled them into believing in the perfectibility of humankind?

The *Centenary Perspective* refuses to engage in any such speculations. The simple truth seems to be that we know we speak out of our situation as they did out of theirs. To judge what they said then, based on the utterly unexpected events which have occurred since their time, is unreasonable. Such speculations can be of value in sensitizing us to our own situation and perhaps in motivating us to face up to the challenges which confront us. But unless we are most careful, they bespeak our pride and a certain hardness of heart.

ACHIEVING A SENSE OF BALANCE

From my point of view the changes in Reform Judaism—except in the area of Zionism—do not involve a denial of our past but a rectification of its sense of balance. Our Reform forebears were not so much mistaken in their ideas as they were one-sided in their emphasis. Stressing what people can do to create the good society, they gave insufficient attention to people's capacity to exploit and oppress one another. Emphasizing Jewish duties to humanity in a post-ghetto age, they did not place sufficient weight on Jewish observance and our duty to our people. Overwhelmed by the opportunity to participate in the universal human march to fulfillment, they were little concerned about our survival as a people and our need for a state in our homeland. In most cases—Zionism being the exception—they gave some credence to the ideas which might have checked their liberal enthusiasm. They knew and spoke about self-aggrandizement and class interest. They understood that history is not unimpeded progress. They cared about the Jewish people, strove to protect its identity, and worked for the development of its distinctive way of life. Only they tended to subordinate these themes almost entirely to their enraptured vision of humanity empowered by education, culture, and democracy utilizing its goodwill for the benefit of all.

The *Centenary Perspective* does not reject their views (except their anti-Zionism) but, on the basis of our experience, seeks rather to restore the balance we believe they lost. Even our rejection of classic Reform's anti-Zionism is not complete, for while we ringingly declare how much the State of Israel means to us, we firmly reject any secular nationalist interpretation of our people or tradition and strongly insist on the authenticity of Diaspora Jewish life and the self-determination of Diaspora communities. Essentially, then, we reaffirm the beliefs of earlier Reform Jews but change the context in which they are held. That is, we happily continue their emphasis on the role of people in shaping their religious life and human destiny, but we balance this by giving stress to the enduring wisdom of our tradition and our duties to our particular people.

Since the older Reform ideas are reasonably well known they are largely taken for granted in the *Centenary Perspective* and are referred to briefly. The committee gave its fuller attention to explicating the new balance of faith which we have gained through recent history.

THE CENTENARY STATEMENT IN PERSPECTIVE

This *Centenary Perspective* itself is not exempted from the Reform need to change when that seems required. The *Centenary Perspective* quite self-consciously speaks from a given moment, based on what its framers know now, not of what Reform Jewish truth must be for all time. The committee acknowledged that history will make new demands upon us in the coming years, as it has done in the past. A living Judaism will then respond in confidence to the issues set before it, even if it must find fresh and thus untraditional ways to meet the new situation. Then this centenary statement will speak more of a Reform Judaism of the past than of the present, and a new declaration of Reform Jewish belief will be in order. To the rabbis who ratified this statement that is as it should be. I am certain the committee and the Conference hoped that these words might, for some time, reflect the reality of Reform Jewish faith, but its primary purpose was to sum up where we stand now. How enduring this formulation will be only the passage of time can tell. But if the fundamental intent of its shapers and supporters is a basis for judging it, then its contemporary vision, not its long-range infallibility, should be the primary measure of its worth.

CHAPTER SEVEN

The Three Pivotal Recent Experiences

One simply could not list all the events of the past century which have shaken humanity, the Jews, and so Reform Judaism. The committee limited itself to mentioning three of the most significant and recent ones: the Holocaust, the creation of the State of Israel, and the spiritual decline of Western culture. Seen from the vantage of the present moment, one might even argue that these are the events which have required the greatest revision in our previous point of view. Be that as it may, the committee not only considered them intrinsically important, but took them to be symbolic of many other social and cultural experiences. Their impact has been so great that we are certain we do not yet fully understand what we have been through and how this ought to influence our lives. We have a continuing obligation to explore what we experienced, for it has been, literally, "extraordinary." Recent events have broken the bonds of the "ordinary" and thus of our normal capacities to explain them or draw forth their meaning. Our theories about humanity, history, and the Jews left us unprepared for what happened, and thus were refuted or shown to need revision, depending upon what we once believed. While the *Centenary Perspective* deals only with Reform Judaism and its need to rethink its faith, the Holocaust and the present state of Western culture have posed profound problems for almost all thoughtful people in our civilization. Together with the living reality of the State of Israel, they have compelled many Jews to rethink their ideas of Judaism and the Jewish people. The *Centenary Perspective* is one aspect of those two greater intellectual efforts. Though its purview is quite limited, I believe it can be properly understood only within the context of the two larger problems of which it is a part.

The document mentions the three events in rough chronological order, but it will be useful to comment on the negative consequence of the Holocaust and our cultural decline together before turning to the State of Israel's positive effect on us.

THE HOLOCAUST

The *Centenary Perspective* speaks of the Holocaust only in terms of what it did to the classic Reform Jewish view of humankind and social advance. Obviously, it also could have been interpreted in terms of what it disclosed about the problems of Jewish survival in the modern world. The committee left that theme to the climactic, summary sentence of the paragraph. It felt that Jewish survival, understood as much in a highly symbolic as well as in a literal way, should now be seen as the culminating concern of this entire period. For economy of diction, then, the bare imperative to keep Jews alive and well is taken for granted here and not mentioned until the word *survival* is used to denote the central Jewish lesson of our time.

The *Centenary Perspective* identifies the Holocaust's specific Reform Jewish impact as its having "shattered our easy optimism about humanity and its inevitable progress." The working draft sent to the Conference for comment had "optimism" unmodified, which drew a number of comments that helped the committee clarify its language. The critics were surprised that we could say our optimism was "shattered" and then proceed to make numerous statements of messianic hope. If the Holocaust made us no longer optimistic about humankind, they contended, how could we still envision and call people to work for a day of universal justice and peace? Such comments made it immediately apparent that the committee had intended one thing by the term *optimism* and that our colleagues had read it in another way. (This is perhaps the simplest case of many which confirmed the wisdom of the committee's decision to circulate an early version of this document.) The questioners equated *optimism* with being hopeful, while the committee had used it in the older, tighter meaning of belief in continuous progress. The present wording, by speaking of "easy optimism" and "inevitable progress," made our intent plain. Personally, I took the decline in expectation associated with the word *optimism* as itself evidence of our new realism about history. An optimist today, apparently, is someone who still has some hope for humanity and its efforts. The notion of steady progress toward perfection is so foreign to our thinking that we can hardly believe optimism once meant that. To assert, if only in the hope of galvanizing one's energies, that "Every day, in every way, things are getting better and better" seems incredibly naive or self-deluding. I do not mean to suggest that Reform Jews of an earlier time were that simplistic in their view of history, yet they had supreme confidence in human progress. We need to recapture something of their positive thinking if we are to see how far the Holocaust has brought us.

OPTIMISM AND THE EMANCIPATION

Reform Judaism's early optimism is most immediately related to the experience of Emancipation. For some fifteen hundred years, roughly from the time Christianity became the official religion of the Roman Empire to the period of the French Revolution, European Jews lived an increasingly degraded, segregated, and imperiled existence. With all that weight of accumulated oppression behind them, with no historic model of a radical social change that might enfranchise

the Jew, our people was almost utterly unprepared for citizenship and equal rights. This may
seem to us to have become fact only by fits and
starts, with reservations and the eventual emergence of political anti-Semitism. Many of our
forebears saw it as something of a miracle, or, if
that is too strong, a wonder. Every time Jews
were treated courteously, every time jobs or
neighborhoods or universities opened up to
them, every time they were allowed to vote or to
debate public issues or to run for and hold office,
something gloriously unanticipated was taking
place. The Emancipation was the "extraordinary
event" of their time. In seeking to "understand
its meaning and to incorporate its significance"
into their lives, they came to a newly positive
sense about humankind. Seeing people do this
for the Jews they had so long despised, and
observing society alter itself despite a mil-
lenium-and-a-half of ugly hatred, made the
possibilities for individuals and nations seem
unlimited. Despite the recalcitrance of some
groups and the resistance engendered by old, bad
habits, the good would win out. One could see
that in one's own lifetime as again and again
another old barrier fell.

This Jewish experience made quite immediate
what was going on in Western civilization at
large. Broadly speaking, the nineteenth century
was a time of general optimism. Life was getting
better, and longer, for many people. There was
increasingly regular evidence of economic

improvement, scientific discovery, technological innovation, and cultural creativity. Though problems remained and others were created, the eventual means of solving them seemed at hand. What people might yet accomplish seemed unlimited—and it all depended on human initiative. For they had discovered a new source of human betterment—themselves and, like them, all other people. Previous generations had trusted God or the church or the king or the wealthy to provide for the general welfare. While each of these had done some good for all humanity, such good was hardly to be compared with what science and democracy, what general education and self-improvement through culture were now accomplishing. As the record of human achievement grew throughout the century, humankind at its best seemed well worthy of the greatest trust.

This was the liberal mood to which the Jewish community, as it modernized, felt drawn and which it then infused with its own euphoria at being emancipated. In my mind it is forever connected with a song in the old, 1932 Union Hymnal, in use in some Reform congregations to this day. Hymn number 230 is set to the tune of the "Ode to Joy" in Beethoven's Ninth Symphony, but I loved it as much for its words as its music:

> Onward brothers, march still onward,
> Side by side and hand in hand;
> We are bound for man's true kingdom,
> We are an increasing band.

> Tho' the way seems often doubtful,
> Hard the toil which we endure,
> Tho' at times our courage falter,
> Yet the promised land is sure.

I think that expressed the faith of many a pre-Holocaust Reform Jew. I know it expressed mine when I was a rabbinical student.

MESSIANISM AND HUMAN POTENTIAL

This faith in human progress was so strong that it displaced the traditional Jewish doctrine of the Messiah. That idea was troublesome to the early Reform Jews because of its nationalist overtones: the Messiah as a king of the Davidic dynasty, establishing his rule in Jerusalem and bringing the Jews back to his kingdom. Moreover, the Messiah-idea had overtones of the miraculous with regard to the end of wars, the resurrection of the dead and the establishment of the Kingdom of God on earth—and these conflicted with modern sensibilities. By contrast, the belief that human beings, acting in harmony to exercise the full range of their newly discovered potential, could create everything that people had ever hoped for seemed a perfectly reasonable idea and thus a proper substitute for the older, supernatural notion. Reform Jews thus spoke of the Messianic Age rather than the Messiah, for they no longer thought in terms of a gifted leader ruling by God's special help, but of an enlightened humanity bringing its own salvation if it would only put its collective will to this cosmic task. This transformation of messianism into a general human project was a powerful corollary of Reform's teaching that Jewish ethics had a universal thrust, and the two ideas should be seen as mutually reinforcing.

We may sum up this evocation of another time by reminding ourselves of one of their slogans, "the perfectability of man." Today this phrase is used largely in a ritual fashion to denote our belief that people can be far better than they now are. That is a far cry from "perfectability" and is another example of what the Holocaust has done to our optimism about humanity. With some qualification, to be sure, our Reform predecessors really *meant* "perfectable"—that with education, culture, psychotherapy, decent housing, jobs, and other forms of proper social planning people can come close to realizing their potential. Perhaps one never could fully close the gap between oneself and the infinite possibilities of being good, but that only meant seeing human perfection as persisting in the quest and understanding human success as getting better and better. And this was as true for society as for individuals. Perfectability and messianism were two parts of one doctrine.

THE EFFECTS OF THE HOLOCAUST

This unbounded faith in humanity was shattered by the Holocaust, but we did not gain this radically new insight into the human condition quickly. Almost all the Jewish community during the Hitler years, and not merely the Reform Jews, so shared this optimistic view of cultured humanity that they refused to believe the early evidence that the Nazis were systematically murdering Jews. In the United States our community required some two decades to be able to face what Hitler had done. A decade or so later we cannot say that we have yet properly assimilated what happened. However, once the consciousness of the Holocaust hit home, the old "easy optimism about humanity and its inevitable progress" had to be given up. What "optimism" now remained would at best be hope, but the notion of inevitable progress, even if modified to allow for occasional regression, was dead. The Holocaust was more than a momentary pause in humanity's onward march. What needed replacement was the one-sided view of humanity that saw only its great capacity for good. Attention now had to be focused on the human capacity and will to do evil. Humankind has a demonic as well as a messianic potential, and so Reform Judaism required a more balanced view of what it is to be a human being.

I think it right for the *Centenary Perspective* to speak of the Holocaust shattering our view of humankind rather than our belief in God. For all the publicity which the Jewish death-of-God movement received, it now seems obvious to me that it was our optimistic faith in humanity and not our alleged faith in God which received a mortal blow from the Holocaust. If we are honest, we will admit that most modern Jews in the period before Hitler cared little about God and expected almost nothing of God in history. We put all our faith in the university and concert hall, the political process and social reconstruction. Piety was for the weak or aged. Relying on God was old-fashioned and medieval. We relied on ourselves, on humanity, to a messianic extent. We need to apply Feverbach's famous rule here: When people talk about God, they are mostly projecting into heaven their ideas about humankind. So when we say God is now dead we do not mean the God of our tradition but rather the one we truly trusted in—humanity. It would have taken a believing community to lose its God. What we ultimately had faith in was human goodness and power; it was that faith we lost.

This explains what seems to me the outstanding religious phenomenon of our time. Once, a few short years ago, it seemed the Jewish death-of-God movement was going to free our community from its hypocrisy of claiming to be a religion yet living by its widespread agnosticism. Though an occasional synagogue proudly gave up God and an occasional nonbelieving rabbi came "out of the closet," the Jewish community has rejected the death-of-God concept. Jews are currently more open to God and Jewish spirituality than they have been in recent generations. I take this as strong evidence in favor of my contention that what had to be surrendered was our virtual idolatry of humankind.

THE CULTURAL WASTELAND

I have not been able to make up my own mind as to the precise relationship of our ability to face the Holocaust and our willingness to see that Western culture was now in a state of decline. The two are closely linked in many minds. With all the unique horror of the Holocaust, it has come to symbolize the demonic elements in Western civilization as a whole. One day, I hope, historians will clarify why it took American Jewry well into the 1960s to face up to the slaughter of European Jews. As I remember it, that was still some time before the Vietnam War had demonstrated to many people the stupidity and immorality of the foreign policy of the United States and before the urban riots made us realize how much injustice we still perpetrated on our minority groups. Yet I wonder if the regular references to Hitler and the Holocaust which were made in the civil rights struggle of the early 1960s did not have their effect on us. We were regularly appealed to not to be like the Germans but rather to take a stand against the social evil which surrounded us. Did this general ethical appeal, which pointed to the German experience as the standard of evil in our time, make it possible for us to realize how great the Nazi bestiality to our people had been?

Whatever the relation between the general and the Jewish social awakening, a decade or more of continual revelations of corruption in our midst since then has left few citizens of the United

States untouched by a deep sense of spiritual betrayal in our country and by the despairing recognition that our situation is symptomatic of Western culture generally. The *Centenary Perspective* is rather high-minded in the three difficulties it notes. (In this instance the committee did not want its words tied too closely to news events of 1976 and thus spoke in terms of more lasting problems in our time.) It mentions "the widespread threats to freedom, the problems inherent in the explosion of new knowledge and of ever more powerful technologies, and the spiritual emptiness of much of Western culture." Each is a major menace to the sort of life we have always hoped to live, yet they make up the substance of much of our daily news. No wonder people speak of living in a paranoid time and that depression has begun to replace obsession as our typical psychic ill. I suggest, however, that there is a special if unconscious irony in mentioning these specific areas of concern to Reform Jews. (I do not recall the committee thinking in these terms.) In each case we are endangered by that to which we looked to bring the Messianic Age.

The threats to our freedom may be the least convincing case. Reform Jews never expected much good from communism, the major threat to human freedom today, though they did hope that social planning and innovation would yield great moral gain. Yet in our country public officials have often sought to justify illegally infringing upon our liberties in the name of the national good. Thus the supposed preservation of democracy is used to constrict the freedom which was the foundation of all our hopes for a better life. So too we once counted on science and technology to give us abundance in all things through mastery over nature. Now information flows so rapidly and with such contradiction that despite an earnest effort to stay informed we find ourselves basically ignorant about most things and uncertain of the present validity of what little we do know. We are completely dependent on our technology to make possible our way of life, yet increasingly it seems to threaten life itself in the name of productive advance. The dangers of the political and material realms might once have been offset by the solace and inspiration to be found in high culture: literature and art, the theater and concert hall, the lecture and the magazine gave us our ideals or reinforced them. We expected the philosophers and writers of our time not only to enlarge our sensibilities but to give us largeness of soul. Being secularized we no longer expected Judaism to teach us very much. The pursuit of culture took the place of what Jews in other ages found in the study of Torah. What else explains the overwhelming statistical disproportion with which American Jews buy books, art, and theater and concert tickets? We looked to the creative spirits of our time to instruct and empower us in our messianic responsibilities. But our contemporary creators make their mark largely by their interesting manipulation of technique, for they have little to communicate substantively. When we turn to them for a deeper understanding of the human condition other than its wretchedness, when, most important, we await some word of hope or seek a compelling call to duty, we find them as naked of idea and inspiration as the rest of us. At their best they help us confront the barrenness of our existence and, since they suggest no way to transcend or transform it, they consequently add to our sense of frustration and futility.

The Emancipation prompted Reform Judaism to place most of its trust in humanity and its spiritual power. The Holocaust and the spiritual decline of our civilization showed that faith largely to have been misplaced. At our present best we are not as good, and at our recent worst we are far more evil than we once believed. We Reform Jews must therefore now rectify our view of humanity and the working out of its destiny. This is one thing recent history has taught us.

THE ROLE OF THE JEWISH STATE

In this same period in which we lost one important component of our faith, we gained another one as a result of the establishment and growth of the State of Israel. Most observers agree that the special attachment of American Jews to the State of Israel became evident during the Six Day War of 1967. Before then the State of Israel seemed only another routine fact of life and, for most American Jews, a rather marginal one. The war brought even Jews who had previously had little attachment to the Jewish community, to the recognition that the State of Israel was important to them personally and thus that they were very much more a part of the Jewish people than they had imagined. The triumph of the Israelis was not only a relief after extreme tension, but a complex inspiration to the Jewish soul. Intelligence linked to courage, morality combined with bravery had won; history could, in special circumstances, reward the righteous. This much might have been expected, but almost no one was prepared for the effect of the capture of Jerusalem and the return to the Western Wall. Reform Jews had for more than a century stopped praying for the restoration of the Temple and its sacrifices; they do not consider places holy, and the Wall is hardly an object to appeal to a group that had for years emphasized modern esthetic values. Yet those stones quickly brought Reform Jews, as it did all Jews, a mystic message of the unity of the Jewish people, of its unbroken historic continuity, and of the reality of the Covenant between God and the Jewish people. Before the Wall, in those days, all the varying strands of Jewish belief and life intuitively came together.

There was no such response among most American Jews to the founding of the State of Israel in 1948 nor to the Sinai Campaign victory in 1956. I do not think there has been any single comparable event to June 1967. Yet the effect of those days has persisted, and the level to which they raised our consciousness of our involvement with the State of Israel has only slightly receded in the ensuing decade.

The *Centenary Perspective* makes no mention of the Six-Day War, for there were many Reform Jews who were deeply affected by the State of Israel from its very beginnings, as well as many others who no longer recall those extraordinary days of June 1967. I mention them here because I think they are the most dramatic example of what is meant when the document says that "the State of Israel, through its many accomplishments, raised our sense of the Jews as a people to new heights of aspiration and devotion." The Six Day War victory was an "accomplishment" of such significance that almost no American Jew was immune to it. Yet the committee also had in mind such outstanding achievements as rebuilding the lives of Hitler's victims, reclaiming the land, welcoming refugees from Arab and communist countries, creating a Jewish culture, maintaining a democracy, relying on arms without becoming militaristic, behaving with dignity and high human standards in the face of terrorism and international insult—in short, setting a splendid example of what Jews do when they come to power despite being under extraordinary pressure. Since the Emancipation we had gained some sense of what individual Jews might accomplish when they were free. Most Jews, some Zionist visionaries excepted, had little idea of what the Jewish people as a whole might create given their own state. From what they have written, the State of Israel outstripped the expectations of even some of those who brought it into being. It has thus drastically changed our perception of ourselves as a group and our potential as a people. The *Centenary Perspective* says our vision reached "new heights of aspiration and devotion." Because of the State of Israel Jews now hope to accomplish more as a people than we ever thought we would and are determined to make those possibilities a full-scale reality.

Nothing symbolizes this as well to me as the inception of an effort, a few years ago, to establish a Reform Jewish kibbutz in the State of Israel. Here the social ethics of classic Reform join with contemporary ecological. communitarian, and noncapitalist sensibilities and the desire to live fully as a Jew to motivate a project that would have been inconceivable but a short while back. True, only a few dozen American and Israeli young adults are involved in this effort, which may never become a going concern. Yet our levels of "aspiration and devotion" for our people and ourselves now reach this far, and very little in the history of the Reform movement or the concerns of acculturated modern Jewry in general prepared us for it.

This positive, ethnic lesson of recent years is

not unrelated to the negative one about humanity. We were inspired by our peoplehood[2] as we
became disenchanted with humanity. Perhaps
the State of Israel would still have had so strong
an effect on our Jewish self-respect had we
retained great faith in humankind and its goodness. With our universal hope dampened, the
appeal of our particular group meant even more
to us. Surely it is fair to say that, in part, we share
the modern American return to our ethnic roots
as a result of our disappointment with our
society. Yet whatever the balance between our
loss and gain of commitment, the result for
Reform Jews is that they now must establish a
new balance in their responsibilities, giving more
weight to the needs of the Jewish people and less
to the concerns of humanity as a whole. Our
situation is captured in the conclusion the document says we derive from the spiritual emptiness
in our culture. The traumatic events of our time
"have taught us to be less dependent on the
values of our society and to reassert what remains perennially valid in Judaism's teaching."
Transposing that emphasis to the level of Re-

---

[2]The word *peoplehood* was used in drafts of the *Centenary Perspective* but does not occur in the final version.
Our consultant for questions of style, Hugh Nissenson,
suggested that it was a clumsy term and persuaded us to
delete it from our text. For further data on the editing
process see the Supplement to *Reform Judaism Today:
What We Believe.*

form Jewish belief in general means that the universal emphasis of a previous time must now be counterbalanced by a strong Reform Jewish concern with the Jewish people. The operative word for this mood is *survival*.

CHAPTER EIGHT

The New Balance in Reform Jewish Commitment

SURVIVAL – OUR HIGHEST PRIORITY

The single dominant lesson of recent years can be put quite simply: "We have learned again that the survival of the Jewish people is of highest priority. . . ." This is the fresh emphasis in contemporary Reform Jewish thought and practice. It is the major motif of the *Centenary Perspective*—or, to be more precise, it is the Reform belief whose new priority must now be balanced against what the previous paragraph called the "essential wisdom of our movement." For we must not forget that the material we are now studying is the second and not the first paragraph of this statement. What Reform has learned in recent years is taken within the context of the century's having "confirmed" its basic teachings. Let us first consider the range of meaning *survival* now has and then discuss why the committee felt this was essentially a rectification of the balance of old Reform Jewish beliefs rather than a radical departure from them.

PHYSICAL SURVIVAL

In its most direct sense, the word *survival* is meant physically. The Jewish people and its tradition begin with Jews, enough Jews that there is a sufficient population mass for us to be a viable ethnic group. To our great pain, the physical survival of the Jews remains a real problem in many places. The State of Israel stands continually imperiled, and on its survival hangs the morale of world Jewry. Soviet Jews are persecuted for daring to assert their Jewishness, and outbreaks of anti-Semitism regularly disturb the lives of Jews in South American countries. In America we threaten ourselves biologically, for our reproductive rate is not great enough to keep our people from dwindling. If the *Centenary Perspective* does not specifically mention the physical aspect of survival, it is not because the committee felt that only the spiritual side of Jewish life was important. After the Holocaust every sensitive Jew will spurn such a distorted sense of Jewish values, and there is no trace of such disembodied pietism in the *Perspective*. It rather takes this primal sense of survival as the basis of its concern for peoplehood and assumes that it will be understood as part of the reaffirmation of ethnicity which is central to its restatement of Reform Jewish belief today.

SPIRITUAL SURVIVAL

Survival also means authentic continuity. We not

only want to live, but we want to live as Jews. We want our lives, even though they differ from those of Jews in a previous age, to show a genuine tie with the history and tradition of our people. We Reform Jews enunciated the premise that survival means change, specifically adaptation to the modern world. The general acceptance of our teaching and the change in our social situation now makes us equally concerned about Jewish authenticity. The Emancipation has largely succeeded; we Jews are mostly moderns. Reform has carried through the first daring part of its program; it has created modes of living by which one can be both Jewish and modern. Only now, under the impact of recent history, we have begun to wonder if we are Jewish enough. Freshly sensitized to our responsibilities to our people, we question whether the old patterns we shaped gave sufficient weight to our Jewishness to keep our people and its tradition vital. What do we need to do, what conception of modern Jewish life do we require in order for our people to survive?

Survival, then, means rethinking who we Jews are and how we ought to live. The *Centenary Perspective* seeks to respond to that need in compact fashion. It is a document of the contemporary Jewish will to survive. It tries to clarify what constitutes genuine Jewishness and applies this understanding to three troublesome questions of contemporary Jewish life.

A SENSE OF ETHNICITY

Jewish survival is here called "of highest priority." I do not see how such explicit language can easily be misread. It says that out of the experience of a century and the torments of the past generation, Reform Jews assert that our peoplehood can no longer be, as it was to prior generations, a subsidiary theme in Reform Jewish life. It is central to Reform Judaism today. Something of this shift may already be seen in the Columbus Platform of 1937, though there, while the same idea emerges, it is thoroughly subordinated to Reform's universal religious teaching. Here, since it is of "highest priority," it is the basis of rethinking the classic Reform affirmations. Yet it must also be pointed out—and this is typical of the way the document balances one belief against another, its dialectical character— that the statement does not say "*the* highest priority." The new ethnicity does not replace the older Reform beliefs, but is now entitled to rank with them. I do not know whether people who today suggest that Jewish survival is *the* highest priority mean what they say literally or merely permit themselves this absolutism because the matter is so important to them. For people like me who are fussy about ideas, "*the* highest priority" means that everything else must be sacrificed to it, that nothing is as important, and therefore one may do or demand anything in its name—anything. Considering what people have made of such priorities in our time, I cannot believe that this is what most people mean when they speak of Jewish survival as "*the* highest priority." If they only wish to indicate that we ought to give the Jewish people a major share of our energies, even making substantial sacrifices for it, I certainly agree. They probably do not mean that anything—say, the three unthinkable acts of classic Judaism, murder, sexual immorality and idolatry—is permissible should it seem necessary to keep the Jewish people alive. Yet I have read and heard people who mean this or something like it, who would readily sacrifice not only decorum but ethical considerations for the sake of the Jews— for example, by calling for the expulsion of Israeli Arabs from the territory of the State of Israel. There is a deeply significant Jewish difference between emphasizing one's peoplehood and chauvinism. The *Centenary Perspective*, for all its championing of Jewish ethnicity, refuses to make survival an absolute. It raises it to the level of a central concern, depicting it quite carefully as "*of* highest priority."

BALANCING OUR PRIORITIES

This reassignment of priorities immediately raises new questions. How does our intense commitment to survival relate to our other major concerns—our loyalty to God, our respect for self, our responsibilities to humanity? The *Perspective* goes on to put these various aspects of our faith in proper balance. In some cases a resolution is relatively clear-cut—the affirmation of God precedes and thus provides the context for the statement on the people of Israel. In some cases a rough rule is given—as in specifying areas of religious duty but leaving the details to the individual will, or in accepting the State of Israel's great importance to us yet insisting that Diaspora life has independent Jewish validity and therefore must be self-determining. And in one case—that of our duties to our people and to humanity—all that could be said is that neither of these obligations, though they may come into conflict, can be given up. This is less tidy and instructive than people might like such a religious document to be, and far more ambiguous than previous Reform declarations. For all that, it reflects accurately the complex nature of Reform Jewish belief today and its new, rather paradoxical set of basic affirmations. When everything in Reform Judaism could be subordinated to ethics and the God who grounded the system, Reform could be clear and reasonably rational. Add the Jewish people in its full ethnicity to those premises and a more dynamic, open-textured faith results.

All of the foregoing, however, relates to but the first half of a sentence. The full sense of this statement emerges only when the new Reform emphasis on ethnicity is dialectically balanced against the old Reform Jewish sense "that in carrying out our Jewish responsibilities we help more humanity toward its messianic fulfillment." Jewish survival is thus seen in connection with a universal human hope, "fulfillment." For all its emphasis on Jewish ethnicity, then, this document retains the classic Reform concern with Judaism as part of the effort of humankind as a whole to work out its God-given destiny. The horrifying events of the past few decades may have shattered our belief in "inevitable progress," but they have not destroyed Reform Judaism's universal messianism (discussed separately below) or its belief that, under the conditions of freedom, Jewish duty mandates intimate involvement in universal human affairs.

An opposing view has been heard in the Jewish community, suggesting that the Holocaust ended the hopes raised by the Emancipation. If that means only that Jewish "optimism" about humanity must be discarded, then, as the document indicates, there is no dispute. But some have been so ravaged by the implications of the Holocaust and the continuing disillusionments of our time that they insist that Jews should no longer have more than the most minimally necessary concern for general society. For them, Hitler destroyed the notion that there is such a thing as "humanity," certainly insofar as it means that Jews must give it anything like the duty owed to the Jewish people. One does what one must do to retain one's rights in society, no more. That is, so to speak, a part of Jewish survival. All the rest of one's energies should go to Jewish survival proper. For such people the Emancipation is over and we are in a new stage of Jewish history. Reform Jews, insofar as this statement represents them, reject this thesis. Replacing optimism about people for realism is not the same as denying altogether that human beings universally can and often do accomplish good. The fate of the Jews being indivisible from the fate of the people among whom they live, universalism is a necessity. Moreover, Jewish faith and ethics make it a divine imperative. Here Reform Jews continue the fundamental thrust of their movement from its earliest days. If anything, the argument can be made—and is, briefly, in section VI, on survival and service—that particularly when we are giving ethnicity great stress it is vital to balance it with proper universalism lest it degenerate into tribalism. Here the dialectical approach of the *Centenary Perspective*, finding the truth in balancing one belief against another, again makes itself manifest.

UNIVERSALISM AND PARTICULARISM

The virtues of seeing our situation as one of righting a balance quickly becomes apparent when one adopts a historical perspective. It would have been folly for the early Reformers to hope to bring Jews into the modern world by focusing their efforts on perpetuating the Jewish people. That was not their major challenge. The Jews they faced were reasonably well acquainted with Jewish tradition, lived in rather solid Jewish communities, were continually reminded of their Jewishness by anti-Semitism or its heritage, and had a strong consciousness of themselves as Jews. The Reformers wanted to demonstrate (while the world remained skeptical) that it was possible for someone adhering to this ancient faith truly to be a modern. Could Jews, wanting to be good Jews, become involved in the burdens of society as well as taking advantage of its opportunities? Did Judaism mandate a significant, ungrudging universal responsibility? No previous Jewry had asked itself that, in part because they had never been asked that question. The Reformers answered it positively; they never lost their sense of distinctive peoplehood. Though they spoke of Judaism as essentially universalistic, they knew they were not unitarians; and though they identified the essence of Judaism as ethical monotheism, they opposed marriage to non-Jewish ethical monotheists. They may have been anti-Zionist and less concerned with Jews knowing Hebrew and Aramaic than their comprehending the ideas of Judaism. This can only be called a subordination of their sense of peoplehood to the task of becoming a participant in society. Their universalism did not become an absolute which dissolved everything Jewish into the sludge of superstition or cultural lag. They knew themselves to be Jews as well as Reformers. And I think it important to reiterate that in their time the projection of a strong Jewish universalism was a major necessity for Jewish survival.

Universalism is surely not the most pressing question of Jewish life today. Survival is. To some extent that is because of the success of earlier generations of Reform Jews which has made it reasonably easy for us to move through our lives as modern and Jewish. There can be little question about our universality today. We are experts in modern living, leaders in its advance and propagators of its styles. Disproportionately, we crowd the university and respond to political appeals designed to benefit humanity. By contrast we are amateurs at being Jewish, inept in religious practice, childlike in knowledge, at best fluctuating in our commitment. Even without the Holocaust and the State of Israel, survival should be "of highest priority" to us. But considering what the world has done and threatens to do to us, what it has done and is doing to itself, to concentrate our Jewish energies on universalism today as the Reformers did for much of the past century would be folly. Our central Jewish challenge is survival and not universalism. Reform Jews, sensitive to the need to change in order to keep Judaism alive, are responding to their changed social situation and in the century document seek to describe their altered sense of the balance between universalism and particularism.

CHAPTER NINE

Continuing Reform's Messianic Hope

AN EARLIER CONCERN WITH UNIVERSAL ETHICS

As the word *survival* sums up the new Reform particularism so the various terms for Reform's messianism must be understood to carry its century-old universal vision. The classic connection of humanity's power with universal ethics and thus with hope for history continues. Reform's messianic language implies, therefore, an endorsement of human activism which conceives of our doing the good as bringing or helping to bring God's kingdom and which understands the Jews as involved with all humankind in working out their common spiritual destiny. The *Centenary Perspective,* concerned with correcting the old imbalance of Reform Jewish priorities, does not expatiate on Reform's ethical and universal teaching. Since a concise document must concentrate on what is fresh rather than on what has commonly been accepted, the text takes Jewish activism, as so much else, for granted. This troubled some members of the CCAR. In the discussion at San Francisco, they indicated that they would have preferred more direct attention to our social ethical obligations. Particularly since some Jews today advocate subordinating ethics to religious practice and focusing our energies largely on our people, they felt such explicit treatment was desirable. I do not see that there was any difference of principle here, only a problem of form.

If social concern is more than New Deal liberalism or left-wing Democratic positions, then the commitment of the Conference to our need to apply Jewish ethics to society as a whole is practically unanimous. I responded to this question about the document by saying that the committee, because of format, preferred to voice our universal ethical concern indirectly rather than as a separate matter and had made it a major motif running through the document as a whole. (Whether my reply satisfied the CCAR substantively or because, in our tight schedule, they did not feel it worth delaying the document over this matter, I do not know, but it was not pressed further.)

A MESSIANIC VISION

The committee consciously dealt with Reform's universalism by referring again and again to our messianic vision. In the final version it appears in five places, one serving as the conclusion of the *Centenary Perspective* as a whole. These references, for all their brevity, provide a balance, perhaps even a context, for the document's concern with survival. Thus at the conclusion of the historical paragraph on "what we have learned," the climactic reference to survival is linked to Judaism's messianic thrust. In section II of the document, "The People Israel," a similar phrase connects our ethnicity with humankind as a whole. In the statement on religious practice, section IV, a phrase reminds us that Jewish duty has cosmic overtones. The several references in section VI, "Survival and Service," give an explicit reaffirmation of Reform Jewish universalism, made all the more significant by its occurring in connection with an acknowledgment of the unresolvable tensions that our social concern sometimes creates in relation to our duties to our people. And the concluding section of the document reminds us that all of Judaism is directed to a universal culmination and that in this despondent era, particular Jewish existence speaks of hope to all humanity. If the implications of survival constitute the dominant theme of the *Centenary Perspective,* then universal social activism is its soft but repeated countertheme.

THE SEARCH FOR A NEW MESSIANISM

The committee faced another problem of form. Trying to write about our messianic hope today, we found ourselves embarrassed by a lack of symbolic imagination. Classic Reform Judaism had substituted the notion of the Messianic Age for that of the personal King Messiah of tradition. That Reform notion was powerfully evocative for times when people trusted implicitly in science, culture, and social planning and confidently expected the onward march of human progress to bring the Messianic Age. Yet this "easy optimism" has collapsed under the battering of modern history. The committee thought, with some misgivings to be sure, that if it used the classic Reform phrase *Messianic Age,* it would be understood as endorsing the classic Reform optimism about people and historical progress. That would be untrue to "what we have learned." Some Reform Jews, most notably Steven S. Schwarzschild in a by-now-classic article of some twenty years ago, have suggested that it is time for Reform to reclaim the traditional concept of the personal Messiah.[3] The committee considered this possibility but quickly agreed that it was unacceptable. There were still too many problems with this idea, and the abrupt introduction of this symbol to a constituency which considered it an outgrown tradition would create more confusion than insight. This left the committee searching for a freshly appropriate way to talk about messianism, one that would reflect a realistic view of

[3] Steven S. Schwarzschild, "The Personal Messiah. . . Toward the Restoration of a Discarded Doctrine," *Judaism* 5 (1956): 123-35.

humanity and history yet project the real hope
which, despite everything, we feel. No contemporary Jewish thinker, to the best of my knowledge, has suggested what such a revised messianism might be or how it could properly be
symbolized. The committee—though this was
hardly its task—could not itself create a new,
major Jewish symbol on demand. While waiting
for some spark of inspiration to touch our
people, the committee decided to employ a
variety of expressions, each of which would
point toward what was meant, yet none of which
was definitive or fully satisfactory in conveying
our faith. So the term *Messianic Age* does not
occur in the document. Instead we have a range
of intimations from the forward-pointing
"messianic expectations" to the generalized
hopefulness of "humanity will be redeemed"
and "messianic fulfillment," to the classic,
almost ritual phrase, "achieve universal justice
and peace," climaxing in "what the prophets
have meant to us" and the quotation from
Isaiah. The last is particularly noteworthy.
Nowhere else in the document is the Bible or any
other Jewish text cited. Unable to find language
of our own, we turned to our tradition to speak
for us, a quite appropriate thing to do, considering our concern for our people. Yet in continuity
with Reform teaching the quotation chosen
makes no reference to a personal Messiah. I
suppose our traditionalists will assume as does
rabbinic literature, that the passage takes the

Messiah for granted, and that our classic Reform believers will see it as pointing only to the "Messianic Age." Were there a better way to bring both of these views together in a new image of messianism, I feel certain the committee would have found it quite appealing.

Interestingly enough, though there were some calls for a specific definition of the document's oft-mentioned messianism, there were no objections to its not using the term *Messianic Age*. Either people felt that the substitute language was a satisfactory equivalent, or they, like the committee, felt that its connection with optimism made it no longer serviceable. From their letters I did not feel that the people who wanted the committee to explain its messianic reference in greater detail were trying to defend the older view. I took them rather as evidence that many thoughtful Reform Jews are searching for a messianic doctrine which is more activist than that of traditional Judaism yet is less trusting of people and more open to the reality of God's help than was optimistic liberalism. The committee shared that faith and that search. As a result, not unlike a good deal of traditional Jewish teaching about the "end of days," it took refuge in relatively open symbols, trusting Jews to fill them out from their knowledge of what they have meant and from their experience of what Jews still hope.

PART III

Living with
Reform Judaism's Pluralism

Reform Jews respond to change in various ways according to the Reform principle of the autonomy of

Diversity Within Unity, the Hallmark of Reform — the individual. However, Reform Judaism does more than tolerate diversity; it engenders it. In our uncertain historical situation we must expect to have far greater diversity than previous generations knew. How we shall live with diversity without stifling dissent and without paralyzing our ability to take positive action will test our character and our principles. We stand open to any position thoughtfully and conscientiously advocated in the spirit of Reform Jewish belief. While we may differ in our interpretation and application of the ideas enunciated here, we accept such differences as precious and see in them Judaism's best hope for confronting whatever the future holds for us. Yet in all our diversity we perceive a certain unity and we shall not allow our differences in some particulars to obscure what binds us together.

From the Centenary Perspective

CHAPTER TEN

How Affirming Autonomy Has Led to Increasing Diversity

Having indicated what Reform Judaism has taught and what it has learned over the past century, the *Centenary Perspective* logically should now turn to depicting the present state of Reform belief. Instead, another introductory paragraph is given, one devoted to diversity in the Reform movement. This material might well have been included in the preceding paragraph on "what we have learned." Reform Jews, particularly in the past few years, have had to learn to live with unusually sharp clashes of opinion in their midst. Indeed, it was the sense that diversity was leading to dissension almost to the point of schism which had prompted Robert Kahn's proposal to the CCAR that a statement of Reform Jewish unity was now needed.

Our committee, appointed as a result of the Conference's concurrence with this suggestion, deemed the topic of sufficient importance to receive independent treatment. There is, then, a shift of focus in this paragraph. Preceding paragraphs are concerned with the Jewish people and with general history. Now an introductory word is said regarding the special contemporary situation in our movement.

THE PRINCIPLE OF AUTONOMY

The discussion begins with a brief mention of the Reform "principle of the autonomy of the individual." This is another instance of taking reasonable familiarity with classic Reform teaching for granted and quickly moving on to the problem of applying it in our time. Yet note the importance assigned to this idea. It is called a "principle" of our movement, the only such usage in the document. Since autonomy is one of the major themes around which the development of the document takes place, adding its own contrapuntal tension to the universalism-particularism interplay noted above, it deserves some extended treatment here.

The term *autonomy* was one of the few technical terms allowed in the text, for the committee felt it conveyed our meaning with unique accuracy and conciseness. The two Greek roots of the word nicely give its thrust: *auto* means "self" and *nomos* means "law." *Autonomy* thus means that people have the right to be self-legislating or, in our vernacular, "to make up their own minds." The term gained great currency during the Enlightenment with its emphasis on using reason, not doing things simply because someone else has told us to.

Consider, for example, some of the people who created the modern temper. Galileo rejected the scientific tradition of his day and the authority of the Church because his mind and observation had taught him the earth moves about the sun. Descartes overthrew all medieval philosophy by insisting he had a right to doubt everything until a "clear and distinct" truth presented itself to his mind, his famous "Since I am thinking, I exist." Rousseau maintained, against all accepted wisdom, that people were naturally good and society evil, and hence people should reshape society to the true common will. From such insights as these arose the notion that all people have an inner sense of right and wrong that they can and should follow.

We have come to know this notion of autonomy as people's right to follow their conscience. Democracy is an effort to create a form of government responsive to individual autonomy. The U.S. Constitution was not acceptable until there was attached to it the amendments we call the Bill of Rights (for individual citizens). Democracy's great problem is how much freedom it can grant to individuals and still have a functioning state. It retains such respect for sincere personal conviction that it will allow extraordinary deviations from the law in its name—for example, conscientious objection to war as a reason for not serving in the military.

TRADITION AS GUIDE — CONSCIENCE AS AUTHORITY

Apply this conception to biblical law and one can

immediately see its appeal to Reform Jews. If rational people should legislate for themselves, then tradition may be a guide or spur to us, but it cannot command our assent. Conscience must be our ultimate authority. When conscience conflicts with Jewish law, Halachah, as with regard to women's rights, Reform Jews feel it their duty—literally—to break with Jewish tradition. Historically, the deed preceded the understanding. The early Reformers knew intuitively that it was right for Jews to become modern even if that required radical changes in Jewish practice.

When traditional Jewish leadership could not see or act upon this vision, Reform Jews did. And as they thought about what they were doing, they found in the idea of individual autonomy the validation of their effort. In the first decades of the movement this idea generally manifested itself in historical terms—that each generation, particularly those that found themselves in new situations, had the right to institute appropriate changes, that is, to legislate for themselves.

CREATING NORMS OF BEHAVIOR

To us, still somewhat astonished at the wild variety of things people do when the times encourage individual freedom, autonomy would seem to lead to anarchy. For many reasons this new personalist sense of Jewish authority did not do so. A century back, one's reason operated with many certainties of science, politics, and culture. For all that people were expected to think for themselves, they could rather easily be satisfied to do what it appeared very many other intelligent people were doing. In religion, conscience might be personal, but one was expected to make decisions in terms of a universally available moral law. All thinking people could know it and act on it. Hence if a person's decisions were regularly nonconformist, it would raise the question how general a moral law one was following. Compactly put, the autonomous individual was nonetheless expected to obey universal reason, hence avoiding anarchic choices.

Such nice philosophic reasoning meant little to most people. They may have talked about individuality but, until relatively recent years, their personal lives were largely ruled by the patterns set by social station. For Jews, the new freedom can be said to have had a paradoxical effect. Liberty made them quite free when it came to Jewish duty but, being insecure in the gentile styles they now took on, made them socially conformist. When German Jews acculturated in the United States they created a fairly stable German-Jewish way of life. They became solid and respectable, people who may have felt free from Jewish tradition but were orthodox about their social norms. A major source of their discomfort at the huge number of eastern European migrants to the United States as the century turned was the immigrants' ignorance and disruption of the recently established American German-Jewish life-styles. Within a few decades a similar process of creating American eastern-European-Jewish folk norms had taken place, eventually becoming the suburban American Jewish style of the 1960s. Not until the breakdown of our general trust in rationality and our new skepticism about society in that decade was a more radical, apparently anarchic effect of personal autonomy seen.

I think these reasons largely explain why, as we look over the history of the Reform movement in America, it seems, for all its espousal of the right to be different, relatively of one piece. Zionism early caused disagreement in the movement, and the mavericks on this issue already appear with Herzl's 1896 call for a congress. Yet except for a faculty flap some few years later at the Hebrew Union College, there was no turmoil over Zionism until the 1930s. The need to be part of the movement seemed more important than the need to assert one's individuality.

Something similar seems to have operated to contain the arguments over increasing ritual in Reform which surfaced in the late 1920s. Yet these two examples point to another factor which was operating to keep Reform Judaism relatively homogenous: a widely accepted, relatively monolithic set of goals. That is, there was little argument over the priorities in Reform Jewish belief. Almost everyone agreed that fitting into the general society, universalism, was the paramount concern. Fostering the distinctive life of the Jewish people, particularism was not unimportant, but it was subordinated to the more comprehensive goal. Thus, while Zionism and ritual could become questions in the movement, not until they threatened the old order of priorities, until they and the struggle over intermarriage became the focus of a movement to put particularism on a par with universalism, did they threaten to break the movement apart. I think that is so important for understanding what Reform is passing through and what this document represents that I want to analyze this recent development at some greater length.

CONFORMITY IN DECLINE

Let us retrace our steps. I have contended that three factors operated to keep Reform Jewish diversity to a minimum despite its doctrine of individual autonomy: a secure and stable intellectual climate, an authoritative social order, and an accepted ideology in which things had a definite place. I now suggest that the underlying reason for the special turmoil in Reform Judaism in recent years has been the weakening or the discrediting of all three factors. Since they no longer function effectively, individuals have been freed to take quite personal positions, even to the point of eccentricity and arbitrariness. Let us see, then, how our intellectual, social, and ideological framework has been shaken in the past decade or so.

There is no general agreement today on what it means to be a rational person. Thinking clearly doesn't mean necessarily taking ethics seriously. Philosophers as far apart as Bertrand Russell, the empiricist, and Jean-Paul Sartre, the existentialist, have discredited the old ideas of ethics as part of natural law or some sort of Kantian moral law.

The social sciences, psychology for example, consider themselves only descriptive and then show themselves divided—Freud, Skinner, Maslow—as to what they think "human nature" really is. They and our writers teach us that all sorts of acts are "human," and so indicate that the gap between the natural and the ethical may be very wide indeed. Thus, reason no longer controls our autonomy. You can be thoughtful today and give reasons for doing all sorts of things. Intellectual relativism reigned during much of the 1960s. This had a strong moral appeal for much that we had been told to do (say, in our treatment of women) which turned out to be socially not ethically based.

Yet rejecting convention also became an excuse for doing "your own thing," even if that meant indulging one's childish fantasies, like having sex without responsibility or taking drugs without caring how much harm they did. The social effects of that time touched everyone. A new permissiveness entered our lives. We now were freer to eat and dress and live and become what we ourselves wanted to become, not what our class or community said we must be. The old American social restrictiveness no longer contained our individuality so tightly. The same was true in the Jewish community.

The neighborhoods to which we moved were less cohesively Jewish. Observance decreased, commitment was low, ignorance and apathy were the rule. What one could do and still be accepted among Jews widely increased. Within ourselves we were no longer sure of what a "good Jew" was. Once it seemed enough to get an education, make a living, establish a family, raise decent children, pay dues to a synagogue, and give to Jewish causes. As the turmoil of the late 1960s shook so much of what we believed in, we began to ask what all our Jewish effort meant and just why it was worthwhile. Even the suburban Jewish style, which for two decades or so seemed to settle the problem of developing a modern American Jewish way of life, began to show its inadequacies.

THE OLD SENSE OF PRIORITIES GIVE WAY

That intellectual and social transition would probably have been enough to deeply affect Reform Judaism. With personal autonomy less channeled by reason or society, deviant individualism was bound to increase. But something greater was at work which exacerbated the tensions within the movement. The old agreement as to priorities collapsed. Universalism was no longer king. Hitler, the spiritual debility of Western culture, and the achievements of the State of Israel showed most Reform Jews this was no time to continue subordinating particular Jewish to universal human goals. One can see most of the Reform rifts of the past four decades or more as skirmishes over this fundamental issue of revising the place of our specific Jewish duties in our religious life. Thus the tensions over Zionism, ritual, the use of Hebrew, the State of Israel, the cantor, the maintenance of a rabbinical school in New York, the introduction of the Sefardic pronunciation of Hebrew, the possibility of prayerbooks opening from right to left, and, climactically, rabbis performing intermarriages all might be considered part of an effort to change our movement from being essentially devoted, as it were, to Reform rather than to Judaism. (Only the sporadic difficulties over the Union's social action program do not reflect this universal-particular polarization. I would, however, argue that if the Union had not been connected with the surge to ritual, ethnicity, and support of the State of Israel, its efforts to put Reform's universal teaching into practice rather than leave it as preachment would not have met such emotional resistance.)

I do not think I underestimate the importance of some of the decisions, particularly the changes, which Reform Jews were considering in these quarrels, yet it has regularly seemed to me that the passions they aroused testified mainly to the existence of their antagonists' hidden agenda. My admittedly subjective analysis of the semiconscious opposing concerns hinges upon my belief that an old consensus came apart. Those who grew up in and loved a Reform Judaism that subordinated particularism to universalism and those who were attracted to the movement by its refusal to be parochial naturally tried to defend the old ideological priorities. They saw in every effort to promote or encourage particularism a threat to their basic faith. As this cumulatively became an effort not for one or another aspect of Jewish tradition or peoplehood but a drive to put particular responsibilities on a par with universal ones, it seemed to them as if the Reform they knew and loved was being radically threatened if not destroyed. At some point this passed over into the unconscious fear that rather than being given equality with universalism, Jewish ethnic concerns were now going to dominate Reform. One step more and the sensitive imagination could see a new parochialism emerging in Reform and with it a move to self-ghettoization. Since Reform had begun out of a positive response to freedom, the movement now seemed headed for self-contradiction, perhaps to the point of self-destruction.

At the other extreme the fears were similarly great. They started from what seemed to their protagonists reasonable judgments. Many people who grew up in the Reform movement and had found it too cerebral, uncelebrative, and other-directed now wanted a Reform that was emotive, ritual-minded, and Jewish community-oriented. There were many too who had come to the movement because they saw the old Reform concern with freedom now linked with a new richer appreciation of the Jewish people and its tradition. These people considered every effort to hold back or oppose the expression of Jewish particularity a threat to their major hope for the development of the movement. As this cumulatively became a struggle to continue the full-scale subordination of Jewish particularity to universalism, it seemed to them that their opponents were refusing to face the facts of recent Jewish history. This led to the fear that Reform would institute only a token concern with Jewish observance and responsibility, thereby continuing its isolation from the rest of the Jewish community and promoting slow assimilation. One step more and the sensitive imagination could see Reform retreating to a Hebraicly tinted Unitarianism, thereby promoting a spiritual Holocaust in the midst of the Jewish people, the unthinkable act for a modern Jew.

I was only dimly conscious of these factors and their interplay until I was well into this intensive study of the *Centenary Perspective*. Yet now that I have gained this insight I can see why it was possible for us, against heavy odds, to write a fairly strong document that gained overwhelming approval. With this hindsight I now see the *Perspective* as an effort to resolve this ideological-emotional conflict, and its opening paragraph on Reform Jewish diversity is a key to understanding the balance between the views which the document suggests as the answer we can all accept.

CHAPTER ELEVEN

The Recent Polarization of Reform Judaism

Reform Jewish diversity reached a new and intense level in recent years over an issue which can be called freedom versus Halachah. It will be easiest, if somewhat oversimplified, to connect each of the divergent views with a single protagonist.

THE POSITION FOR PERSONAL FREEDOM

Professor Alvin Reines of the Cincinnati school of the College has been at work on a position which may be characterized as a radical affirmation of personal freedom. His view of personal existence seems philosophically similar to that of Jean-Paul Sartre, who in his early writing held that the only human good is personal freedom. People should therefore resolutely fight any effort to infringe upon their autonomy no matter how subtle or allegedly well intentioned it claims to be. Thus intellectual or religious movements which are not satisfied to merely set their claims before us but insist upon our allegiance or compel our compliance are evil. Reform Judaism behaves paradoxically in this regard. It declares itself an advocate of freedom,

106

but then seeks to indoctrinate its adherents and otherwise gain organizational discipline. It thus betrays our human dignity and shows itself to be inconsistent and irrational. The failure of the movement in recent years to excite the many people who are searching for a proper faith may be laid to the unwillingness to act boldly and consistently to uphold its fundamental commitment to personal freedom. Reform Judaism should acknowledge that the introduction of Reform into Judaism was, in effect, the creation of a new religion, one which asserted that in the modern world individuals were going to be the final authority in their lives. Reform could only narrowly be defined as being free to choose against the Jewish past; positively it insisted, albeit without having the courage to say so plainly, that people were free to choose whatever future they found valuable. Reines thus advocated fulfilling the old Reform agenda by turning us into a group the only principle of whose association would be the commitment of the members to seek their own free choices and not to infringe upon the freedom of their fellows similarly so engaged. For himself, he felt that there were a number of symbols in the Jewish tradition which might be useful in helping people feel the many wonderful dimensions of freedom and endure the pains which existence in a world of limited possibility make inevitable. Religion is humanity's response to its finitude, and Reines has sought to create an idea of God appropriate to the human condition yet fully acceptable to the rational mind.

In Reines's theory neither the Jewish people nor Jewish teaching exerts any independent authority over us. Since freedom is the one great good, Judaism may not make any claims upon us that would infringe upon our will, which must remain utterly unrestricted until we choose to give it a direction. As a Jew, Reines is willing to draw on the Jewish tradition where it helps him in his universal search, and he suggests this pattern as a possibility to others. Yet in utilizing Jewish symbols Reines seeks to remain thoroughly consistent to his radical affirmation of the self and its freedom. So even those aspects of the Jewish tradition he uses in his quest are thoroughly reinterpreted, emptied of any Jewish particularity, and considered to be ways of speaking about being, as finite humans confront it. Thus "Judaism" is now only one historic way of speaking about "Reform" which, though it seems to have started out as a modifying adjective, is here raised to the status of a substantive. The resulting full-blown universalism would seem to have more in common with existentialism than, say, with Conservative Judaism, and, to the best of my knowledge, there is little or no place in Reines's interpretation of Reform teaching for any significant relation to the State of Israel.

THE POSITION FOR HALACHAH

At the opposite pole stands the thought of Professor Jakob Petuchowski, also of the Cincinnati school of the College. (That these two positions are represented on the faculty of our major rabbinical school is indicative of the commitment to diversity in our Reform movement.) In a number of his articles Professor Petuchowski has suggested that Reform Jews, to be more intimately a part of the people of Israel, should rethink their attitude toward following at least some critical matters of traditional Jewish law, the Halachah. His major concern is in the areas of personal status, conversion, and divorce. Here we have cut ourselves off from the Household of Israel by using our own standards. While following the Halachah might cause us some pain—because of its rules about witnesses, contracts, and such—most of the law poses no special problems for us. We should shoulder the extra burdens involved in abiding by Halachah so as not to continue separating ourselves from our people. Petuchowski has hoped that if the Reform movement indicated its willingness to live under at least some aspects of the Halachah, traditional Jewish authorities might then be willing to make some liberal constructions from within the system, thus expanding the areas where all religious Jews operated in common.

Petuchowski's argument should be linked with the view of some rabbis, which he seems to share, that what Reform Judaism needs most today is a return to Jewish discipline. Adherents of this position talk of the need for a "Reform Jewish Halachah" or for the return of Reform Judaism to some measure of traditional Halachah. Negatively, the argument proceeds from deep dissatisfaction with what is termed the "anarchy" in Reform Jewish life. Positively, it is pointed out that the chief concern of Judaism has always been action, that in not defining its expectations of its adherents Reform has de facto abandoned them to their individual resources, which are largely non-Jewish and secular. Judaism created and strengthened the life of the spirit through a personal and communal regimen of action. Now that the fight for modernity has been won, our people are ready to be more Jewish. By not telling them what is required of them we are failing to meet their present felt needs. Besides, Jews want to be part of the Jewish people as a whole, and nothing so separates Reform Jews from the rest of religious Jewry as our refusal to acknowledge the authority of at least the central provision of the Halachah.

INTERMARRIAGE: FORUM FOR DEBATE

The intellectual incompatability of the Reines and Petuchowski positions is readily apparent. From the former standpoint, any effort to introduce discipline into Reform Judaism would violate the most fundamental of Reform principles, that of personal freedom, and thus is anathema. From the other point of view, to encourage people to be so self-legislating that they can claim the religious right to violate some of the most sacred remaining practices of our people is an utter perversion of the title Judaism. The polarization of Reform Judaism in recent years tended toward these extreme, contradictory positions.

The actual issue which raised matters to a new height of acrimony in the early 1970s was intermarriage. It became the battleground over which the banners of freedom and discipline were variously raised. In 1909 the CCAR had passed a resolution discouraging the practice by some rabbis of performing marriages between a Jew and non-Jew. As this practice increased during the 1960s, a number of rabbis felt it was important to take a stronger stand on this matter in the hope of reversing the trend or, alternatively, accepting the inevitable and seeking to win the families to Judaism, to mitigate the old condemnation, and give guidance as to what best might be done in the case of an intermarriage. The issue became explosive, for behind it lay hidden the worries about the future of Reform Judaism outlined above. After some years of trying to avoid a showdown, the CCAR in 1973 passed a resolution reaffirming its previous stand and calling upon its members to refrain from officiating at intermarriages. Read today, the wording of the resolution may seem relatively mild, yet the Conference had so rarely expressed an opinion about the beliefs or actions of some minority of its members that the passage of the resolution was seen as the beginning of a new era of Reform Jewish discipline, dolefully by some, gleefully by others. Freedom, autonomy, and the continuity of Reform Judaism were the battle cries on one side. The need for Jewish discipline, for strengthening our loyalty to Jewish tradition, and consideration for the Jewish people as a whole were the rallying calls on the other side. The minority went so far as to organize into a group called the Association for a Progressive Reform Judaism. Though the Association in due course said it would only operate as a caucus within the Conference, nonetheless its existence threatened to split the Reform rabbinate into two warring armies. This was the situation in which Robert Kahn, president of the Conference, proposed in his opening address at the 1975 annual meeting a compromise platform. The Conference accepted Kahn's idea and proposed that a committee be appointed to use Kahn's proposal as a basis upon which to draw up such a statement of contemporary Reform Jewish unity. Though Kahn had not directly dealt with the issue of diversity in his document, the committee decided that, despite the intellectual and emotional difficulties involved, it was important to do so as a prelude to anything substantive which the document might then go on to say. This was the problem, then, to which the third of the *Centenary Perspective*'s introductory paragraphs is a response.

CHAPTER TWELVE

The Response, I: Ten Affirmations of Autonomy

The committee made a strong, even ringing affirmation of the Reform commitment to individual freedom. I know of no Reform document which does so this plainly and this positively. I see ten separate espousals of this position in this paragraph and I want to point out each of them.

1. A COMMITMENT TO PERSONAL FREEDOM

"Reform Jews respond to change in various ways, according to the Reform principle of the autonomy of the individual." The paragraph begins with an assertion that is unparalleled in the rest of the document. Without qualification or hedging it says flatly that there is a "Reform principle of the autonomy of the individual." All that follows in these sentences on Reform diversity is derived from that statement and, I would argue, much of what follows in the document as a whole. Rather than reiterate what has been said above about the meaning and importance of autonomy in Reform Judaism, let us concentrate our attention on the various ways this "principle" is elaborated in what follows.

114

2. AN INCLINATION TO DIVERSITY

"Reform Judaism does more than tolerate diversity; it engenders it." The intellectual stability and social conformity of earlier generations masked this reality. Yet if Reform proclaims the autonomy of the individual, it thereby fosters a variety of views in its midst. People are diverse and therefore will often see with a unique vision. In changing times when their situation is unclear and confusing, they are likely to wind up with many different ideas as to what ought to be done. True, most of us fear being thought different, and institutions find that efficiency of operation demands a limit to diversity. Thus we surrender our peculiar notions for personal serenity or social quiet. At best, then, we are fortunate when there is some tolerance of difference. However, if Reform is serious about individual autonomy, it must positively encourage dissent and pluralism. (I think there are some limits to this "principle," but in the next few pages I intend to set aside all such qualifications and show how strongly the *Centenary Perspective* supports personal freedom in Reform Judaism. The reader who cannot stand seeing this theme out of context should read the next chapter before continuing with the discussion of the eight other statements affirming autonomy.)

3. AN UNDERSTANDING OF THE COMPLEXITIES OF OUR TIMES

"In our uncertain historical situation we must expect to have far greater diversity than previous generations knew." Perhaps each era sees itself as more complex than previous ones. We certainly feel that the gap between our ideals and the plans by which we might try to put them into effect has grown frighteningly large. Our Reform predecessors not only had greater intellectual and social stability from which to proceed, but they were reasonably confident about the projects which would realize their dreams. So much has failed that we once counted on that we are increasingly skeptical of all nearly utopian proposals. We have come to see old problems—ignorance, prejudice, exploitation—as far more complex than we thought. Wherever we turn new and disturbing problems face us—Jewish survival despite democracy, world hunger despite productivity, overpopulation, the depletion of resources and ecological disaster. Worst of all, we now have to believe that new and unsettling problems await us no matter what we do. In such an uncertain time we cannot expect the relative agreement which characterized our movement for so many decades. A historical situation of diverse and shifting currents will move us in many different ways.

4. AN ACCEPTANCE OF DIVERSITY

We need to learn to "live with diversity without stifling dissent." The easiest response to make to those who differ with us is to use our power to silence them, or to coerce their assent. That is a daily reality everywhere from family life to government. Most institutions are ambivalent about individualism. They proclaim its worth but normally put organizational needs above individual expression. Parents invoke experience and the power of the purse, governments prate of national security. Since Reform Judaism makes personal autonomy a principle, it cannot stop listening to voices of conscience raised in its midst or margins without self-negating inconsistency. For it to silence individuality by administrative manipulation or coercive legislation would be heinous.

5. A BELIEF IN PROCESS

"We stand open to any position. . . ." A special frame of mind is necessary to live with freedom, particularly in a time when the range of opinions radically widens. The skills which our forebears evolved when they first came in contact with democracy and applied it to Jewish life were apparently adequate to the variety of expression of their day. They hardly seem so in our time of greater clash of ideas. Decorum does not work as restrictively for us as it did for them. We need greater patience, more stamina, even a deeper faith in the process if we are to be receptive to Reform's contemporary range of opinion. We need to learn to give an honest hearing to positions we deeply oppose and to listen to points of view we would sooner ignore than refute. With greater diversity in its midst, Reform requires a broader openness of its adherents.

6. A BROAD STANCE

". . . open to any position . . . advocated in the spirit of Reform Jewish beliefs." The breadth of this statement is noteworthy. It speaks of positions consonant with the "spirit" of Reform, a characterization that explicitly refuses to restrict licit ideas to those consonant with some official document—say, the Columbus Platform or the services in *Gates of Prayer*. Moreover, "spirit" modifies a phrase which is purposely plural, "Reform Jewish beliefs." Here great enough latitude is given to reflect the pluralism in Reform Judaism today. (If my memory is reliable here, it was Rabbi Ronald Sobel who, in one of our redrafting sessions, called this possibility to the committee's attention and received their immediate, unanimous agreement.)

7. AN ALLOWANCE FOR INTERPRETATION

The committee then applied these strictures to

its own work: ". . . we may differ in our interpretation . . . of the ideas enunciated here. . . ." There is no claim, explicit or otherwise, that this document provides an unequivocal, one-leveled definition of what constitutes a proper Reform Jewish belief. The *Centenary Perspective* may be an official document of the Central Conference of American Rabbis, but like all documents—and by specific design—it will speak to different people in different ways. It was often phrased to allow for multiple interpretation, for the committee knew that on a number of issues there are varied Reform intellectual positions. And with changing times the text will be asked different questions and be read from fresh perspectives, most certainly producing impressions that cannot today be anticipated.

8. A CALL FOR ALTERNATIVE ACTIONS

The same is true of the "application of the ideas enunciated here." The move from ideas to specific courses of action almost always involves a greater variety of opinion than the mere intellectual interpretation of a text.

9. A REJECTION OF RIGID EVALUATION

Having endorsed diversity to this extent may disturb some people. They will find such liberalism emotionally unacceptable and organizationally regressive. The document rejects any evaluation, saying, "we accept such differences as precious."

10. A COMMITMENT TO THE VALUE OF DIVERSITY

The document even specifies just what it is about vigorous differences of opinion that is so valuable: ". . . we . . . see in them Judaism's best hope for confronting whatever the future holds for us." Is this not the central faith of Reform Judaism, that as times change new ideas are needed to meet them? If we do not stand open to them, Judaism will petrify. Not every hour demands a modification of thought of practice, and not every fresh proposal is a better way of keeping Judaism vital. But since our certainties are few and our times so unstable, we need to be open to the new ideas which, as the idea of Reform itself did, make possible the faithful continuity of Judaism.

I reiterate: I do not know of a more forthright organizational avowal of Reform Jewish individualism. For all that the document can be read in many ways, I do not see how this heavily supported personalism can be interpreted out of the document.

A REJECTION OF TRADITIONAL HALACHAH

If that is so, then the document must be understood as rejecting the possibility that traditional

Jewish discipline, Halachah as it is understood in Orthodoxy, can be a part of Reform Judaism. For Halachah says that, regardless of personal will, the individual must do what the Torah says. Such a doctrine is incompatible with Reform Judaism's teaching about personal autonomy. I am not saying that Reform Jews find no value in tradition, or that they cannot personally accept its laws as binding upon them, or that they may not decide for the sake of peace in Reform Judaism or among all religious Jews, to abide by some of its provisions. I also am not saying that such people, particular congregations, or even our movement may not, based upon this view of individualism, create some sort of Reform Jewish "Halachah." I think using the traditional term but not intending its sense of an authority which overrides conscience is so radical a shift of meaning that one must use quotation marks to signify this reinterpretation. Anything less is intellectually irresponsible, perhaps even deceitful.

Just what sort of discipline a community committed to personal autonomy might have is difficult to say, which is why our thinkers have had trouble trying to clarify what might be meant by a Reform Jewish "Halachah." In any case, I read the *Centenary Perspective* as saying that the concept of Halachah, as that term is traditionally understood, is not compatible with Reform Judaism. This passionate espousal of freedom, however, must be taken in conjunction with another theme which sounds through the document's response to the problem of Reform diversity: the limits placed on intellectual autonomy.

CHAPTER THIRTEEN

The Response, II:
Six Limits to Intellectual Autonomy

The *Centenary Perspective*, for all its affirmation of autonomy, sets certain limits on its legitimate Reform Jewish exercise. This is the most sensitive area, for liberals are loathe to impinge on anyone's freedom. Nonetheless, for all the tentativeness with which they are given, I see the *Perspective* indicating six conditions for the proper Reform Jewish use of personal freedom.[4]

1. PREVENTING A PARALYSIS OF ACTION

We need to learn to "live with diversity . . . without paralyzing our ability to take positive action." One can spend so much time remaining open to diverse views or gathering data that one never does anything else. If Judaism is a religion of deed, that is sinful.

---

[4]This paragraph of the *Perspective*, of course, deals only with intellectual matters. Section IV of the document deals with the limits of autonomy in relation to acts, that is, religious duties. The conditions laid down there are specific, perhaps because the abstract notion has already been dealt with here, perhaps because action can be spoken of much more concretely than can ideas. See *Reform Judaism Today: How We Live*, Part II.

At some point there is a Jewish obligation to act which supersedes the need to attend to every conscientious view. That is true of organizations as well as individuals. Our religion is a communal as well as a personal matter—see section II of the *Centenary Perspective*, "The People, Israel." At times the need of the Jews to take combined action takes precedence over our commitment to diversity. Obviously this can become the basis for organizational tyranny. Leaders often think that getting their programs approved is far more important than listening to different and deviant opinion. Our organizations, particularly our massive conventions, have a democracy that leaves us feeling frustrated, even violated. Yet for all that there have been abuses of our autonomy in the name of the Jewish people, of the corporate good—which is a significant value in Judaism and must not be ignored in our movement. Though we should make a continual effort to have our institutions and leaders be more responsive to the rights of the individual conscience, our community also legitimately lays some claim upon the single selves who comprise it.

2. SETTING LIMITS TO UNINFORMED DEBATE

"We stand open to any position thoughtfully . . . advocated. . . ." Perhaps that should not need statement. Yet all of us in Jewish life have had to bear with people who insist on expressing their conscience without using their minds. On many matters requiring decision there is a substantial body of learned opinion, sometimes even facts. One owes it to oneself and equally to one's community to know something of what has been said on a given topic and what data is relevant to it. Conscience is no excuse for ignorance or mental sloth. It does not excuse us from knowing something substantial about the Judaism over which we are standing in judgment. I do not mean that only rabbis and professors can make proper decisions or that only they have a right to speak in the Jewish community. I do think that opinions whose major attraction is that they are new or different are not thereby always deserving of serious attention. The use of freedom to differ with others presumes that one will bring as much learning and wisdom to bear on a matter as one can reasonably muster. The idea that so long as Jews feel they are sincere Reform will accept their mindless, willful choices is refuted by this statement.

3. DEMANDING CONSCIENTIOUS ADVOCACY

Positions ought also to be "conscientiously" advocated. This is a far more difficult criterion to apply. It calls on us to ask whether the person offering the unusual view deeply and truly believes it. In recent years we have seen much dissent, and almost every large organization has a member or two who disagrees with everything out of neurosis or willfulness, not as a matter of the most ultimate commitment one can make. It is one thing to claim our attention to your conscience and another to say we must be open to your hostility or exhibitionism. To dismiss those with whom one vigorously disagrees as sick or self-serving can easily be a form of repression, yet at some point the personal judgment must be made. And in religious matters it is of special importance.

4. REQUIRING A REFORM JEWISH PERSPECTIVE

These general considerations, which might apply to almost any social group concerned with affairs of the human spirit, lead on to the specific circumstances of our diversity, namely that they take place within the Reform Jewish movement. We therefore must limit the exercise of freedom in our midst to positions which can be advocated in "the spirit of Reform Jewish beliefs." As noted above, that phrase deliberately lays down a very broad spectrum within which acceptable opinion may be found. It is stated with such openness precisely because it sets a limit on our autonomy. It does not say we must accept anything anybody might thoughtfully and conscientiously advocate. There are other Reform Jewish beliefs than that of a personal autonomy, and they set the context within which our autonomy is legitimately exercised. To keep those limits as open as we can, we refuse to try to be precise about what these beliefs are or include. That would be dogma. Still, we know we have them. Again, we shall certainly want to be most cautious in arguing that some proposals go beyond the spirit of our beliefs. That would be to declare them heresy. Still some ideas are out of our world of faith. Reform Judaism is not just a cipher which one fills in as one pleases. We will show extraordinary forebearance to all sorts of eccentric views, for we are genuinely committed to personal autonomy; but we are also committed to continuity of the Jewish tradition, and we see the former limited by the latter even as Reform has always stressed that the latter is limited by the former.

5. OPERATING WITHIN REFORM BELIEFS

The *Centenary Perspective* is not a creed or a statement of dogma, but it is also not without high Reform Jewish significance. It may be open to a number of interpretations, but its sentences have content. Indeed, if it is believable when it speaks of autonomy, it must be equally believable when it speaks of its limits. The phrase "the spirit of Reform Jewish beliefs" is paraphrased in the next sentence by the words "the ideas enunciated here." What follows in the document is, in fact, the beliefs of Reform Judaism, at least those that the overwhelming majority of Reform rabbis, organized in the Conference, formally consider to be basic to our movement. They have not approved such documents often. They did not take this one lightly. They gave it a greater measure of support than anyone had guessed that they, in all their diversity, could grant it.

Moreover, there should be no confusion about what is the preface to the document and what constitutes its body. Autonomy and diversity are prefatory, not substantive concerns of Reform Judaism. God, the People Israel, Torah, and questions of our obligations constitute the major content of our religion. The *Centenary Perspective* by its very form implies that Reform Jews should exercise their personal freedom in the context of the Reform Jewish beliefs "enunciated here," or, if you will, in their spirit.

6. MAINTAINING THE THREAD OF UNITY

When all the talk of diversity is done, the paragraph concludes with the assertion that Jews have more in common than there is that separates them. We are an identifiable movement. We may be fractious and idiosyncratic, but we hang together. We can argue with each other in special intensity because we know we share special ties. As the statement puts it, "Yet in all our diversity we perceive a certain unity and we shall not allow our differences in some particulars to obscure what binds us together." Since that sentence introduces the body of the document, since this was the specific aim of drafting this document, what follows may be taken as a statement of this "certain unity" which "binds us together." But if we are together, we are not merely single, autonomous agents. Reform Jewish freedom must somehow operate within the ties which render us a community. Even to make possible our special communal brand of diversity, individuals must agree not to contradict the premises, as loosely specified as they may be, on which our community organizes itself.

BALANCING FREEDOM AND CONSTRAINT

Again, I do not see how it will be possible to read this text as placing no limits on personal freedom. Rather I see it as a forthright rejection of the view that Reform Judaism is committed only to autonomy, that the individual will is the unrestricted good of the Reform Jew. Considering the height of emotion over this issue at the time the committee came into being, the reception accorded this paragraph was phenomenal. In response to the working draft a few rabbis wrote to the committee opposing the wording of this paragraph on diversity or that of section IV on religious duties on the grounds that the document presumed to suggest limits to Reform Jewish choice. The number of such advocates of absolute freedom, three or four, was much smaller than anticipated. By contrast, there were very many expressions of support for the statement from people who had in the previous tense years advocated either the freedom or the "Halachah" positon. The committee thus felt that its balance between freedom and constraint represented the position of the overwhelming majority of Reform rabbis and so, while improving its language, continued on with the substance of its working draft. No additional comment was received when the final draft of the document was sent to the rabbis a month prior to the Conference, nor did anyone raise any questions on this topic in the floor discussion. I do not think any member of the committee dreamt when we first met in January 1976 that we would be able to speak to this explosive issue and gain such widespread approval.

Since above we divided our analysis of this paragraph in terms of its two contradictory themes, in the next chapter we will turn our attention to the balance revealed when the paragraph is taken as a whole.

CHAPTER FOURTEEN

The Response, III:
The Reform Jewish Dialectic

OUR TWO COMMITMENTS

The special challenges diversity sets before Reform Jews are described in this manner: "How we shall live with diversity without stifling dissent and without paralyzing our ability to take positive action will test our character and our principles." We propose to live with diversity and proudly call it, in the rubric for this paragraph, "the Hallmark of Reform." Yet we cannot give a rule which will cover all the difficulties that will arise as we bring our differences of opinion to bear on our problems. The sentence only clarifies the polar dangers we must avoid, stifling dissent or being unable to act. However, we are reminded that our response in troublesome instances "will test our character and principles." The last term deserves our immediate attention. One would think that one's principles would settle what one ought to do. What is implied here is that Reform Jewish principles actually raise difficulties, for we begin with partially conflicting beliefs. We have autonomy, but there is a God whom we should follow and a living, historic Jewish people who stand in special relation to God, of which we are a part. Though we make our own choices, we do so as faithful Jews; or, if you prefer, though we are Jewish, we propose to be self-legislating. We are free individuals; and we are Jews. Not one without the other, at least not in the Reform Judaism described here. The very words *Reform Judaism* bring together the two basic commitments of our movement. We can reform because we assert our autonomy, where necessary against Jewish tradition and where desirable in support of our creativity; yet we are part of Judaism in an equally deep and rooted way. In all our individuality we know ourselves to stand in relation to the God of historic Jewish experience as part of the people of Israel.

Much of the time our setting out from two premises causes us little difficulty. We accept Jewish ethics both because they speak to us as free persons and because we are Jews. We observe the Passover Seder because it celebrates what we most deeply believe about being free and because it is our tradition's rich celebration of God who freed us from slavery to be a people specially devoted to God. Reform Judaism was founded on the intuition that people in the modern, post-Enlightenment world would properly insist on their autonomy and that Judaism could be reinterpreted so as to give proper scope for personal freedom while guiding it in authentic Jewish ways.

I have already indicated my belief that much

of Reform Jewish practice was created to harmonize these two principles. In some periods over the past century it looked as if a happy balance between these faiths had been worked out and Reform Jews seemed to have a stable sense of what it means to live freely and Jewishly. In recent years that adjustment has given way. For all its subordination of our Jewish duties to our free choice, some find the Reform way still too parochial, giving insufficient room for self-expression and self-development. Very many more, however, have felt that the older Reform style did not take our Jewishness seriously enough and made one of our primary concerns a matter of only secondary interest. While that may have made great sense a generation or two ago, recent history requires that Jewish survival be "of highest priority." To some extent, the presence of each of these tendencies in recent Reform thought prompted the opposing view to be more radical and led to the recent polarization of the movement.

ONE FAITH – TWO INCLINATIONS

The *Centenary Perspective* rejects the effort to turn Reform into a one-premise faith, whether that premise be autonomy or tradition. Rather it roundly affirms the dual basis of our movement. It vigorously asserts the autonomy of the individual to choose the right--yet for all that it is leery of restricting freedom, it insists that autonomy be exercised within a Reform Jewish sense of God, the people of Israel, Torah, and our obligations. And for all that it proclaims our Jewish faith and duties it says Reform Jews approach them in personal freedom. The *Centenary Perspective* thus dissociates itself from the recent rhetoric in Reform Judaism which has sought to identify autonomy of particularism as the single imperative of our movement. The centenary statement takes the position that absolutizing either thrust is wrong and that what makes Reform Judaism unique is our insistence upon both these premises at once. Balance, not which should dominate, has been our problem, particularly because we have had to raise particularism to a higher level than a previous generation had given it. I believe that the extraordinarily speedy and phenomenally widespread acceptance of this paragraph came because, once the Conference saw the two faiths expressed in proper juxtaposition to one another, they recognized that though they might wish to emphasize one or another side of the balance, this tandem affirmation expressed their basic faith, Reform and Jewish at once.

Rabbi Joseph Glaser, executive vice-president of the CCAR, said at the Executive Board meeting of April 1976 (which I attended to discuss the response of the membership to the working draft and elicit further comment) that he thought the tenor of the draft had already helped create a new sense of unity among the rabbis. Insofar as his judgment was correct, I think that the paragraph on diversity was particularly responsible for it. Yet I am also convinced that some of the combativeness of the Conference had already begun to wane as a result of the debate between Rabbi Gunther Plaut and Professor Eugene Mihaly which took place at the June 1975 Conference in Cincinnati. It was a confrontation between one of the leaders of the Halachah/"Halachah" group and one who had articulated many of the feelings of those who emphasized personal freedom. The program had an unusually large turnout of members and guests and, despite a late start and lengthy presentations, there was a concentration on the proceedings unusual for Conference sessions. The evening demonstrated, in my opinion, that when the rhetoric of tradition or autonomy was pared away, little separated the two men.

Rabbi Plaut was not prepared to require Reform rabbis to follow religious rules—Halachah—laid down by the Conference, though he did want Reform Jews, out of their freedom, to have a greater sense of religious discipline, thus favoring a Reform Jewish "Halachah." Professor Mihaly expounded the importance of individual decision to Reform Judaism but then linked that with a statement he had made to the Conference some years before that "there is no Judaism without Halachah." I do not know how many people heard the debate the way I did, but it seemed to me that much of the intellectual underpinning for the supposed division of our movement had been washed away by a confrontation that turned out to be an encounter.

TENSION AS A CONSTANT: THE DIALECTICAL STANCE

For all that, there are tensions today between the call of autonomy and of Jewish responsibility. The *Centenary Perspective* says we must hold fast to them both and limit the expression of the one by our simultaneous concern for the other. Just this causes our special Reform Jewish problem with diversity. As difficult as it is to live consistently with a single-premise faith, so it is more than doubly complex to try to move from two, occasionally conflicting, beliefs to build one life or movement. We Reform Jews are so diverse in our understanding of the implications of our faith because we hold fast to two fundamental commitments to which we can give different emphases in different situations. This is the root of our three major difficulties with Reform Jewish obligations—religious duties, the State of Israel and the Diaspora, and duties to our people and to humanity—to which the document gives its major attention. We would not have such problems were we single-minded about our freedom or our Jewish loyalty—or at least we would not have them with the special intensity they take on among Reform Jews. This explains why the centenary document is characterized by a continual balancing of the one faith against the other, of one set of responsibilities against the other. The technical term for dealing with beliefs held in tension is *dialectical.* The centennial document is dialectical in tone, for the nature of our contemporary Reform Jewish faith is dialectical, two-premised. Our belief literally requires two terms, *Reform* and *Judaism.* The more monolithic, autonomy-ethics-universalism-dominated Reform Judaism of previous generations logically produced more monochromatic documents. Such deductive consistency may have spoken their faith quite adequately. After "what we have learned," such a single-themed statement of Reform Jewish faith will not do for us. We can no longer claim that ours is a rational religion whose only essential premise is ethical monotheism. We are too deeply, fundamentally committed to the Jewish people and to God through the Jewish people for such a view, though it means sacrificing some consistency and any claim that our religion is philosophically based. Logic despises conflicting premises and abhors paradoxes, but people mostly live by them. We grow as persons largely by learning to live with the clashing demands made upon us. That is why the document speaks of diversity testing our "character," for precisely in those situations where reason cannot compel decision one must reach deeply into one's human resources in the hope of responding decently. No one can yet say what problems will confront the

Reform movement in the next few years or what clash of interests it may have to face. Sometimes intellect or conscience may enable most of us to see where we must take our stand. But if the trials of recent years are any guide, we shall regularly be thrown back beyond our reason to who we are and what we truly believe. That is not an unreasonable basis from which a religious movement should seek to meet the issues before it. And it should therefore give much of its energy to the development of the spiritual life of its members so they will have rich personal resources upon which to draw in such circumstances.

THE DIALECTIC IN ACTION

Perhaps, too, some people will see in the work of producing this centenary statement something of a Reform Jewish model of living with diversity. The committee represented most of the major shades of opinion represented in the Conference. They were, when they began, deeply divided about matters of procedure and substance, indeed even about the wisdom of producing a statement at all. Yet in the process of working with one another, respecting one another's differing faith and person, in the effort of reaching out to all our colleagues in the rabbinate, not passively but with active concern for every differing opinion we could elicit, we managed to create a document which, as it turned out (and to the surprise of many), spoke for ourselves and the overwhelming majority of the Reform rabbinate. For those of us on the committee it was a profoundly moving personal experience. We had ourselves come to "live with diversity without stifling dissent and without paralyzing our ability to take positive action." We felt that this effort had indeed tested "our character and our principles" and that, by God's grace and our earnest effort, we had not been found entirely wanting. We emerged with new faith in ourselves, in our commitments and to our movement, knowing that what we had managed to do in this effort others could do, perhaps better, in the many other difficult matters which today crowd the Reform agenda.

REFORM
JUDAISM TODAY

Book Two
WHAT WE BELIEVE

Book Two

WHAT
WE
BELIEVE

REFORM JUDAISM TODAY

Eugene B. Borowitz

BEHRMAN HOUSE, INC. New York

Library of Congress Cataloging in Publication Data

Borowitz, Eugene B.
  Reform Judaism Today.

  CONTENTS: Book 1. Reform in the process of
change. Book 2. What we believe. Book 3. How we
live.
  1. Central Conference of American Rabbis. Reform
Judaism, a centenary perspective. 2. Reform
Judaism—United States. I. Title.
BM197.B67   296.8'346   77-24676

Published by Behrman House, Inc.
1261 Broadway, New York, New York 10001

Produced in the U.S. of America

CONTENTS

PART I

An Introduction to the Principles

The paragraph on God in *Reform Judaism: A Centenary Perspective* opens the major portion of the statement, consisting of six numbered paragraphs, that rather naturally falls into two sections. Each of the headings in the latter section, paragraphs IV-VI, begins "Our Obligations," a theme examined here in terms of three contemporary concerns: religious duties, the State of Israel and the Diaspora, and service to the Jewish people and to humanity at large. The headings for paragraphs I-III, however, do not include such a phrase in common. Rabbi Jack Stern, Jr. pointed out in one of the last meetings of the committee drafting the *Centenary Perspective* that these paragraphs also have a common focus. He called them the "principles" of the statement, since they treat of God, the Jewish people, and Torah, and these constitute the basic beliefs of the Jewish community. There is, then, a nice balance to the substantive section of the document, with three paragraphs on principles balanced by three paragraphs on obligations. The symmetry was not consciously intended by those who

3

worked on or contributed to the shaping of the document. It was, however, a most congenial result of the drafting process, since it seemed to the committee to give balanced expression to their sense of Reform Judaism. Yet it was decided not to use a thematic title for these first three paragraphs. The terms *principles* and *beliefs* seemed rather grandiose, perhaps even somewhat dogmatic, and the committee preferred to avoid making such authoritative claims for their work.

The sense of proper balance was further borne out by the discrepancy in size between the exposition of the beliefs and that of the duties. The first three paragraphs are each much shorter than each of the last three. One might expect a religious document to stress theological principles, especially in so complicated a time as ours when belief does not come or stay easily. But historically that has not been true of Judaism. Our religion has always emphasized our duties more than any philosophy which might serve as their basis. This traditional Jewish concern with action more than creed is reflected here and is explicitly referred to at the beginning of the section on obligations, paragraph IV, on religious practice (on which, see chapters 12 to 15). This stress on what Jews should be doing was a conscious response to what seems the major interest of concerned Jews in our time. There is some spiritual search in our community, and a good

deal more questioning about Jewish identity—that is, just what being a Jew means
today. Most Jews, however, express their
Jewish intent in a rather Jewish way, by asking
what they should do. So books like *The Jewish
Catalog* or the Central Conference of American
Rabbis' *Shabbat Manual* are very much more in
demand than books on Jewish theology. Since
the *Centenary Perspective* is directed to a given
moment—the centenaries of the Union of
American Hebrew Congregations and the
Hebrew Union College-Jewish Institute of
Religion—it speaks to the present situation,
seeking to respond directly to its needs.

It should also be pointed out that these hundred years of nationally organized Reform
Judaism have yielded a certain measure of
agreement in the area of beliefs. Or, to put it
more precisely, we have arrived at a good working consensus as to what we hold in common
and what we can reasonably (though not
always comfortably!) leave to personal decision. Through the many months in which
hundreds of people commented on the various
drafts of the document there were no major
philosophic differences over what the text said
or did not say. The overwhelming majority of
Reform Rabbis—and, I suggest, Conservative
Rabbis and American Jews generally—shares a
common sense of modern Jewish belief. This
commonality is quite limited in its content, to
be sure, and it most certainly allows for variety

and development in Jewish faith in ways that go far beyond what our tradition knew or, more certainly, ever put in explicit form. The brevity of these first three paragraphs reflects the consolidation of that consensus; most fortunately, the committee was able to put it into words early in its work. Had it tried to say very much more, it would have passed into the realm of controversy. Knowing what is to be left to individual opinion is also a major part of reaching social agreement.

There was an additional reason for being brief about matters of basic Jewish belief. In this sort of format one cannot hope to say very much to begin with. Would expanding the section on God from five sentences to eight or even twenty suffice to make a major difference in answering our questions about God? Further, saying more, not being brief almost to the point of terseness, might make it seem as if enough *had* been said, that this was somehow as much as most people needed to know. By keeping these paragraphs as short as they reasonably could be, the committee tried to signal the reader that they are but a bare introduction to the most important matters of Jewish faith. Their very form calls for more study and investigation. Having said only about as much as one can say to someone standing on one foot, they carry with them Hillel's legendary closing dictum—is it not also part of his concise description of Torah?—"Go study!"

PART II

God

The affirmation of God has always been essential to
our people's will to survive. In our struggle through the

I.
God

centuries to preserve our faith we have
experienced and conceived of God in
many ways. The trials of our own time
and the challenges of modern culture have made steady
belief and clear understanding difficult for some.
Nevertheless, we ground our lives, personally and communally, on God's reality and remain open to new
experiences and conceptions of the Divine. Amid the
mystery we call life, we affirm that human beings,
created in God's image, share in God's eternality
despite the mystery we call death.

From the Centenary Perspective

7

CHAPTER ONE

Jewish Survival and Our Sense of God

RELYING ON INTUITION

When people do talk about belief in God in our time they tend to do so in personal terms, often quite personal, referring to their innermost feelings and the like. In part that has to do with the Protestant influence on our culture. Against the authority of the Catholic Church, Luther emphasized what individuals knew to be true as God gave them, personally, the truth. Over the centuries, particularly in the United States, this Protestant teaching has become associated with the notion of conversion as "seeing the light" and with the phenomenon of revival movements. This way of being religious, with its emphasis on the emotions and the change effected on one's personality, has generally been uncongenial to Jews. Conversion in Judaism is a matter of education and will, not the result of a special gift of God. Besides, most Jews are born into the Jewish relationship with God. They may know moments of great personal intimacy with God—the Psalms show how far back this goes in our tradition—but what goes on *inside* the

9

Jew is not the major focus of the Jew's religious life.

For cultural and philosophical reasons, too, Jews have been uncomfortable with the stress on subjectivity. Being so much a part of big-city, secular life, they find it bringing God too much into the foreground of existence. Being largely university-trained and intellectually oriented, they are skeptical of religious claims that seem so much based on emotion and so little attuned to reason. Nonetheless, when modern Jews have talked about God, they too have done so in personal terms—though, I hasten to add, these have generally been philosophical. The individual or individual experience has been the starting point of most modern Jewish religious thought. The most common way of pointing to God has been to refer to the person's conscience, to insist that its mandates derive from something greater than what we have been taught by our families or our society, that its ultimate source is God. More rigorous intellectual arguments work from the order we intuit in a highly complex universe, or the way our search for all-embracing ideas is the summit of all our thinking, and the testimony that behind all things is the God who is One. Or, beginning with the feeling aspects of being human, we describe our awe that anything exists, our wonder that existence is so grand and thus our sensitivity to God who is its ground. We then regularly use interesting

verbs to describe our faith: we "sense," or
"feel," or "know" there is a God, all in ways
that we do not commonly use these verbs (and
thus my quotation marks). In each case the
way to God, whether more rational or more
intuitive, is personal and inner.

UNDERSTANDING OURSELVES
THROUGH OUR BELIEFS

There is good reason for modern Jewish thinkers to follow this line of thought while recognizing its possible Protestant background. In
the late eighteenth century a crisis developed in
humanity's thinking about religion—about
science, too, I should add. Previously people
had little difficulty believing that if we could
think about the world quite clearly in our
minds, then we could be fairly certain of what
the world itself was. The crisis came when it
was pointed out, in ways which have been
practically impossible to ignore ever since, that
what we think about the world might say more
about us and the way we think than it says
about the world. For religion that meant that
our ideas about God—more specifically, our
proofs that God was "out there,"—also said
more about us than about reality. Since then,
reasoning about religion has had to start with
what we know about ourselves, how we think
or what we experience, our ethical or esthetic
sense. Whatever certainty we can have must
start with us. Such belief as we will affirm must

first convince us personally. We feel we not
only have the right to question those who
come to us asking us to believe things, but that
we have a duty to do so if we are to be true to
ourselves, the one thing we really have and
know. Skepticism is part of our modern sensibility; it is thus a necessary part of modern
believing. We have faith and question it,
moving on thereby to deeper, clearer faith and
to more searching questions. Our sort of believing cannot for long stand still. So all modern
religious thought, general and Jewish, focuses
upon the individual, working from the individual to God, or, for traditionalists, showing
how the individual is fulfilled by God's
revelation.

THE SCOPE OF PERSONAL AUTONOMY

Individualism has been fundamental to Reform
Judaism. The earliest Reform Jews thought
mostly in terms of the rights of their generation as against those of the tradition. Specifically they felt they were as entitled to define
what a Jewish life meant in their radically
changed social situation, as previous generations had been in their time and place.
Gradually this became the right of individual
Reform Jews to determine for themselves what
they would believe and, more importantly,
what they would do, continuing the tradition
or creating new patterns of Jewish life. The
century of Reform Jewish history which the

Centenary Perspective has in view cannot be understood without this growing emphasis on individualism, what contemporary writers often term personal autonomy. The first historical paragraph of the *Centenary Perspective* mentions this as one of the things that Reform Judaism has taught many modern Jews, that "Jewish obligation begins with the informed will of every individual." This is the basis for the diversity in Reform Judaism, discussed in the last of the historical paragraphs of the *Centenary Perspective*, and it shapes the special problems and opportunities involved in defining the Reform Jew's religious duties (section IV, paragraph III). Giving such power to the individual is the basis of Reform Judaism's difference not only from Orthodoxy but from much of Conservative Judaism as well.

In Orthodoxy, what God has made known in the Torah and the Torah tradition is more important than what the individual comes to believe is true—or, to put it more precisely, the complete fulfillment of one's individuality as a Jew is to be found in the Torah as given by God and interpreted by our modern sages. In Conservative Judaism the individual mind and conscience may be granted greater influence, but individuals should not define Jewish observance for themselves but should, as in the past, follow the leadership given a modern, observant community through an official body of its scholars. Reform Jews, agreeing that the Torah tradition provides invaluable guidance and that scholars are uniquely equipped to discern the lessons of the past, nonetheless emphasize the right of individual Jews to make the final decision as to what constitutes Jewish belief and practice for them. The Reform respect for personal autonomy carries that far.

JEWISH IDENTITY AND JEWISH SURVIVAL

Yet this distinctive Reform Jewish emphasis on individualism is absent from the opening of this paragraph on God. Mostly that is because it can be taken for granted. Years of Reform Jewish teaching about thinking for oneself may be counted on as the background readers will bring to this statement. Since it is concise and directed to the immediate, centenary situation of Reform Judaism, it concentrates on the relation of the Jewish people's age-old will to survive and its affirmation of God. The emphasis is communal, not individual, for this has been the special concern of recent years. The Holocaust, the accomplishments of the State of Israel, and, more dramatically, the threats to Israel's existence have made most American Jews realize how much their precious individuality is tied to the Jewish people. And Jewish identity has again largely become a question of Jewish survival, whether that of the State of Israel, of Jews in the Soviet Union or other oppressive countries, or of Jewish life in the United States darkly threatened by apathy, ignorance, and intermarriage. Even as individualism highlighted Reform Judaism's development through much of this past century, so the responsibilities and hopes of Jewish peoplehood have since the 1950s and '60s come to the fore of Reform Jewish consciousness. As the second historical paragraph notes, Reform Jews have learned from recent history "new heights of aspiration and devotion" to the Jewish people and that its survival ... is of highest priority."

Paradoxical as it may seem, we see in this survival of the Jews despite everything an indication that God is real. That the Jews have endured these many centuries in dignity and service; that they continue to be a living presence in history while many of their oppressors have effectively died; that they have refused to stop being Jews and linking their lives with the Torah despite prejudice and persecution; that in the face of the unprecedented tragedies of our time they remain humanly undefeated and Jewishly determined; that regardless of their widespread and manifest faithlessness they remain recognizably loyal to the Jewish tradition and its messianic outlook—all this is not mere biological urge, historical quirk, or sociological oddity. Jewish existence reflects something far transcending itself. We are skeptics, yet we know Jewish history says something about God. We do not believe much, but in the presence of the indomitable Jewish will to be and be Jewish, we sense God's power. We care about the Jews because— quietly, to be sure—we care about God. When we worry about the Jews and their future we naturally wonder where God is and why God doesn't do more to help us. This is not some childish remnant in our psyche, merely an infantile hope that Daddy/Mommy will save us. It is our deep, bedrock sense that, odd as it may sound to say it so plainly, the Jews are involved with God. And the *Centenary Perspective* points to the fact that in our time we gain a special sense of God's reality by our intimate involvement with the Jews.

SEEING GOD'S ROLE IN JEWISH SURVIVAL

More, *The Perspective* says that Jews have always known that their existence had more than tribal worth. So they took courage from knowing that their struggle to exist and to do so in decency was substantially for God's sake. And they hoped that as they put forth their effort so God would, in the mysterious ways that God affects human affairs, help them. Many individual Jews and Jewish communities were lost in the process. The Jewish people has survived. In inexplicably roundabout ways God's protection has manifested itself. We today are far less likely to await God's active providence. Yet we also believe that as we work for our people, we work for what is most precious and significant in the universe and draw its power to ourselves.

Here, as in so much of the *Centenary Perspective,* a balance is struck between two themes, in this case devotion to God and devotion to our people. Seeing diverse aspects of our faith in relation to one another keeps them from being taken in isolation and thus extended to unfortunate extremes. Thus to concentrate one's Jewishness so fully on belief in God that one has no room left in one's heart or will for the Jewish people strikes us as so self-centered an individualism as hardly worthy of consideration for the title *Judaism.* Yet, similarly, to be so devoted to the survival of the Jewish people as to forget that there is a God and that this people takes its significance from its relationship with God seems an odd way for the people of the Torah to hope to have a future—though considering the threats to the Jewish people in our time errors on this side of the spectrum are easy to understand and forgive.

THE PHILOSOPHICAL PROBLEM

Incidentally, this contemporary Jewish concern with corporate identity sets a special problem before modern Jewish philosophers. Thinkers of a previous generation clarified the individual aspects of being a Jew. Much of their teaching remains valid and is indispensable to any future philosophy of Judaism. It is, as noted above, the accepted background for all the topics treated in the *Centenary Perspective*. But now the problem arises, how can we balance their individualism with our sense of equally being members of a people? Can we find a way to describe our intuition that Jewish history testifies to God's reality which will be as convincing as the ways preceding philosophers moved from individual experience to God? The problems are formidable, particularly as modern philosophy gives almost no credence to group experience or group authority. The *Perspective* therefore leaves this matter, as so many others, to the scholars and their deliberations.

CHAPTER TWO

The Different Ways of Knowing God

FAITH AND DOUBT

There is a tendency to think that Jews of other eras had unfaltering faith and never were troubled by doubts about God. Mostly that is romantic nonsense. There is hardly a major Jewish book in which problems of belief do not come to the fore. Philosophers like Saadia and Maimonides write in the introductions to their works that they were prompted to set down their ideas because Jews in their time were so confused and doubting.

The major difference between previous ages and ours is that once most people and cultures were religious. Today religion is on the defensive in intellectual circles, and faith seems more the exception than the rule. Yet, while understanding God is particularly difficult in our secular time, it has always been something of a problem. Our questioning is not utterly unprecedented and thus not thoroughly un-Jewish. If anything—and this is the reflection of our modern view of life and history—we cannot imagine that any great idea could stay alive and meaningful if it had not been subject to doubt

19

and change. Jews lived among many religious groups: idolaters, Zoroastrians, Christians, Muslims. They lived in many climates, cultures, societies, economies, governments. It is inconceivable to us that they were never influenced by these experiences, that their basic ideas always remained the same. Were someone able to show such stability over several thousand years we would immediately guess that what survived had very little validity.

A DYNAMIC SENSE OF TRUTH

Premodern people did not look at change this way. They thought permanence was the mark of truth. Something that was true never changed, or never did so in any significant way. We still retain something of that sense. If truth changes, that implies there must be several truths, which seems a contradiction in terms. Jewish faith would say that, as there is one God, there is ultimately only one truth. The problem we face, however, is whether anybody but God can know it—the one, whole truth. Even if the premoderns didn't think they knew it all, they thought they knew much of it. We are more modest. We think the most we can claim is that we are growing toward such comprehensive understanding—though every once in a while it looks as if what we thought was a better sense of truth turns out to be a lot less than that. Our sense of truth is dynamic, moving, and we do not see why, whether previous generations were conscious of it or not, it should not have been that way in the past.

A major revolution took place when this notion of truth-as-growing—that is, of change—came into our understanding of Judaism. For if Judaism had changed in the past, then there was no reason why it could not change in the present. More, if change was the means to Jewish survival, then those who refused to change Judaism were dooming the Jewish people. There is, then, a moral, divine imperative to change when it is needed to meet the exigencies of the time. This was the intuition which sustained the Reform Jews of the early nineteenth century. They knew that a westernized, participating Jewry could not merely adapt a few of the patterns and practices of a Jewry that had been segregated for centuries. They knew some major changes were required, and boldly they set out to make them. In the arguments which ensued they proved that this was what had been done in Judaism in the past. They created the "Science of Judaism"—our poor translation of an important German term—*Wissenschaft des Judentum*—by rigorously applying the notion of change to the history of their people. In the hands of an early Reform Jewish master like Abraham Geiger the idea so illuminated the past records of the Jewish people that, as the opening paragraphs of the *Centenary Perspective* testify, its place in Judaism has by now been accepted by almost all Jews.

The Jewish sense of God has been no exception to this rule. Some things seem to have remained relatively stable. Chief of these is the notion that God is one. Yet scholars have pointed to places in the Bible where it seems as if God rules only over the Land of Israel, implying that there are other gods elsewhere. Another supposition has it that there were other divine beings, though these did not reach God's status. Another stable feature would seem to be God's own name, which we regularly do not pronounce, substituting instead *Adonai,* "My Lord." Yet almost everyone knows that there are other names for God in the Bible and that the rabbis and the mystics invented other titles by which to call God. As we now study the record of the way Jews historically have talked about God it seems quite clear that time and temperament, culture and personality have always had a part in shaping Jewish views of God.

EXPERIENCE AND CONCEPTION

The *Centenary Perspective* points to both what we have "experienced" and what we have "conceived" of God. The difference between them is important enough to merit some attention. Experience covers a great range of what people go through. What they conceive is limited to that to which they give intellectual form and expression, generally their concepts and ideas. For a religion as sophisticated and intellectual as Judaism, conceiving of God can be quite important. Yet most people find such abstraction beyond them. They believe in God and, insofar as that is based on something in their lives (or the life of their people, like the giving of the Law at Sinai), we say they have experienced God. It once would have seemed self-evident that some sort of religious experience is part of most people's lives, but contemporary society is quite stringent in getting us to repress our sense of the sacred. Nonetheless, many people can remember occasions when God was real to them. But few people are theologians. They do not try to create a pattern of ideas which will adequately explain what they have felt. Somewhere between the many who experience and the elite who philosophize are the poets and storytellers who put their sense of God into words that very many people can respond to and be inspired by. We are more likely to recognize God as a Process than as a Shepherd, yet there is something in that ancient way of depicting God that still moves us, and it is not clear how many of our modern terms for God will survive for centuries, not to ask about millennia. Modern Jews of whatever personal bent can be grateful for the extraordinary variety of the Jewish effort to get close to God, for it gives them courage in their own quest and guidance in making their own formulations.

Reform Jews of an earlier period were somewhat less open than this to the diversity of Jewish relationships with God. They thought of Judaism, and certainly of Reform Judaism, as a rational religion. By this they meant, at least, that modern people, wanting to think for themselves and accepting only what they felt was believable, would find Reform Judaism's appeal to the mind more than to tradition particularly appealing. They also believed that Judaism addressed itself essentially to the intellect—in which they included the moral and esthetic senses—and that its chief contribution to humanity was its way of thinking about God, what they called Judaism's God-idea or concept of God. One can give good reasons for their taking this position. In their day it was critical to demonstrate that superstition and magic were not essential to Jewish belief and practice, that the fundamental truth of Judaism was equal to and compatible with the best of modern science and philosophy. Their emphasis on ethics as a chief manifestation of Jewish piety and their demonstration that Jews share in the universal concerns and responsibilities of humankind were crucial to generations of Jews emerging from ghetto segregation, and they remain important teachings today.

Yet identifying Reform Judaism so closely with rationality also caused problems. If our religion is mainly a matter of the mind, then what happens to our heart and its devotion, to the prayer, the ritual, the simple human trust that once were such important parts of Jewish piety? As people are more than rational beings, so religion is rightly more than an intellectual affair. This critique is less than fair to those early Reform Jews who courageously pioneered the new forms of being Jewish from which we all still derive. These rationalists, it should be remembered, fostered the development of modern Jewish music and liturgies. They were not so narrowly philosophical as to refuse to speak to the heart. Yet they were very much more concerned with conceiving of God rather than with experiencing God. With God essentially an idea, later Reform Jews found their practice of Judaism somewhat cold and unmoving. The present generation, while not denying the validity or value of the intellectual approach to God, recognizes that Judaism has been and today should be equally hospitable to those whose relation to God is of that more personal, inexpressible, varied sort we call experience.

CHAPTER THREE

The Special Problems of Belief in Our Time

Though Jews have always had something of a problem finding or conceptualizing God, we can identify two special sources of difficulty in this regard in our time: the events of history and the challenges of culture. As recently as the late 1950s the religious literature of the Jewish community would have emphasized the latter rather than the former.

HISTORY AS AFFECTIVE EXPERIENCE

When we speak of the trials of history now, our minds immediately move to the Holocaust and to the traumas in the United States and the world of the early 1970s. Yet the Holocaust did not emerge as a major Jewish religious issue until the mid-1960s. No one is quite sure why. The facts were known in 1945 as the war in Europe came to an end, and in the next year or two pictures and documents regularly circulated in the American Jewish community. They had some effect upon us, yet there is no equivalent in the literature of that time to the debate concerning the "meaning" of the Holocaust which took place twenty years later. The

26

easiest explanations are psychological. The pain was too great and we wanted to forget it. We felt so guilty at having survived, even at a distance, or at having done so little, although almost all American Jews knew nothing of what was going on, that we wanted to forget what had happened. Or, more positively, we channeled our feelings into doing things for the survivors. There were European refugees to care for, a State of Israel to be founded and then supported, immigrants to the United States to help. We were caught up in America's gigantic social relocation, its economic expansion and consequent rush to suburbia which plunged us into forming new Jewish communities and building new Jewish institutions. Was there something about the civil rights movement of the early '60s that roused us to what had happened when good people in Germany stood idly by? Or was it the capture and trial of Eichmann? Or the development of a Christian death-of-God movement which made it socially acceptable for American Jews to raise doubts about God? Or were we finally secure enough in our Jewishness and Americanism to raise such questions? The answers are by no means clear. Until the mid-1960s, however, it was culture, not history, which disturbed Jewish belief most.

THE CHALLENGES OF CULTURE

The challenge had come first from the triumphs

of science. Through the post-World War II period there were many American Jews who felt that the Jewish sense of God needed radical reconstruction in terms of what science said about reality. They worried about the Genesis story of creation as against current astronomical speculations and the theory of evolution; about the miracles of the Bible as against the scientific implausibility of such stories; and about the biblical images of God as having a face, an arm, or emotions. The standard liberal response was to invoke the idea of change. The Bible spoke in its language and we would speak in ours. Some of the Bible was "myth," a symbolic story, in which one used everyday events to describe a reality beyond the human—and so the stories of the Creation, Adam and Eve, and the Flood. Thus the facts of these tales may be faulted, but we cannot complain about the sense of ultimate reality contained in them. The miracles, too, seemed easily explicable as the exaggerated way people would tell of great events, particularly when they believed God had helped them at critical moments in history. And the Bible's anthropomorphic portrayals of God could be seen as an early and still appealing symbolism. This liberal way of reading the problem passages of the Bible became rather widely accepted among American Jewry. Nonetheless, to this day there are people who emerge from their religious education—or the lack of it—and are shocked

when they try to take some of the passages of
the Bible or prayerbook literally. This continuing experience has prompted some American
Jewish thinkers to call for a thoroughly revised
way of speaking about God. They suggest
talking of divinity in thoroughly scientific
terms, most usually in terms of the ordering
process in nature.

Similar problems arose from other aspects of
culture. Psychoanalysis reduced all inner experience of God to wish fulfillment or the projection of father/mother into the universe to
love/judge us, depending on our psychic needs.
Sociology and anthropology came along to
show us how many of the ideas and practices
we had thought unique in Judaism were paral-
leled in other cultures and were therefore best
explained as human needs rather than God's
commands. The Marxians insisted that religion
was fundamentally a means with which the
upper classes keep the lower classes from rebel-
ling, and exposed Judaism as more concerned
with maintaining the etiquette of the newly
arrived upper-middle class than with serving
God with any seriousness. In general, the
vibrant, exciting cultural activities of our time
were secular—that is, they were nonreligious,
when they were not antireligious. This modern
culture made religious faith seem primitive or
regressive. For all Reform Judaism's efforts to
show that one could be fully modern and
Jewish at the same time, for all its philo-

sophical expertise, its moral passion, and its esthetic concerns, belief remained an odd way for a serious person to face reality.

QUESTIONS RAISED BY HISTORY AND CULTURE

Something of these challenges still remains in the Jewish community, but it does not seem to have the force today that it once had. I am convinced that the reason for this emphasis is a major shift in our center of confidence. Once we knew that whatever the university, the bestseller, the important magazine told us was true. Judaism would have to adjust to it—though it never managed to catch up. As long as we put our trust in high culture, we had doubts about Judaism. Only we have increasingly begun to doubt culture. We have been shocked by a science which wanted to know about things but set aside questions of right and wrong, by a technology which used science for profit yet at great human cost, by a psychiatry which rarely cured, by writers and artists who exposed but could not exalt the human condition. Jews remain disproportionately involved in all American cultural activities. They do not, as they once did, seem to make it their substitute for religion. As culture has become only important but no longer our major source of truth, its challenge to religion, while real, has tended to decline.

By contrast, we have been more shaken by

what we have seen happen in human history. Permit me, for a moment, to defer comment on the Holocaust and speak instead of more recent events. We can hardly believe what we have seen, again and again, revealed about human nature. The Watergate exposures were only a part of a whole series of disillusionments. The Vietnam War taught us America could be as stupid and self-righteous as any other nation, that its leaders would sacrifice lives and an economy rather than admit their errors, that though the calamity was evident to the overwhelming majority of Americans, the bloodshed was prolonged. Assassination and riot; pious preaching about civil rights, wars on poverty, aid to the powerless, while all remained the same; corruption in business; FBI and CIA illegalities; benign recessions; muggings and rapes; cynicism and self-serving; a society was going pagan. Internationally, the same tragedy was played on a larger, distant stage. No community had put more faith in the United Nations than did the Jews. We thought it would bring reason and justice into international affairs. We dreamed of peace, perhaps even of a more equitable world economic order where nations would begin to live out the common humanity of people. Instead we got Yasir Arafat appearing with gun in holster and the denunciation of the State of Israel for rescuing its citizens from Uganda but not of the terrorists who seized them or the government which abetted the terrorists.

In such a time it has been difficult to believe in anything—reason, morality, people, God. Almost all the institutions in which we placed our trust, the very human nature on which we counted eventually to bring justice into the world—these have betrayed us. They have turned out to be unworthy of the confidence we placed in them. What sort of God would create, or order, or abide, or not do something about such a world? If God is good, then why do such terrible things regularly happen and why does not God work for the good?

This is the same range of questions which are raised by the Holocaust. I thought it best to mention the contemporary issues first because I wanted to make certain that we did not consider the Holocaust merely a historical or parochial matter, one significant only for another time or only to one people. I do not deny these particular elements in it, but what happened to European Jewry in World War II forecast something of how the following decades have assaulted the entire human community. What the Nazis showed us about the possibilities of human behavior has been repeated in smaller and less stupefying ways, yet ones which reflect a similar decadence if not depravity. The *Centenary Perspective* does not specifically mention the Holocaust in speaking of history's challenge to faith in God. It seemed wiser to recognize how many other events have deeply troubled us and to link the

Holocaust with them as part of our continuing trial.

The *Perspective* also notes that not everyone was moved to skepticism. "The trials of our time and the challenges of modern culture have made steady belief and clear understanding difficult *for some*" [italics mine]. Those whose belief or understanding of Judaism was deeply shaken attracted much community attention with their dramatic protest against the tradition and their search for a new way of facing reality. For many others the difficulties were much more modest. "Steady" faith gave way to moments of doubt which often enough were then followed by fresh belief. The "clear" understandings of a previous day gave way to confusion and not infrequently moved on to new and more satisfactory conceptions of God. For such people we cannot speak of a loss of belief, only of a time of insecurity and fluctuation in faith, one which sometimes was as much a period of growth as it was of pain. And for a small minority none of this mattered. Somehow their faith was never touched. They knew what was happening around them, and to them, and yet they believed. Eliezer Berkovits has called our attention to the fact that many people who went through the Holocaust never raised the questions that some people who were far from it popularized. He argues that we should be less concerned to follow the doubters, a common human category in this secular time, than to keep faith with the believers, an uncommon group in any time, but one which, considering the circumstances of their steadfastness, is worthy of our awe and emulation. I myself have always marveled that Leo Baeck, the great Liberal rabbi of Berlin, the only major modern Jewish thinker to have spent the war in a concentration camp, emerged from his experience without the need to question or revise what he had written about Jewish faith many happy years earlier.

CHAPTER FOUR

Responding to the Challenges

UNANSWERED QUESTIONS

Having described our difficult situation, the *Centenary Perspective* then responds to it in only one word, "Nevertheless." This is not an answer, at least in the intellectual sense. A number of people have tried to give such answers. Some have suggested that God must be thought of as limited in power, perhaps growing with our help. I have noted that what we really lost was our faith in humanity and, since that had effectively taken the place of our faith in God, we thought that our loss of faith in the human race meant the death of God. Still others have suggested that the Holocaust was a unique event, hence inexplicable. If that is so, to try to explain why it happened or what it meant is to deny the horror and thus is itself a sin. There is much to be learned from this ongoing discussion, but it is clear that there is no consensus among Reform Jews or the broader community about what is to be said about the Holocaust. What can and should be said philosophically must therefore be said elsewhere.

35

Yet one may well argue that this nonintellectual "Nevertheless" is a Jewish answer, for it asserts a faith that drives one to a Jewish life. The Book of Job ends somewhat in this way— though, to be sure, Job has experienced God speaking to him and as a result gives up his questions and confesses his faith. Those of us who have had Job's questions have rarely had his experience. Yet Job's model is not without its traditional Jewish implications. Job never has his questions answered. At the end of his suffering he does not know any more than when he began to question. Despite his lack of understanding, he trusts. Jewish law does not require a Jew in the face of evil to deny the evil or to consider various philosophical explanations as to why evil occurs (though rabbis, philosophers, and mystics have offered them). Instead, it mandates a blessing. The response to evil is an act, something done, not merely thought. One is commanded, amid the trial, to acknowledge God's rule and thereby to deny that this evil event has broken God's order for the universe. Jews may not understand how God permits such things. They are entitled to question and challenge God, as Job did. They are encouraged by the helpful records of their heritage to search for intellectual explanations which may help them relate this trauma to what else they know and believe. But while such philosophy is honored, an act of affirmation is required.

I do not mean by this reference to Jewish law to say that this practice has been easy for traditional Jews or that we moderns can simply follow the old pattern, particularly in the face of so monstrous an evil as the Holocaust. I only want to show that while a philosopher might not consider this Jewish "Nevertheless" an answer, it is a good Jewish way of responding to the problem of evil. In this respect the older Jewish rationalists are a worthy model. They, too, never explained how a good God could have evil in creation. They regularly argued that we must see evil as a challenge to our ethical capacities and answer it by doing the good, by creating righteousness. They thought this was a perfectly rational response to the question of evil, and in some ways it is. But it involves saying that a thinking person can ignore the question of why evil is there, in the world, and not just in the result of a person's faulty will. I am not sure that it is "rational" to have such devotion to duty regardless of one's understanding, but I can easily see its Jewish grounding.

A SENSE OF BELIEF

If we can manage to say "Nevertheless" today, it is, I believe, precisely for historical and cultural reasons. For some time now, ever since Jews in large numbers became university-trained and culturally sophisticated, we have thought of ourselves as essentially agnostic. We preferred mostly not to discuss our lack of belief and often not to act upon it, particularly when we became parents. We set the question of God's reality to one side for the sake of our children and the Jewish community. We liked to think of ourselves as being open to any new evidence for the possibility that God is real, but none ever convinced us. It probably couldn't have. We were always armed with many arguments as to why the evidence couldn't bring us to God. We thought of ourselves religiously as believing, ultimately, nothing. This didn't bother us as long as we could put our trust in culture and see our hopes working out in history. They were our substitute faith. Only now we see (as many Christians do) that history can easily end in ugliness and that culture no longer provides the appropriate values by which people are moved to transform history.

The death-of-God movement of the late 1960s did the entire religious community an unexpected good turn. It announced that God was dead in this culture—but then it could not tell us where a compelling sense of humanity's dignity and destiny was to come from. We were suddenly faced with the possibility that the universe is, at best, neutral and that our goals and standards for human behavior were merely our own idea and nothing more. If that is so, we will not for long do very much about them. We cannot even stay on a diet—because we know we made its rules. But to think of transforming the powerful forces operating in society on the basis of a mere personal inclination is quixotic. Yet, it turns out, we care about people and what happens to humanity. We want our children and our families and our communities and, if at all possible, our country and the world to be humane. We believe in the importance of high human attainment, and we know that this concern is not just our own idea, a childish hope, a cultural remnant, a class interest. Our sense of values, for all that it is shaped by our particular situation, reflects something real and lasting in the universe itself.

It turns out that we do not believe nothing. We are not nihilists. Rather, having come face to face with people who really believe nothing, we have discovered, often to our own amazement, that we believe something. And that is the ground of our "Nevertheless." We do not understand very much indeed about what we mean when we say we have a sense that a transcendent claim is laid upon us—or to put it in simple, traditional language, that there is a God who commands us—but, after all the terrifying experiences of recent decades, that is what we know we believe and probably have believed all along.

I do not deny that there are many other ways for people to find their way to some sense of personal belief and many people whose agnosticism remains in force. But it

seems clear to me that the pattern I have
described above is characteristic of the recov-
ery of faith by very many people in the Jewish
community today.

WHAT BELIEF MUST MEAN

A few additional comments must be made with
regard to the content of this affirmation. To
have some sense of God means to build your
life on it. God is either that important or what
one believes in is not God. A religion must be
taken that seriously, which is another way of
expressing the *Sh'ma*'s "with all your heart,
with all your soul, and with all your might."
Here the two aspects of modern Jewish living
are made explicitly "personal and communal,"
for to believe as a Jew, while a very personal
matter, must likewise include being one of the
people of Israel. The foundation is thus laid
here for what follows in the *Centenary Perspective* about the Jewish people and one's responsibilities within and to it.

The *Perspective* does not use the term *God's
existence* but rather speaks of *God's reality*.
The two terms overlap, and the former is
avoided in part because it has become something of a cliché and is therefore often treated
as if it had no real meaning. There are also
some interesting problems raised in modern
thought (and incidentally, in his own way, by
Maimonides) about what we mean when we
speak of God's "existence." The existence we

know is of things—but we surely do not mean to imply that God is another thing, just a bigger and better one. So some thinkers have urged us to talk about God as the basis or ground of all existence. That is an elegant point, but the drafters of the *Perspective* had something much simpler in mind: we wanted to say that God was not an illusion, not merely something we imagined, not just a wish of ours. Our God is real, so real that we base our lives on God's reality. By this affirmation we did not mean to close out the possibility that in the future we might draw closer to God in experience or idea. In one sense we remain agnostic: we know we do not know all we can or would like to know about God, and so we remain open to new insights. Even in faith, change remains part of the Jewish experience of God.

CHAPTER FIVE

Of Life after Death

The *Centenary Perspective*'s paragraph on God concludes with a sentence on our belief in life after death. The committee decided to include it here only after some deliberation. Since our hope for an afterlife derives largely from our trust in God, the juxtaposition of the two topics seemed desirable.

TWO INTELLECTUAL PROBLEMS

Most theological matters are not easy to talk about, but the theme of life after death presents two very special problems to modern thinkers. While they may not believe that science knows all about reality, they cannot easily ignore the scientific view of life and thus of death. At present life seems to science essentially a matter of proper chemical combinations. When the right chemicals come together under the right conditions, living matter results. The forms and sizes and structures and capacities of life can grow to extraordinary ranges of complexity, yet they remain, at their base, chemical arrangements. By extension, death is simply the breakdown of a chemical structure which is living. The elements continue on in other configurations, and there is no loss in the total energy in the universe. What is gone is a certain order to which we give the evocative name *life.* As there were only chemicals to begin with, so there are only chemicals afterward. Thus there is no special thing present to survive the death of that most wondrous complex example of life we call a human being. This scientific way of looking at life is dramatically confirmed with every new discovery in molecular biology, and it has made of most religious liberals skeptics if not confirmed disbelievers in life after death.

There is, however, another difficulty related to this topic. In the case of all other religious realities we can claim some personal experience, be it of a rational or of a more feeling variety. There is nothing analogous about our hope for life after death. Of course, this is what makes research into psychic phenomena so intriguing, particularly when there is contact with someone who has died or with a person's previous existence. Were we able to validate such data, we could then not only affirm the reasonableness of religious belief in an afterlife but we could insist that scientists acknowledge this data and rethink their theory of human life so as to account for it. Thus far the results of research in this realm have been inconclusive. They surely do not seem to warrant basing one's religious faith on them. While leaving the question of possible personal experience open, then, one finds oneself without a basis upon which to base one's belief.

THE NEED FOR A STATEMENT

These two intellectual problems are reinforced by the Jewish tradition's reluctance to say much about life after death and by the modern religious thinker's concern to keep the focus of religion on this world and our responsibilities in it. The result has been that most Jews in our time avoid speaking about personal survival after death. Mostly there is talk about living on in the memory of those who knew one or, for those of a rationalist bent, one can speak of people living on in the ethical deeds they did. It came as no surprise, then, that the question was raised in our committee (and by several rabbis who responded to the first draft circulated) as to whether this topic required a statement at all. For many people it is a matter of little or no importance. Since many matters could not be commented on, the absence of a statement on life after death would not prove disturbing. The committee, though conscious of the intellectual problems it faced and how little it could honestly say in their face, decided it could not pass this matter by. Though many Reform Jews are agnostic or disbelieving in this area, the committee felt that such positive faith as could be given utterance deserved a place in the statement.

DESCRIPTIONS OF LIFE

Those who affirm life after death emphatically reject the notion that human life can ever adequately be described in chemical terms alone. No one denied that analyzing life in terms of its chemistry has had many useful results or that great benefits would yet result from extending chemical research into life. The delicate question is not whether talking about human life in chemical terms is useful, but only whether one can go on from what we know to say, "It is only chemical." Yet we have no alternate way of talking about human life that tells us very much about its origins, maintenance, or end.

In this respect the Bible and the thinkers of the Middle Ages (who reinforced the Bible's views with certain philosophical notions) were very much better off than we are. They believed that a human life resulted from the combination of two parts, a body and a soul. For them the soul was a thing, what in the Middle Ages was called a substance, which was eternal. When one died, God took the soul back to a special realm, at some later date to be inserted into the restored body at the resurrection for the final judgment and the disposition of the person.

Whether one wishes to replace the concept of resurrection with that of the immortality of the soul or not, our present difficulty is that the notion of such a substance as a soul is no longer intellectually tenable for most modern thinkers. If one wants to talk about survival after death, it would be helpful to be able to say just what survives, what it is beside chemicals (or somehow extant through the chemicals) which makes up the unique thing we call human life. Earlier in this century it was still possible to use the term *spirit*, for it had some status in the German philosophical world on which America drew so heavily. From this came the heavy Reform Jewish emphasis on immortality. But by now *spirit* has gone the way of *soul*. We still use both words—but only poetically, to point to what we think we believe but have very little idea of. So with regard to the "mechanics" of life after death we have almost nothing to say and, at the moment, we have no good prospects for explaining life so as to clarify why we believe it does not end for us once we die. No wonder so many Jews have given up this belief.

LIFE AS MYSTERY

Yet a positive sense of an afterlife can be derived, if not from ourselves then from our relationship with God and our sense of God's reality. We are indeed creatures, but creatures of a most exalted capacity. We are conscious not merely of our own reality but of that of God, the supreme reality of all existence. There is something about our life which can respond to, and in that sense participate in, God's reality. We know ourselves to be called upon by God in ways that, so far as we can tell, extend to no other creatures. We are God's coworkers in nature. So, in our limited way, we share in God's purposes and power. All creatures share in God's reality; we do so in special measure. Through the phenomena of our consciousness, our intellect, our will, our personhood we come to know ourselves as especially close to God's own reality. There is something God-like about human beings, and God does not die. We have no name for this special character of human life. We do not know its relationship to our chemical nature. Indeed, science and Judaism seem to be talking in two radically different ways about what it is to be a person, and this may necessarily prevent any synthesis of them. Yet even as we have good reason for not denying the chemical understanding of much of our existence, so we have good reason for not denying the reality and greater significance of our special relationship to God.

In this Jewish view, life is seen as a mystery. When we understand it with the greatest precision, chemically, it is utterly different from our immediate personal experience of it. The elements have no will or consciousness, yet from them is supposed to derive our inner life. They are utterly amoral and apparently unesthetic. We consider people without a moral sense and devoid of appreciation for beauty somehow unhuman. Perhaps there are scientific ways of explaining how multiplying and ordering packets of programmed energy eventually yield persons. The topic of how matter yields spirit is still hotly debated. To the religious mind the idea that chemicals, in no matter how complex a configuration, should ever have been spoken of as possessing a soul is indicative of a mystery built into creation. Taken at its fullest, we do not understand life. We accept its mysteriously given limits and opportunities and try to work within them.

DEATH AS MYSTERY

Death is a greater mystery. We do not know life without a physical base. We have no experience of what existence the other side of death could be like. Against that ignorance we balance our recognition that life itself is mysterious, that death is part of life and the creation God ordained. Death, like life, comes from the God whom we know daily showers goodness on us. We trust God's goodness even in death. We cannot believe that having shared so intimately in God's reality in life we do not continue to share it beyond the grave. Our creaturely existence, having risen to the level of participating in the ultimate reality in the universe, God's, now may aspire to extend and fulfill that greatness it came partially to know in life. Having reached such heights precisely in our personhood, our individuality, we trust that our survival likewise will be personal and individual.

Searching for a way of pointing to the intimate relationship between God and people, the committee gave up its normal use of modern terms and utilized a biblical metaphor: human beings are said to be "created in God's image." The phrase is familiar enough to convey our sense of the closeness between God and people. Yet its biblical provenance is sufficiently well known that this sudden, unusual metaphorical reference should signal a special form of religious affirmation. What *image* means cannot be defined, but after centuries of significant usage the term is not empty of content. We cannot say very clearly what we believe, yet we do not propose to abandon our faith that the God who gave us life will yet give us life after death.

This is a most modest affirmation—one sentence with its several evocative but limited terms. For all that, it is an important belief for those of us who share it to acknowledge and articulate. Perhaps that is the way of modern Jewish faith. We find ourselves unable to say very much. But we are able to say something. So what we do say is very important.

PART III

The People Israel

The Jewish people and Judaism defy precise definition
because both are in the process of becoming. Jews, by

**II.
The
People
Israel**

birth or conversion, constitute an uncommon union of faith and peoplehood. Born as Hebrews in the ancient
Near East, we are bound together like
all ethnic groups by language, land, history, culture,
and institutions. But the people of Israel is unique
because of its involvement with God and its resulting
perception of the human condition. Throughout our
long history our people has been inseparable from its
religion with its messianic hope that humanity will be
redeemed.

From the Centenary Perspective

CHAPTER SIX

Why Is There No Statement on Human Nature?

BEGINNING WITH THE PARTICULAR

The second paragraph of the *Centenary Perspective*'s "principles" again shows how this document stresses the social side of being Jewish. This impression arises not simply because this is a paragraph on the Jewish people or because so ethnic a matter immediately follows the discussion of God. Almost everyone would expect a Reform Jewish statement today to have a positive feeling for the Jewish folk, and it seems natural to us to talk about the Jewish people after talking about God. Yet this means that nothing much has been said—certainly it is not one of the principles—about human nature generally, about people as a whole and their relationship to God. The document speaks only about the Jews, this one group and its involvement with God.

The liberals of another day would have followed a different pattern. They regularly started from universal human experience and then worked their way up to a belief in God. Since all people were capable of knowing God and none had special ability or unique experiences, whatever was to be said about the Jews had to derive from the general possibilities of being human. Humanity logically came before the Jewish people—as it did in many liberal lives—and that is the order which is followed in the first great modern book on Jewish theology, Kaufmann Kohler's book of that title. (Since Kohler was president of the Hebrew Union College, his formulation, about the time of World War I, was highly influential among Reform Jews, though other liberal thinkers held similar ideas.) Anyone familiar with the previous point of view might well wonder why the *Centenary Perspective* speaks of the Jewish people without first clarifying the universal human situation.

PERSONAL COMMITMENT

The response is substantially the same as that given to the parallel question: What happened to individualism in the paragraph on God? There, the focus was on God's place in the people of Israel's will to survive rather than God's relationship with all humanity. Here, rather than speaking of what individuals in general—humanity—can know about God and do in God's service, the concern is again the Jewish people. With space limited, the message of this hour is highlighted, much else being taken for granted. What is critical to Reform as to all Jewish experience in our time is the involvement of the individual Jew with the Jewish people. This major theme of the *Perspective* is reiterated here to special effect. With reference to universal humanity left in the background while Jewish ethnicity is given center stage, a rebuke is administered to those who insist they can be Jewish in utter privacy. Instead, the rabbis are here saying that a proper Jewish life is not limited to what one does in one's heart, though one should put one's heart into it. As against Whitehead's maxim on being religious, Jewish existence is not what one does with one's solitariness, even though it obviously starts with the individual. To be a Jew is to be part of a people, and without involvement in Jewish peoplehood one can not be much of a Jew.

Fortunately, this folk encourages all sorts of individuality, so that having a mind of one's own and doing things in one's own style has long largely been honored among Jews, and certainly so in modern times. But trying to be a Jew without benefit of our folk history or tradition or present community but only as some sort of person-in-general is rather a contradiction in terms. Of course one can be a "kosher Jew" on a desert island or in some other situation where isolation is enforced. Thus without a minyan, one can still pray—but, symbolically enough, one prays what the minyan would be praying, with some exceptions, and, preferably, about the time a normal minyan would be praying it. You may be forced to be all alone—yet you live your life in relation to the community of Israel. Going further, you may certainly say your own, private prayers to God whenever you want to (and in a special part of the regular service), but that is no substitute for the common Jewish duty; an individual Jew must join with the community in the shared, corporate action of his people.

THE EXAGGERATED INDIVIDUAL

At this centenary hour the old Reform Jewish emphasis on the individual seems so secure—it is so fundamental a premise it comes up again and again in the *Centenary Perspective*—that it did not seem to require fresh, explicit treatment. The opposite rather seems to be the case. Individualism has come to dominate our self-consciousness to the point that our social nature and responsibility are often ignored. In America today the widespread criterion of value is "What's in it for me?" The old counterbalancing sense of the common good has substantially been given up in the name of an alleged realism. What begins sensibly enough as an education that tries to meet student needs expands by inescapable, seductive advertising into the subconscious expectation that the world centers around us and exists for our gratification. Operating on the basis of such a fantasy one can hardly understand why marriage, the synagogue, or the community makes such great demands; illusion blinds us to the simple truth that our vaunted singleness would not amount to much if there weren't a whole culture and society to give it a basis and context. Totalitarianism has sacrificed the individual to the nation, but one often has the impression in the democracies these days that the world and society exist mainly to nurse us.

The Jewish equivalent of this exaggerated individualism is the radical separation of one's self as person from oneself as Jew. Then one can believe that what one really cares about and hopes to achieve has little to do with one's having been born into the Jewish people. So one takes up the consumer's stand toward Jewish life, asking always, "What's in it for me—now?" Obviously, the *Centenary Perspective* does not mean to assert a totalitarian Jewish standard, that the individual Jew exists for the sake of the Jewish people whose corporate dictates should supersede all personal concerns. It rather hopes to correct the mistaken notion that most of us would be what we are as individuals without our Jewish background—consider how critical ethnicity is to our odd statistics of social achievement—and that the Jewish tradition exists only to serve our needs and not, legitimately, also to make certain claims upon us.

As long as one keeps a gulf between one's essential self and one's merely accidental Jewishness, one will never have a healthy sense of what it is to be a Jew. Thus what needs attention in the present stage of American Reform Judaism is not so much the loss of our general individuality to the social mass, as bad a problem as that is, but the erosion of our self-identification with the Jewish people as the result of an overblown individualism.

CONFLICTS OF CONSCIENCE

Stressing so the ethnic side of our individuality, the *Centenary Perspective* might very well have gone on to explore the problems which arise for a sensitive Jew when personal fulfillment conflicts with group responsibility. On the everyday level such issues come up whenever hobbies, excursions, or fatigue conflict with services, study, or community meetings. Sometimes a Jewish conscience is torn between the sense that two children are all that this family rightfully should bring into the world and another that this number is at least one less than replenishing the Jewish people makes mandatory.

No conflict of duty to self and to community in our time is as classic as that raised by the possibility of intermarriage. If one is essentially responsible to one's self, and if one's fundamental duty is self-fulfillment, then, in this trying time, one should marry whomever one might reasonably hope to live out one's life in happiness with. Naturally, both partners being Jewish might make that somewhat easier, and it would surely be more rich ethnically. But if the self is primary, and if being Jewish is nice but marginal, then the future spouse's non-Jewish background will not matter much to us. However, if our individuality and Jewishness are closely interrelated, then not to marry a Jew would be a betrayal of self. Of course, the *Perspective* does not discuss the intermarriage issue. I have only brought up this thorny topic to illustrate how the emphasis on individualism can lead to certain tensions in Jewish duty. Since the majority of Reform rabbis are on record as opposing the performance of intermarriage, I imagine they will interpret the weight given here to the group rather than the individual as an endorsement of their position.

Yet if, as the *Perspective*'s paragraph on diversity noted, people should interpret the statements here in their own thoughtful and conscientious Reform Jewish way, another view will certainly be forthcoming. This document is not against the individualism long emphasized by Reform Judaism. It rather takes it for granted in most of what it says. With regard to intermarriage, the ethnic concern of the document means only that people who approach things in terms of themselves should also consider at the time of marriage their relationship to the Jewish people and their obligations to it. Many rabbis who perform intermarriages certainly hope that such considerations will be part of a couple's thinking in approaching marriage. Such rabbis conduct an intermarriage in the hope of gaining a family and their children for the Jewish people. They thus see themselves as no less loyal to the Jewish people and no less concerned with its importance in the lives of individuals than are their nonintermarrying colleagues. The paragraph on "The People Israel" also bespeaks their view, though they draw different consequences from it than do the majority of their colleagues, including me.

This is a good example of the diversity engendered by the double affirmations of Reform Judaism—here self and people. Though this is an unusually emotional and disturbing matter to those in the antagonistic parties, it also illustrates with unusual clarity how unity often lies behind Reform Jewish dissension. All the disputants affirm the significance of the Jewish people in the life of the individual Jew and feel that it deserves more emphasis in our time than it received in the recent past. Yet everyone also agrees that the believing, knowledgeable self-determining individual is the basis of Reform Judaism.

CHAPTER SEVEN

Why Is Defining the Jews so Difficult?

COMPLEX HISTORICAL DATA

Trying to explain who the Jews are or what Judaism is becomes troublesome for two reasons: the variegated data and the descriptive terms available. Consider the Jews of Bible times. They began as a family which eventually grew into tribes and clans. They wandered in the wilderness like bedouin, then settled as a loosely federated group of tribes living in a land they occupied. Then they were, in turn, a nation under a king, a few tribes in exile, a small group of returnees living as a special religious group as part of a great empire—and they show other social patterns as well. Racial, religious, and national factors all play a role in these portraits of the Jews, though in an extraordinarily varied mix. The result is that one historically continuous group took on many forms, at times quite different one from the other.

One must then add to the biblical data the utterly unexpected historical phenomenon that this people was then detached from its ancestral land for nearly two thousand years and scattered all over near Asia, Europe, North

Africa, and the Americas. In these millennia there was no single continuing center of physical existence, but only shifting points of religious preeminence. Already the problem of simple description is well out of hand. But then the Jews reconstituted themselves as a nation in the Land of Israel, though Jews around the world have no political share in it!

Thus to say that the people of Israel has been a dynamic phenomenon, changing and adapting its social nature over the centuries, is an understatement. But definitions are static. A word which was adequate to the Jews in one time is rarely accurate to describe them a while later. Today, with Jews thinking of themselves in many varied ways, definition is all the more hazardous.

COMPLEX RELIGIOUS DATA

Matters are equally complex when one tries to find a simple word with which to describe the relationship of this people to God. In their classic period their God involves them with a land, in the creation of a certain kind of society, and is deeply concerned with their politics as well as with a cult in a great central sanctuary. Then all of this disappears and is replaced by a religion of lawyers—and preachers called rabbis, some of whom are wonder-workers and others of whom are mystics, though mysticism is later challenged by a philosophical development that considers the nonrational dangerous. In modern times this construction substantially gives way when the majority of Jews no longer observes rabbinic law or respects rabbinic authority. Equally difficult, some modern conceptions of a proper Jewish relationship to God go far beyond the admittedly wide range of rabbinically permitted interpretations, while a very large number of Jews claim not to be believers at all. If, then, this is a "religion," it is a most odd one.

JUDAISM AS "RELIGION"

The variety of Jewish social and religious experience is staggering. Our culture simply has no word to describe so multifaceted a phenomenon, almost certainly because our language has been shaped so strongly by Christianity. Its particular experience of God is adopted as the model for people's relationship to God. The affect of this Christianizing of our general language is widespread. A good deal of what seems the essential similarity of world religions often derives from our translating the texts of other faiths, including primitive ones, using English terms with a Christian conception of God and piety behind them. So other sacred books naturally come out sounding reminiscent of the Bible.

The most immediately appealing English word we could use to describe the Jews, particularly in terms of their concern with the life of the spirit, is *religion*. In many ways that gives a good sense of the historical Jewish experience, but only if one does not press the notion very hard. There is the odd biblical involvement with land, society, and government; there are the anomalies of contemporary Jewish disbelief and the secular but Jewish State of Israel. The problem with using the word *religion* for the Jews is that it customarily implies a "church." Christians have a special sense of religion, and it derives logically from the unique events which gave rise to their faith. The Christ comes into the world to begin transforming the normal perception of affairs and to save people. Hence Christians are those drawn forth from humanity by their faith and the grace of God. Obviously, that is too limited a statement of a great and complex doctrine. Still, it will serve to indicate how, for a Christian, religion is a matter of having the right faith and, variously understood, being part of the right group, the Church. In such a view, *religion* implies accepting the creed or the dogmas which clarify what constitutes a saving faith and participating in the group created on the basis of finding faith, the Church.

Not every *religion* is easily understood as a *church*. The Buddhists may more easily be described as sharing a rather rationally arrived-at philosophy, and they are socially organized around their monastic brotherhood. For Muslims, religion is not so much located in a separate activity—which, to be sure, is supposed to influence all of life—but is really coextensive with cultural and national life. I think it fair to say that in the history of religion the Christian way of thinking about believers and their relationship to God is somewhat unusual. In any case, the Jews are not a church. They are not organized around a saving faith, and efforts to identify a Jewish creed of Jewish dogmas have normally met with intense debate and little acceptance. Moreover, the Jewish group is far more inclusive of activities and interests than what we normally expect of a church. Thus, the word *religion*, which is our normal English term for a relationship to God, is somewhat misleading, even in that limited focus, when applied to the Jews. When one adds to this spiritual inadequacy a full acceptance of what we have come to call the ethnic realities of Jewish life, *religion* covers perhaps a major dimension of Jewish existence, and that with some possible distortion, but surely not the whole thing.

THE ETHNIC-RELIGIOUS SEPARATION

This split of the religious from the ethnic side of being Jewish demands special comment. Even in the few biblical examples given above it was clear that faith and nation were utterly intertwined. As a result of the Emancipation, the usual source of our modern Jewish problems, they were radically separated. Had the

Jews come out of the ghetto into a world where religion was, as it had been, a major ingredient of culture, the issue might not have arisen. In the medieval period, the nature of the Jews as a group was not a serious question. Maimonides in his thirteen principles of Jewish belief does not mention the Jewish people. (Check the *Yigdal* hymn or its translation in the prayerbook the next time you are at services for a song version of Maimonides' "creed.") Maimonides and other Jewish thinkers did not have to talk directly about the Jewish people, because in their day the major divisions among humankind were seen as essentially religious or, to be more precise, as the result of different revelations. The Torah had its followers, as did the Koran and the New Testament. Philosophers were therefore mainly concerned with explaining how revelation could occur and arguing why one's group had the true one. Only when religion is not taken seriously and revelation becomes problematic do thinkers shift their focus from what God did in order to separate humanity into groups to what sorts of divisions have naturally arisen among human beings. Secularism set the context for the emancipation of the Jews and thus the possibility of thinking of them as a natural social group on the one hand and as a church-like religious group on the other.

The people who created the idea of a secular state, one where religion is separate from citizenship, did not know whether Jews could take part in such an arrangement. Before the French Revolution most people knew that the Jews lived separate from the general populace. Jews had been, so to speak, a nation within the nation, conducting their own law courts and collecting their own taxes for the government. Gentile society did not realize how much this was due to its segregation and persecution of the Jews over centuries. Instead, the non-Jews projected an image of extreme clannishness, even of the hatred of humanity, onto the Jews. When they had to face the issue of equal rights for Jews, they wanted to know, with varying levels of anti-Semitic hostility, on what basis Jews were now to take part in the state. There were no longer to be separate groups within the free, western European nations, but only one people—say, the French or the British, and somewhat later the German. One could legitimately maintain one's separateness only on a religious basis—that is, if one was a Protestant (in varying denomination) or a Catholic, the major religious divisions. If the Jews wished to fully partake of the new national life—a possibility of incredible promise to the ghetto dwellers—they could be separate as a religion but not as another nation. When Napoleon asked leaders of French Jewry for an official Jewish community response to the offer of citizenship, he specifically asked them whether their religion permitted or placed barriers in the way of their full participation in the new French nation. In effect, he wanted to know if they were a religion sufficiently like Protestantism and Catholicism, to be granted the private privilege of separate existence. They answered as have the Jews of almost every free country ever since that time. They identified themselves as such a religion. In due course a word was coined for this; in English, it is *Judaism*. We could avoid a number of misconceptions if we remembered how recent that term is and under what circumstances it came into being. I am not sure how much of an "ism" the Jews have had—but saying we were *Judaism*, a religion, made the social side of being Jewish even more difficult to describe.

EQUALITY AT THE EXPENSE OF ETHNICITY

The very way the question is now put produces both the benefits of the new situation and its problems. Dividing the state and citizenship from religious belief—specifically, making it non-Christian—means that Jews can be part of it and yet carry on as a separate religion. But splitting nationality and religion also makes it impossible for Jews to say that in their religion the believers are not a church but an ethnic group, what Europeans might call a nationality. To gain entry into the Western world the Jews had to suppress a part of their Jewish identity. This was so sensitive a matter while the Jews were struggling for their rights that the Reform Jews turned their relationship to the Land of Israel and their concern for the coming of the King-Messiah into empty symbols rather than historical expectations. Subsequent history has convinced most Jews that our attitude toward our Land and to self-government should not be so abstractly idealized, but is something Jews can and should do something about here and now.

What have remained troublesome are the limits this modern sense of being a Jew had imposed on our community life. We have synagogues and voluntary organizations as Christians do. We go beyond that to organize community councils for defense, fundraising, some coordination of activity, and a bit of joint planning. But the concept of our being another religious community and the limited role for ethnic groups in a democracy do not allow for very much more than that. If the Jews, however, for all their religious tradition, are also a people with a rich folk tradition and need to live out their religiosity in diverse corporate ways, then they lost a good deal while making the gains of coming into the democratic state.

THE RESTORATION OF ETHNICITY

The Jews of the nineteenth and early twentieth centuries who were struggling to win equality could not say, as we do so easily today, "We are another religion, but we happen to be organized as an ethnic group and not as a church." In their day such words hadn't yet come into general use, because the concept of maintaining separate ethnic groups was utterly unacceptable. Jewish thinkers groped for modern words that could usefully describe the Jewish group. They were quite interested when, in the latter part of the nineteenth century, the concept of race came into intellectual fashion. Here was a scientific term which explained differences between peoples in a way which didn't interfere with their participating in their states—at least until the Germans began to apply race to nationality. By the early part of the twentieth century it had been adopted by Jewish thinkers as diverse as Kaufmann Kohler in the United States and Franz Rosenzweig and Martin Buber in Germany. Today we shudder at their use of such terms as *Jewish blood*—which they believed transmitted the genetic information. But we are speaking out of the horrors we saw done in the name of race, while they were speaking out of the relatively harmless, limited, social vocabulary of their time.

Our present vocabulary is the result of something of a revolution in the American consciousness. As long as Americans thought in terms of democracy as a "melting pot," ethnic diversity seemed culturally backward. Then to have described the Jews as *ethnic* would have meant that they were still attached to their immigrant roots. But as Americans began to value group existence—as it became clear that Blacks and Indians, Poles and Italians, Greeks and other nationalities had a right to preserve and foster their specific heritage, thereby enriching our democracy—one could use the word *ethnic* to describe the Jewish group and expect that it would be positively received.

AN IDEA OF WHO WE ARE

This still doesn't settle our problem of defining the Jews. Even if we are a most peculiar group. Other such groups are primarily racial or national, but we still claim to be a religion. In the modern, democratic sense we are a religious group, but our social base is ethnic. Thus we seem to have two parts to us, which have become separated and which we somehow cannot put back together. The Western world has no good term for such a group, mostly because there aren't very many of them. (Below I shall discuss an Asian group with similar characteristics, the Sikhs.) The problem set for us by the Emancipation remains: our nationality derives from our citizenship and our separateness essentially from our religion, though this happens to have an ethnic, not a church, base. This is a clumsy way to try to understand oneself, and it is clumsier still to use in trying to explain it to someone who has not lived it. No wonder we have such difficulty making clear to Christians why we are so involved with what they see as only a political entity, the State of Israel. Nonetheless, though we cannot be precise or elegant, we now have some words which give a fairly adequate idea of who the Jews are—at least for the time being.

CHAPTER EIGHT

The Double Affirmation: Faith and Peoplehood

BEING BORN A JEW

Perhaps nothing so well demonstrates what seems to the Christian mentality the strange double nature of the Jews as the two ways one becomes a Jew, birth or conversion. Birth is not easily thought of as a way to enter a church where accepting a saving faith is critical. Some Protestants insist that one cannot properly join the church until one is mature enough personally to accept the Christ. (Catholics deal with this by the sacrament of confirmation.) Other Christians, basing themselves on the New Testament accounts, accept infants into the church by baptism. This can lead to the troublesome status of the child born to Christian parents who dies before being baptized. In Christianity the biological act of being born cannot substitute for baptism or accepting the faith. But a Jew is born Jewish, traditionally, if born to a Jewish mother. The biological nature of this is borne out by the analogous case of the Jewish male infant who is not circumcised for legitimate reasons (e.g., health) and who then dies. There is no question of the status of that child. He died fully a Jew and has as much hope for the afterlife as any other Jew. Circumcision is a major law, but it is not a condition of being a Jew (and certainly not a sacrament, an act in which God fully participates, since Judaism has no such rites). Neither the traditional naming ceremony for girls in the synagogue nor the circumcision of males makes children Jewish. Birth does.

Entry into a group by birth is natural for an ethnic group. Americans easily understand that the child of Italian parents, say third-generation Chicagoans, is "an Italian." Obviously that child is not a citizen of Italy but of the United States. Yet if the family is at all concerned with its origin and the perpetuation of the customs connected with it, the child will have the sort of ethnic background implied by the term *Italian.* This is so common that it seems somewhat old-fashioned, because unnecessarily defensive, to hyphenate the child as an Italian-American. So in terms of normal entry into the group the Jews are obviously ethnic. But then, too, people become Jews by conversion.

CONVERTING TO JUDAISM

By contrast to the birth route the conversion path of entry into the Jews is easily understood by Christians. Leaving aside now the difference between the special Christian sense of "seeing the light" and speaking merely of the notion of gaining a faith one did not have before, conversion is the classic Christian way of entering a religion. So converts to Judaism seem to follow a well-known path and Judaism appears to be a religion. One can make something of a case that conversion to Judaism is more like changing ethnic groups than like accepting faith in a Christian way. Traditionally what one does for would-be proselytes is to remind them of all the problems the Jewish people undergoes and then, if they persist, to instruct them in the Jewish way of life. Once they learn what Jews do and agree to do this wholeheartedly, they are accepted in our midst, a process not dissimilar to becoming a citizen of another country. But while one may want to distinguish the Jewish sense of religion from the Christian and thus emphasize its ethnic aspects, one cannot ignore the relationship to God which lies at the heart of sincere Jewish observance. If the traditional pattern of conversion did not include direct theological instruction, that was because it could be assumed that Jewish practice would carry the message of Jewish belief to the convert as it did to Jews. An insincere convert, a mechanical, unbelieving *mitzvah*-doer, could not properly be called a convert to Judaism. Ruth, the Moabitess, whom the rabbis considered the classic model of a genuine convert, put the dimensions of being a Jew beautifully when she is described as saying to her mother-in-law, Naomi, "Thy people shall be my people, and thy God, my God."

SPIRITUAL AND BIOLOGICAL

If, then, the spiritual component is critical to being a Jew, it is reasonably clear how an act of conversion can bring one to it; but then what has biology to do with it? Being born to Jewish parents may bring you into an ethnic group, but can it automatically bring you into some sort of relationship with God? The matter can be taken to what seems, to the outsider, an almost absurd level. A woman born to gentile parents is not Jewish. She then, by learning and will, converts to Judaism. But then, purely biologically, her child is born Jewish. The child gets by birth what the parent received only by will—yet it seems inconceivable that the mother's decision to be a Jew had changed her biology and made it "Jewish"! Incidentally, something of a similar oddity operates in the opposite direction. Though you may become a Jew by conversion, you cannot remove yourself from the Jewish people by converting to another faith. You may lose certain rights and privileges within the Jewish community as a result of your apostasy, but when you are ready to come back we will not ask you to undergo conversion. You may have to undertake some acts which indicate the genuineness of your return, and some authorities have been known to impose penalties for such sinfulness. Still, the rule usually applied here is "A Jew who sins is still a Jew." (The case is slightly different with a gentile convert who later leaves

Judaism. They are generally not still considered Jews but rather people whose conversion was probably not truly sincere to begin with. Decisions on such cases will vary, but often the ethnic tie does not hold them when the religious tie lapses.) It is also remarkable how often when Jews convert to another faith their Jewish identity clings to them. Perhaps this is due to the anti-Semitism of those who refuse to forget the Jew's origins. Yet it is also testimony to the special ethnic way one is a Jew and should not be utterly discounted.

A UNION OF PEOPLEHOOD AND FAITH

With all this in mind the *Centenary Perspective* calls the Jews an "uncommon union of faith and peoplehood." *Unique* would have been too strong a term. Among those whom anthropologists once used to call primitive peoples, the union of religion and ethnicity is the norm, not the exception. What makes the Jews radically different from such groups is the universal nature of the Jewish God and the almost worldwide experience of the Jewish people. Most other groups whose religion was coextensive with their culture had a rather limited sense of God and lived in one small area. Already in biblical times the Jews believed that there was one God in all the world and that God was the God of their people in a very special and intimate way. Even when the Jews left their native land through exile and dispersion, they still retained this faith. Losing the normal attributes of nationality, they did not give up their ethnicity.

At least one other group has had so comprehensive a sense of God, what historians of religion have termed "a high God," and yet insisted that the group who served this God most appropriately was fundamentally national in character. The Sikhs are a people of India who in the sixteenth century were brought to a new religion by the guru Nanak. The ethnic character of their faith is most readily seen in their distinctive dress. Sikh males wear turbans, have beards, and carry some metal on them. While one can join the Sikhs, their own children are born into the Sikh "faith" as into the Sikh nation. The similarities with the Jews are quite real. Defenders of Jewish uniqueness will insist that the Sikh experience is too short to be compared to that of the Jews and that the Sikhs have never undergone the ultimate test of the ethnicity of their religiosity, namely the destruction of their major institutions in their homeland and dispersion from it. The two cases are somewhat different. With all that, the Sikhs show that the sort of union the Jews have between ethnicity and religion is not otherwise unknown in human religion.

To people growing up in a Christian environment it may seem somewhat odd that faith and peoplehood, will and biology, can interact the way they do among the Jews. Nonetheless, that is the Jewish way and it has its parallels among other peoples. There have not been enough cases to make such groups worthy of a distinctive descriptive term. This leaves one with the need to create special coinages for Sikh-Jewish-type groups. We are left with such hybrid usages as *religioethnic* or *ethnic-religious,* and thus the vocabulary of the English language itself turns out to be a special Jewish problem.

CHAPTER NINE

Some Ways
in Which We Are Ethnic

HEBREW—THE JEWISH LANGUAGE

Aside from entry by birth, ethnicity operates
among Jews in a number of ways, some of
which the *Centenary Perspective* specifies. The
first is language—most obviously, these days,
Hebrew. If one compares the role of Hebrew
among the Jews to Latin among Roman Catholics, the ethnic factor quickly emerges. No one
has ever suggested, to the best of my knowledge, that the cause of Catholic Christianity
would be much better served if all Catholics
could be gotten to speak, read, and write in
Latin, but that surely has been the goal of
Jewish Hebraists. Indeed, I think ·nost American Jews would agree that were it possible
somehow easily to achieve it, we would have
far better Jews in this country if all of us were
fully at ease in the Hebrew language.

Of course in Protestant Christianity, a
special language plays no role at all. Perhaps
the issue would be put more clearly if I distinguished between what Protestants have called
an ethnic church and the sort of ethnicity
which is critical to Jewish religiosity. An ethnic

church is generally identified as one that largely utilizes the language of the immigrants who founded it—German, Swedish, or the like. When the immigrant generation passes, some traces of the old ethnic style may linger on. Generally this is not the use of the old language, since most Americans tend not to use their parents' and grandparents' native tongues. Rather, what remains is the style of the church, its celebrations, special events and foods, perhaps too a special concern with the interpretation of Christianity current in the old homeland. But when the church is fully Americanized, when English is spoken and the children of this church move on to other churches without these old-country ties, one cannot say that the church or its wandering offspring are now less Christian. The ethnicity was not critical to the religiosity but an addendum to it. Among Jews a similar case would be the use of German in the synagogues of the late-nineteenth-century American immigrants. It was a functioning part of their Jewishness, but they could give it up and still remain quite authentically Jewish.

Whether one could give up Hebrew completely and for all time and still remain significantly a Jew is quite doubtful. Better than such theoretical speculations, however, is the experience of Reform Judaism in the United States. There were some rabbis and congregations early in the century who almost

completely dispensed with the Hebrew language. Their argument was that one should not
pray in words one did not understand, that
God would surely accept prayers on the basis
of intention rather than in consideration of the
tongue in which they were uttered. Yet despite
the logic of these statements, the Reform
movement has since the turn of the century
steadily moved in a more Hebraic direction
Prayer should be heartfelt, but Jewish prayer
includes joining one's heart with the hearts of
one's people and, through their words, to the
hearts of those Jews who by their faithful continuity made possible one's own Jewish life. So
for some years now Reform Jews have
generally asked that their services include a
number of Hebrew prayers whose words they
may not directly understand yet which they
want to hear. They know that Hebrew binds
them tightly to the Jewish people and thus is
intimately related to Jewish belief and practice,
a good instance of the uncommon link of ethnicity and belief among us.

OTHER JEWISH LANGUAGES

The linguistic factor in Jewish ethnicity is not
limited to Hebrew. The Jews have had a pro-
clivity for creating languages down through the
ages. Of these mixtures of Hebrew with a
vernacular, American Jews are most familiar
with Yiddish, though the Sephardim among us
will speak or remember Ladino. There are good

records and occasional speakers of other Jewish languages—Judeo-Persian, Judeo-Arabic, and such. That is hardly the sort of thing a religion, in the Christian sense, should have been doing, yet the Jews regularly created distinctive literatures and folklores in a number of such special languages over the centuries.

Maurice Samuel had a delightful theory about Yiddish which, if true, lends extra testimony to the Jewish mix of ethnicity and religion. He suggested that Yiddish was invented, so to speak, to keep a measure of Hebrew alive in the everyday lives of Jews. Yiddish has been variously estimated as carrying about 20 percent of its vocabulary in borrowed Hebrew words. A Jew who speaks Yiddish already is in touch with a substantial Hebrew vocabulary. Though the sacred tongue itself had been limited to religious life activities, it was carried over into the secular activities of Jews by being incorporated into a special Jewish language.

ISRAEL—THE JEWISH LAND

The Land of Israel has long occupied a special place in the Jewish religion and its life. The Bible has made Jerusalem more than a city for countless people around the world and Zion more than a hill therein. These ordinary places have been transformed by Jewish and Christian experience into symbols of the transcendent, locales where God and people came into special

contact. How much the more have they meant
to Jews whose folk had its origins on that land,
who considered it part of their unique relationship with God, and who looked to it as the site
where the redemption of their people and all
humanity would center.

Reform Jews of an earlier time had difficulty with this classic Jewish emphasis on the
Land of Israel. Facing the suspicions of the
new nations who cautiously gave them rights or
of neighbors who wondered if Jews were not
congenital aliens, the early Reform Jews elimi-
nated prayers for a return to the Land of Israel
from their prayerbook. But they did not
eliminate—could anyone?—the Land of Israel
from their Judaism. They still cherished the
Bible and thus retained steady contact with its
strangely evocative places. They maintained the
Jewish calendar with its associations with the
agricultural cycle of the old homeland. Thus
Reform Jews made no effort to do away with
Sukkot but took great pride in its relation to
the Puritan and later American festival of
Thanksgiving. Yet in these latitudes, giving God
thanks for the harvest in late September or
early October made sense only if one explained
that we celebrated here now as our people did
in Bible days in the Land of Israel. It took the
horror of the Hitler years and the joys associated with the establishment of the State of
Israel, as well as the new American appreciation of ethnicity, to let the Land of Israel come

to a fuller place in Reform Judaism. The *Centenary Perspective* seems to take for granted that acceptance of the Land of Israel as one more facet of the rounded-out Reform Judaism of our times. Since a common land is a major factor in ethnicity, it is listed here among the things that Jews, in their ethnic aspect, share.

THE JEWISH STYLE

The *Perspective* goes on to list "history, culture, and institutions." It could have added a good deal more, and these must be considered merely a few major indications of Jewish ethnicity. Each in turn could be broken down into many parts. So in a discussion of institutions we could discuss those peculiarly interesting creations, the Jewish family or school or community structure. All ethnic groups have them and give them their own distinctive twist. And so have we, shaping them in a way as much spiritual as folk. The elaboration of similarities and differences, the effort to disentangle the religious from the ethnic in each instance, could go on endlessly (itself one of our ethnic traits, the love of analysis and argument).

Which brings me to the matter of our style, of that elusive approach to living one finds so widespread among American Ashkenazi Jews. Sometimes you recognize it by a shrug or a gesture, more frequently, a few years back, in one's intonation or turn of phrase. We associate it with that mysterious interpersonal "radar" science tells us cannot exist and is notoriously unreliable but that most Jews still utilize to detect the presence of other Jews—with occasionally striking results. Even the ways Jews try to hide from their Jewishness or shield themselves from detection by other Jews is part of our ethnic heritage. Overeating instead of boozing, an addiction to the verbal, jokes, a sensitivity to changing fashions—who knows how far the modern Jewish style, for all its varieties and personal embellishments, goes? Yet it clearly derives from Jewish group experience and only peripherally from the Jewish religion. Any serious-minded Jew will find it difficult to attach great spiritual significance to Jewish style, yet without it we would lose something precious. It grounds our ethnic life and is therefore part of us in a way it could never be if we were merely a church.

THE CULTURAL IMPERATIVE

This understanding of our group nature owes much to the thought of the great American Jewish philosopher Mordecai Kaplan. He was the first person, who, in the 1920s and 30s, tried to apply to the Jews the insights of the new science called sociology. In place of race and blood he taught American Jews to speak of peoples and their civilizations—what later more commonly came to be called culture. The first thing a sociologist notices about humanity is that it is divided into different groups. This led Kaplan to argue that the Jews are another such natural group and that no supernatural choice was needed to set us apart from other peoples. Just as all other groups developed a way of facing the world and elaborated it into a multi-faceted life-style, so too did the Jews. And since religion was only one part of a people's culture, even if the pivotal part, so the Jewish religion needed to be seen as but one aspect of an entire range of ethnic activities. Much of the revival of Jewish music, art, dance, and other cultural activities among us in recent decades has been due to Kaplan's insistence that we are an ethnic group and need to take up the full gamut of cultural responsibilities which derive from that identity. Kaplan had gotten this idea from the cultural Zionists before him, specifically from Ahad Haam. Yet he must be given special credit for Americanizing their rather narrower, European sense of nationality and for utilizing the insights of Durkheim and some other early sociologists to help Jews gain a rich, full sense of their group nature. This section of the *Centenary Perspective* should then be particularly pleasing to those Reform Jews who have found Mordecai Kaplan a guide to their sense of a modern Judaism. Yet for all Reform Jews it expresses the conviction that Jews are not a church but, odd as this may seem, an ethnic group. Had the document said only this, it would have pleased no one, probably not even the Kaplanians. The statement on ethnicity must be kept in balance with what went before which spoke of the union of peoplehood and faith, and therefore with what follows, a statement of this people's involvement with God.

CHAPTER TEN

The Religious Side of This People

THE JEWISH NATION

The Bible considers the Jews a nation in the same way that the Hivites, the Hittites, the Egyptians, and the Babylonians are nations, yet it makes a major distinction between the children of Jacob—Israel—and them. The other peoples came into being when God dispersed the peoples of the earth into tongues, lands, and nations after they tried to build a tower at Babel which would reach up into the heavens where God resides. Nationhood commonly results, therefore, from human sinfulness and God's punishment. The Jews became a nation in an entirely different way. God came to Abraham and told him that he was to obey God in special ways, as by leaving Ur of the Chaldees and going to a land that God would show him. In return, God would eventually make of his children a great and multitudinous nation.

After three generations the numbers began to grow, and four centuries later a mighty people existed—the Bible counts six hundred thousand. To them, at Sinai, in a mighty act of fulfillment and new agreement, God gave the Torah. No other people had anything like it. No other people was expected to give God the special obedience and loyalty that the people Israel now owed God. At the same time, no other people could hope for the special gifts of God, such as the Land of Israel, the protection of God amid the trials of history, or, as it was eventually understood, the ultimate vindication of Jewish constancy when the King-Messiah arrived to rule the world and demonstrated the truth of the Jewish assertion that their God was indeed the one Lord of all the universe.

THE CHOSEN-PEOPLE CONCEPT

Until modern times it was quite clear: God chose the Jews. They were a nation because God wanted them to be a nation and this was unlike anything any other people could claim. Their nationhood was also unique because it was based on their having the Torah, the God-ordained laws and teachings by which they were to guide their national life. I do not see that one can deny that the Jews were therefore understood to have a special status in relation to God, one closer to God than anyone else had and therefore a better one. This did not imply that other peoples had no relation to God or that the Jews therefore deserved privileges in this world. They would indeed get special rewards in the life of the world to come, but in this world chosenness was closely linked with Torah and its commandments and thus implied special standards of obedience.

Modern Jews have found it difficult to affirm the doctrine of the chosen people in the ways their ancestors did. With regard to God, they shy away from ascribing to the Divine such explicit intervention into history. It is one thing to say God's power moves through nature and even makes itself felt in human affairs. It is quite another thing to say, so flatly, "God chose us." Moderns prefer to talk about religious reality from the human side, emphasizing the initiative of people. Religion seems to us as much our work as God's; it seems easier to understand as more human discovery than God's gift. Now, too, as we Jews for the first time see humanity in worldwide perspective, we recognize that most human beings are very much alike. We do not believe that the Jews are as different from all other peoples as previous generations thought, though, with all that, most of us do not think that they are just another culture. Besides, the democratic view of humanity assigns equal status to everyone. For these and other reasons, chosenness seems dangerous or anachronistic or in need of reinterpretation, though some still maintain it is true.

THE MEANING OF CHOSENNESS

The *Centenary Perspective* sidesteps this issue. This is another instance of no single theology satisfying the overwhelming majority of rabbis. Some of them want every vestige of the idea purged from our Judaism. Others use Zangwill's phrase of some decades ago, "a choosing people," which though acknowledging that we have no specially assigned place in the universe says we have distinguished ourselves as a people by our unique effort to live up to our sense of God's will. Some supplement that with the contention that historic peoples, like individuals, have certain talents. The Jews have a genius for responding to God. I once heard George Steiner, the famous British critic, suggest the possibility that perhaps there was something peculiar in the genetic chemistry of Jews, an odd structured DNA and RNA which gave them their special capacities.

Others prefer to emphasize the message rather than the Jews.

Early Reform Jews, basing themselves on the special affinity they felt existed between religious liberalism and Judaism, proclaimed that the Jews have a special mission to humanity: spreading the idea of ethical monotheism. The idea now seems somewhat pretentious and is not often heard. Some rabbis feel these liberal notions of chosenness reduce God to a passive bystander in the affairs of humanity, including the special quality of Jewish life. Believing that God is personally present to people, at least at certain moments, they speak of the Covenant between God and the Jewish people, the sense of mutual agreement which arises from moments of special insight, when people love. There are also those who, despite their appreciation of the human role in religion, simply accept God's greatness as beyond them and therefore reaffirm the traditional teaching that "God chose us from among all peoples and gave us the Torah."

OUR "INVOLVEMENT WITH GOD"

The *Centenary Perspective* covers all such possibilities with the words "involvement with God." It says further that the uniqueness of the Jewish people comes from this involvement. One may understand this in two ways. The more traditional way would be to say that there is something in the content of the involvement with God which makes the Jews unique. It is the Torah or the Covenant or something about the relationship between God and the Jews which distinguishes the Jewish people. The more humanistic way of reading the sentence would be to ascribe uniqueness only to the Jewish historical experience. One might argue that no other ethnic group has ever been so concerned about bringing God into its civilization as has the Jews. There is no claim here that the relationship of the Jews to God is special, for the universal God treats all people alike. Everyone could have done what the Jews did; in fact, they didn't. The uniqueness of the Jews is merely a historical fact, and one can raise no moral objections to that, since all historical experience is unique.

Regardless of which position one takes, Jewish ethnicity, all agree, is uniquely religious. It has to do with God. It has not and does not exist in and of itself. The paragraph rejects the notion that ethnicity alone can ever furnish a satisfactory understanding of our people. It denies the validity of all purely secular interpretations of the Jews. Thus for all its previous strong assertion of the significance of Jewish ethnicity, the *Perspective* now equally strongly insists that the Jews and their ethnicity are irredeemably religious.

IMMEDIATE CONSEQUENCES

The *Perspective* adds two further considerations. First, the involvement with God is linked to a "resulting perception of the human condition." Relationship with the Divine has immediate consequences for what it is to be a human being. The Jews are not concerned with just worshipping or being in the presence of God. Jewish intimacy with God results in: commandments to follow, a society to build, temptation to confront, sin to atone for, forgiveness to seek, judgment to confront, and hope that the God who we know is real will eventually become a reality in all human life upon the earth. The particular religious experience of the Jews has given them a vision of the universal possibilities of humanity. Some will want to assert that this view of the human condition is itself unique among the religions of the world. Surely the age-old devotion of the Jewish folk in bending its ethnicity to this vision is without parallel among the cultures nations have created.

Jewish faith in God and thus in humanity climaxes in the Jewish messianic hope. The Jews may be a quite particular ethnic group, with all the concrete, historical individuality that goes with peoplehood. Yet Jewish ethnicity is indissolubly joined to Jewish faith which moves on inexorably from God to people to a messianic vision of sin overcome and God's will as the inner law of every human heart. So in its particularity the people Israel reaches out to all humanity. Again the *Perspective* has repeated its familiar theme: the particular and the universal coexist in contemporary Reform Judaism.

CHAPTER ELEVEN

The Perils of Splitting Faith and Folk

POLARIZATION

I must add a personal word to this interpretation of the *Centenary Perspective*'s paragraph on the people of Israel. What emerges here, as does so often in this document, is the problem of finding a proper balance between two commitments which partially conflict. What regularly causes difficulty in Reform Judaism is such devotion to one of the affirmations that the other one is as good as forgotten. Then those who are concerned about the other belief stress it all the more in the hope of counteracting the protagonists of the first belief. Instead of healthy tension, polarization results. One is forced to choose between positions which, isolated from their counterbalancing view, are not what you really believe. The older Reform Judaism occasionally stressed the religious side of being a Jew to such an extent that our peoplehood was almost lost. Today one might call this religion without *Yiddishkeit*. The ethnic factor, understood in their case as the specifically German-Jewish style, was utterly subordinated to the Protestant religious model.

So early Reform Judaism came to seem very much like a church.

Criticism of that adjustment is quite easy in a time when ethnicity is acceptable, perhaps even a positive value. American social moods moving as fast as they have in our time, we cannot assume that change is permanent. Still, from this vantage point one can wish they had been stronger in their affirmation of a distinctive American Jewish community style. Yet it is not clear, particularly when I think back to the early 1930s and the pressures upon us—I was growing up in a medium-sized Midwestern town, Columbus, Ohio—that it would have been very easy for those trying to win a place for the Jews amid the general community to insist on greater Jewish distinctiveness.

Today I occasionally feel that the opposite sort of single-mindedness is becoming a problem. Some Jews are so proud of our new Jewish ethnic self-consciousness that they seem content to forget that we are also a religion. The reasons for such an exaggerated attention to our peoplehood are easy to appreciate. We have real enemies and they threaten us harm, less seriously on the domestic scene where there is more threat than reality, but radically on the international scene where we see the isolation of the State of Israel and continuing pressures upon it. We must be on guard; we know that in an emergency we must depend primarily upon ourselves alone. The needs of the Jewish people then summon us to duty, and no self-respecting Jew will say no to that call. In such a situation it is not difficult to overlook our simultaneous responsibility to God and thus to humanity. Our energy, our money, our concern go overwhelmingly to the State of Israel, with some funds reserved for our struggle against bigotry and anti-Semitism. By contrast, synagogues, Jewish education, and the fostering of Jewish culture make do with what can be spared. The example is somewhat unfair, but I hope it puts our problem of perspective into immediately recognizable terms.

SOURCES OF THE STRUGGLE

This concentration on ethnicity has strong forces behind it. We turn to our immigrant roots out of nostalgia for the warmth and closeness of an earlier day. The great accomplishments of the State of Israel appeal to our need for heroes and our disgust with most governments. Besides, ethnicity, though nice, cannot make many demands upon us. American Jews overwhelmingly resist the implication that rich ethnicity depends on knowing Yiddish or Hebrew. By contrast, Jewish religion means facing the claims of God and the commandments, even if these are understood in a liberal way. Our need to help our people may get us to attend meetings, organize activities, and give money, but that is a much easier kind of authority to deal with.

The ethnicity-religion issue can be more sharply drawn. There are cases in our community today where ethnic concern reaches the level of chauvinism. Some Jews think of general society or world problems only in terms of how they specifically relate to Jewish needs. When we use our community for what it can do for the Jews but refuse to contribute to its welfare, when we are effectively only for ourselves, then something precious in the Jewish balance between duties to self and duties to others has been lost. I am not saying Jews should sacrifice their ethnic rights for the sake of mankind in some gross parody of Christian self-crucifixion. Rather I am deploring a Jewish ethnicity which ignores God and our active responsibility to humanity. I do not deny that there are still sick Jews who wish to be so pure that they cannot abide the taint of selfishness they fear is involved in caring about their own people. Yet I am far more troubled at the moment by the growing number of Jews whose resurgence of Jewish ethnicity means the rest of the world can, as far as they are concerned, go to hell.

THE FLAW IN KAPLAN'S UNDERSTANDING OF GOD

Intellectually, one may find some vague parallel to this problem in a common, thoughtless appropriation of Mordecai Kaplan's theories about Jewish peoplehood. Kaplan, in clarifying the nature of the Jewish group sociologically, argued that the people was the motive force in the creation of Judaism. For Kaplan, God can play no independent role in this process, for Kaplan's God has no independent status. Rather Kaplan sees the religious component of a civilization, as critical as it is, arising from a need of human nature and responding to it in ways appropriate to that social setting. In the hands of people less subtle than Kaplan this can easily become a way of reducing religion to ethnicity. If a people creates its religion and in due course its idea of God, one can legitimately give all one's energy to helping the people live a healthy ethnic existence. When the group is strong enough, it will get around to religion. This theory can easily be appropriated by atheists and agnostics to justify avoiding religious questions while yet claiming to reconstruct Jewish life. I have often met educators and social workers, and to a lesser degree rabbis, who used Kaplan to validate an ethnicity that had as good as given up on Jewish faith.

From my point of view Kaplan must take some responsibility for this, though his own writings treat positively of religiosity as part of Jewish ethnic life and of the sort of God we might today believe in. The problem has to do with what the preceding paragraph in the *Centenary Perspective* called "God's reality." For Kaplan this means the "reality" that human nature—as science, Kaplan thinks, has shown—is involved in a purposive relation with nature. We are full of plans and projects, and thus really trust that our universe is so constructed as to allow us to achieve our goals. We necessarily believe, therefore, that there are real processes in nature which support our hopes for our lives. We base our existence on these natural realities. They are the reality we term *God*. Our God is therefore as real as the reality in nature on which we rely. But God, then, has no independent reality. God is, so to speak, no "thing," no being, no entity in itself. God is only a word we use to describe many discrete natural processes. God's reality therefore cannot ever stand over against us and make independent claims on us, though for Kaplan we should obviously not hope to do what nature cannot support. So weak a sense of God as Kaplan's, I believe, can easily be swallowed up in individual and ethnic human activity. "What supports me is my God" easily becomes "Doing what I want to do is being in touch with God." Or, ethnically, since the people creates its religion and shapes its idea of God, ethnic activity becomes the equivalent of directly religious acts, the familiar problem of why pray rather than study or meet which has dogged Kaplanians for years. Kaplan, in giving us a rich sense of our peoplehood, has extended it to the point of denying the independence and thus the counterbalancing role of God in Jewish existence. Kaplan is no chauvinist, and his own, unexplained sense of moral absolutes, gives him a broad sense of Jewish responsibility. But his humanism is so rigorous that he cannot give us the strong counterfaith in God which sets limits to Jewish self-love and places it in the sanctifying context of universal responsibility.

OUR PARTNERSHIP WITH GOD

The overwhelming majority of Reform Jews acknowledge that they hold a double premise as the foundation of their faith: there is one God for all the world, and their ethnic group, the people Israel, is intimately and inextricably involved with that God. The inevitable result of such a two-part affirmation is that some Reform Jews have always been more concerned with emphasizing the universal, religious side of Reform Judaism, while others have done the same for the ethnic, particular side. This, as well as the staunch insistence on personal autonomy, has engendered much diversity in the Reform movement. The *Centenary Perspective* here points out that these points of view need to be seen as part of a partnership: God with the people of Israel, the people with its God. That will not by any means eliminate the differences of opinion and practice which result from stressing one side of the balance or the other. But it will at least help us develop a sense of what, in all our diversity, we hold in common with regard to religion and ethnicity.

PART IV

Torah

Torah results from the relationship between God and the Jewish people. The records of our earliest confron-
      III.   tations are uniquely important to us.
   Torah   Lawgivers and prophets, historians and
poets gave us a heritage whose study is a religious imperative and whose practice is our chief means to holiness. Rabbis and teachers, philosophers and mystics, gifted Jews in every age amplified the Torah tradition. For millennia, the creation of Torah has not ceased and Jewish creativity in our time is adding to the chain of tradition.

From the Centenary Perspective

CHAPTER TWELVE

Reform's Radical Idea: A Dynamic Sense of Torah

THE "PEOPLE OF THE BOOK"

The chief symbol of Judaism is the Torah scroll which proclaims that the one God of all the universe has given instruction to the people joined to God in Covenant. The scroll itself contains only the first five books of the Bible, but upon this rests our entire sacred tradition, the rest of the Bible, the rabbinic literature, and the teaching of Jewish sages to our own time. In a sense, the word *Torah*, comprehensively taken, is synonymous with *Judaism* — and, since the latter term is only a century or so old, may be considered its predecessor. Many religions have sacred books and all have traditions, some book-based and some essentially oral. Judaism is uniquely centered on God's having communicated in words, even in books. Scholars have seen this as the root of the Jewish emphasis on intellect and education. If God has given us a book of divine truth (really a collection of books), only fools would fail to study it with the closest attention. Since interpreting the book and drawing forth its implications for situations unspecified there gained the authority of the text itself, Judaism became a religion heavily based on tradition. Mohammed was so impressed with this conception of religion that he called for Muslims to treat those who were "people of a book" differently from those who were not. One quick way of distinguishing between the general character of Eastern religions and those of the West, Judaism and its daughters, is still this notion of revelation, of God giving the faithful rules for and an understanding of life.

THE DEFINITION OF TORAH

Because *Torah* is a term so rich in meaning to Jews it has resisted translation and made its way into the vocabulary of the most un-Hebraicized modern Jews and of non-Jewish students of Judaism. The common English translation, "law," is wrong and misleading in a way that tends to disparagement. A good deal of the Torah scroll books, for example, is not law, and that certainly holds true of most of the Bible and the midrashic side of rabbinic literature. Law is a central category in Torah, but to equate the two gives rise to attacks on the character and worth of Judaism which go back to the writings of the apostle Paul in the New Testament.

What *law* commonly means to people is a set of rules, detailed, difficult and annoying, by which one is judged and generally pronounced guilty of some infraction or another. Religion, which begins by loving God with all one's heart, soul, and might, ends up as a set of performances to be done, and thus rather dry and mechanical. Anyone who has suffered through hearing Judaism denigrated as an arid legalism will shudder at the implications of translating *Torah* as "law." (Paul may have gotten his distorted view of Torah—as other Christians certainly did—from using the Greek translation of the Bible which renders Torah as *nomos*, "law.")

The Hebrew root of the word Torah is *y-r-h*, whose most concrete usage is for casting something in a certain direction, as in shooting an arrow. More abstractly it comes to mean "to teach," as in the first words students beginning Hebrew learn when they are told to call their teacher *moreh* or *morah*. We should probably translate *Torah* as "The Teaching." While that has some nice religious associations and could include much besides law, it seems far better simply to use the Hebrew term untranslated and thus not lose any of its unique connotations.

A DEVELOPING SENSE OF TORAH

Reform Jews initiated a new movement in Judaism by their new sense of Torah. Biblical Judaism is centered around a decisive act which took place at Mount Sinai. There God fulfilled and completed the Covenant made with Abraham and his descendants, by speaking

directly to the nation derived from the Patriarchs, making ten unparalleled personal utter-
ances, and, when that proved frightening to the
people, giving the rest of the Torah to Moses to
transmit to them. The Bible understands other
prophets to have followed Moses and communicated special aspects of God's will. It also has
poems, proverbs, speeches, and narratives
whose relation to God is not clearly specified
but which are apparently considered to be
derived from God and thus sacred.

By the time of the rabbis the Jewish idea of
revelation is more fully elaborated. God uses a
"holy spirit" with which to inspire some
people to write. The rabbis judged the Song of
Songs to have been written under the influence
of the holy spirit and included it in Sacred
Scripture, but said the Book of Ben Sirach had
not so been written and barred it from the
Bible. More important, the rabbis said that
what Moses had received from God was not
only the Written Torah, the first five books of
the Bible, but the Oral Torah as well. The latter
consisted of relatively independent traditions
concerning Jewish life and values. It also
included the rules for the proper way to interpret the Written Torah or extend the Oral
Torah to meet new conditions of Jewish existence. The rabbis could not conceive of a
conflict between the two kinds of Torah and
considered them only two aspects of one,
complex, consistent, living heritage. As we now

read what the rabbis of the first and second century of the Common Era did to keep Judaism vital, particularly in the wake of the destruction of the Temple, previously the central institution in Jewish religious life, we marvel at their flexibility and ingenuity. Their doctrine of the Oral Torah appears to us an extraordinarily creative way to keep Judaism from becoming chained to a text set down a millenium or so previously. Through the Oral Torah they developed biblical Judaism so as to meet the difficulties and opportunities of a new time. Since these processes of change could be carried out by any generation of learned Jews, Judaism now had a method for meeting the unexpected and staying alive.

STAGNATION OF THE PROCESS

Had the flexibility of these early centuries of rabbinic creativity continued into the modern period, there probably would have been no need for the creation of a Reform movement. In theory, the Oral Torah puts such power into the hands of the rabbis that, using it to a maximum, they could have introduced many of the changes we now take for granted as desirable in a modern Judaism. Many things prevented this from being the case. Rabbinic law works largely in terms of precedent, and by modern times there were so many precedents and such respect for predecessors that it was difficult to authorize modification of traditional practice.

Jews had for centuries lived in segregation and under oppression, making trust in general society and radical accommodation to its mores appear imprudent if not sinful. Besides, the demands being made of Jews to alter their life-style seemed intolerably greater than anything Jews had ever experienced in the past. And the Jewish community had been spiritually exhausted by the strenuous effort to survive the difficult years from 1500 to 1800. So the response of the traditional rabbinate to the possibilities of the new freedom of the early nineteenth century was almost uniformly negative.

Yet everywhere freedom was offered them, Jews moved to accept it and willingly paid its price. If survival as such is a primary Jewish value, one may say that in some measures they acted from Jewish motives—they sought a decent life for themselves and their families. One senses something of this unexpected manifestation of Jewish loyalty in their response to the temptations of society. When it turned out that the cost of full participation was conversion to Christianity, only a minority, though not an inconsiderable one, were willing to change their faith. Imagine their unpleasant choice. They wanted to be modern, yet that seemed to entail being Christian. To be Jewish implied identification with a life-style stubbornly oriented to the ghetto and its relatively medieval culture.

A NEW SENSE OF TORAH

This dilemma was broken by a courageous few—lay people, it should be understood—who insisted, against what their sages said, that it must be possible to be modern and Jewish, to be Jewish in a modern way. If the authorities would not lead the move to such a Judaism, they would create it themselves. Thus Reform Judaism came into being. It was an effort to accept Western society without accepting Christianity, to create a form of Jewish life appropriate to the conditions of Emancipation.

These first-generation lay tinkerers with Jewish form seem to have had little conscious sense that they were breaking with the traditional doctrine of Torah, that the Oral Torah authorized only certain kinds of change and then only when sanctioned by the leading rabbis of the age. I think they reformed Jewish practice in the same intuitive Jewish way that the ghetto dwellers rushed out into general society. They knew, somehow, that it was right for Judaism not to stagnate, that one could change the modes of being a Jew and still remain true to one's Jewishness. I doubt that their sense of what they were doing went much deeper than that. Not until the second generation of Reform Jewish leaders, rabbis versed in Jewish lore, some university-trained, was it possible to state the new sense of Torah which lay behind their innovative continuity. They were not philosophers, so they created no rigorous new concept. Nonetheless, they evolved a way of talking about what they were doing that remains characteristic of most modern Judaism. They said that God's will can be known by people in every age and not merely through the documents and precedents of ages past. In a time of radical transition Jews have a right to act on what they believe God wants of them in their altered situation. Torah can change—if necessary, radically.

Then the Jewish historians came and proved that the content of Torah teaching had indeed been modified over the centuries. The very books of the Torah scroll were themselves seen as the result of human creation moving through a series of four major phases. This dynamic sense of Torah seemed completely confirmed by many cultural developments, including the theory of evolution and the belief in social progress which accompanied the economic growth of the nineteenth century. What happened at Sinai was extraordinary, but only one of a series of historic occurrences continuing into the present. How Jews should serve God could not be restricted to one pattern authorized by one group but had to come more directly from the people itself and accord with what its conscience found appropriate.

MODERN JEWISH APPROACHES

This basic position has undergone much refinement since. (Below we shall explain four modern ways of understanding Torah-revelation.) Despite the elaborations it remains the basis of contemporary Reform Judaism. Somewhat playfully, though provocatively, one may say that it created "Orthodox" Judaism. Before Reform proclaimed a relatively unrestricted right to change Jewish practice, there was hardly any need to defend tradition's theory of authority. But in the face of the Reform challenge a vigorous defense of the classic position had to be made, bringing the traditional doctrine of Torah to self-consciousness and creating "Orthodoxy"—"the right opinion"—in the place of what had heretofore only been traditional Judaism. Other modern Jewish movements derive their special concerns from this issue. Conservative Judaism and Reconstructionism accept the Reform premise that Torah is dynamic. They differ from Reform only in how the flexibility of Torah should be controlled or directed. Reform Jews have come to be resolutely individualistic, arguing that for all the virtues of the tradition and the benefits of scholarly guidance, the individual Jew must be the final arbiter of what is living Torah. Conservative Jews have insisted that change take place slowly, with concern for the bulk of observing Jews and under the guidance of a body of scholars knowledgeable in Torah and committed to using its procedures when instituting new Jewish practices. Recon-

structionists, believing that the Jewish people is
the creator of Torah—which they equate with
Jewish culture—call for some democratic body,
representative of loyal Jews, democratically to
vote what the standards for contemporary
Jewish living should be. One may therefore
argue that, intellectually, Conservative and
Reconstructionist Judaism are sects of Reform
Judaism, for they derive from its fundamental
break with Jewish tradition and build on its
insistence that Torah can be freshly developed
in every age.

THE REFORM POSITION

In the nineteenth century many a traditionalist
Jew, Orthodox or proto-Conservative, would
have argued that Torah was substantially static
and had not developed in response to historic
situations. Thus we hear worries in the Midrash
how Abraham, though he lived before the revelation at Sinai—of the Oral as well as the
Written Torah—could, as Genesis says, think of
serving the three men who came to visit him
the unkosher combination cheese and meat.
Since one God had given one Torah, every
great Jew must have known it and little could
have altered in it despite time. Today the language of evolution, adaptation, and social
responsiveness is simply part of the self-
understanding of most Jews, even of modern
Orthodox scholars, the first five books of the
Bible excepted. As a result, when our com-

mittee came to formulate the section of Torah it found itself confronted with very few problems. A century ago—even a couple of generations back—the Reform sense of Torah would evoke polemics and argument. In our time there is virtual Jewish consensus; the acceptance of Reform Jewish teaching has been that complete. The curious consequence of this situation was that, in the draft presented to the Conference in San Francisco, the statement of Torah was only two sentences, namely, "Torah results from meetings between God and the Jewish people. The records of our earliest confrontations are uniquely important to us; yet Torah continues to be created even in our own time." There had been a longer paragraph on Torah in the working draft* mailed to the rabbis in March, but since that version seemed verbose the committee undertook to prune every excess word from it and what we needed to say about Torah was finally contained in those few words. They said that Torah was as much a human creation as it was God-given and thus dynamic in a more-than-traditional sense. They indicated it was essentially a folk, not an individual matter. And while they asserted the unique value of the Bible and, by implication, rabbinic writings, they emphasized that what is created today may also be entitled to the

---

*For a discussion on the procedure and process involved in arriving at the final document, see the Supplement to this volume

dignity and authority of being called Torah.
Since by now these Reform Jewish attitudes
were widely understood and accepted, the
committee thought not much more needed to
be said.

When this draft came to the floor of the
Conference, objections were voiced to the
brevity of this section. Our colleagues did not
object to what had been said, and it was not
clear that they thought anything truly significant had been omitted. My feeling was that
they believed saying so little implied that
Torah had accordingly little significance to us.
Of course, the opposite is the case. The doctrine of Torah as dynamic determines the
unique position of Reform Judaism, and thus
anything which seems to make Torah relatively
unimportant detracts from the value of Reform
Judaism itself.

Another possible misunderstanding the
document's brevity might engender was that
Reform disparaged the value of tradition,
particularly the multifaceted development of
Judaism in the postbiblical, premodern period.
That, too, contradicts our teaching, for we
insist that not just Sinai or the Torah books
dominate Jewish thinking, but that Torah is
produced in every age. There was no difference
in principle here, only one of form. As a result
it was agreed that the paragraph on Torah be
expanded based on the working draft's longer
text and on the discussion by the Conference.

Some additional suggestions were received after the San Francisco meeting, and a draft was submitted to the committee which resulted in the present section on Torah. It specifies some of the various forms in which Torah has been created, connects the possession of Torah with the need to study and to practice, and removes what some saw as an invidious comparison between the Torah created in our time and that of a previous age.

CHAPTER THIRTEEN

How Torah Arises: Four Modern Views

Reform Judaism transformed the classic Jewish doctrine of Torah by drastically increasing the role people played in its origin. For the Bible, Torah is something God gives, and when Moses or the kings do not know what God wants them to do, they inquire of God quite directly. Some rabbis could even speak of Torah as having existed with God before Creation. The liberal view, by contrast, concentrated on human discovery often to the elimination of any special act of God. This emphasis on the human aspect of Torah is understandable as a response to the historic problem modern Jews faced. They knew Judaism must change if it was to survive. Since the traditional authorities insisted that the Torah system could not make the radical adaptations apparently required by the modern world, the Reformers made them themselves. Human action was the basis of Reform—and, as they saw it, the basis of Judaism's possibility to survive. If they were right, human initiative was a critical element in Torah.

HUMAN INITIATIVE AND TORAH

Two consequences followed from this assumption. First, as the dynamic sense of history grew in the nineteenth century, the Reformers saw human initiative as the motive force in much of the Jewish religion's development. The Jews, like all other people facing new situations or compelling new ideas, humanly made the adjustments that seemed required. Quickly it seemed so obvious to them that Jewish life had always been shaped and re-shaped in this way that they did not see how anyone could deny that a substantially independent humanity had created the Torah and its subsequent traditions.

Some qualification is needed here. The Bible and Talmud do not deny the Jews a role in relation to Torah. The Bible pictures them accepting it out of their free will, agreeing to receive and live by the Torah as a matter of positive choice and commitment. For the rabbis, human participation goes even further, though some rabbis emphasize God's dominance in the relationship. Their Judaism focused largely on the Oral Torah with its manifold procedures for developing new laws and values. They stressed the human factor for the power to decide what Torah now said was in their hands. The rabbis' "humanism" is strikingly illustrated in two passages in the Talmud much beloved of liberal preachers. The annual Jewish calendar, specifically the dates of Rosh Hashanah and thus of Yom Kippur, must be fixed by a human court. Thus we are told that when, in one talmudic tale, the angels ask God when the New Year will fall, God says, "Why ask Me? Let us both go down and see what the rabbinic court has determined." The other tradition tells of a Heavenly Voice pronouncing Rabbi Eliezer right though he is the only one disagreeing with the rabbis over the purity status of a certain sort of stove. The rabbis then remind the Heavenly Voice—with a biblical quotation, to be sure—that it is their responsibility, not Heaven's, to rule on what are the authoritative implications of Torah. Later, Elijah meets and tells one of the rabbis that in that hour God laughed and said, "My children have conquered me."

For all the charm and, by some standards, religious audacity of these stories, Jewish tradition basically thought of Torah as God-given and limited the human role in reinterpreting it to the patterns which God has prescribed and the precedents the masters of prior generations had set. Thus the possibility of granting women equal rights to men in Judaism hardly comes within the sphere of human initiative in traditional Jewish law but seems to many of the earliest Reformers exactly the sort of thing they must and should do. To be precise, we should say that there is only a relative difference between the role of people in defining duty in Orthodoxy and Reform, but it is great and radical enough to make for a major new direction in Jewish history.

Liberal Jewish thinkers have proposed a number of theories explaining how Torah arises from among human beings. In such a situation the *Centenary Perspective* avoids endorsing any one view and presents a general statement agreeable to proponents of the various theologies. Thus to say that "Torah results from . . . God and the Jewish people" is, by contrast to the classic "God gave the Torah to the people of Israel," to give the Reform Jewish view. The two partners in Torah are mentioned, but no specific role is assigned each, thus allowing people to utilize whichever liberal understanding of Torah they accept. The committee had a problem, however, in trying to find a suitable neutral word to describe what it was between God and the Jews that engendered Torah. In the working draft the committee vetoed the word *encounters* as seeming to endorse the interpretation of Martin Buber. It then settled on the admittedly clumsy locution *meetings* between God and the Jewish people. That seemed to be open enough for various interpretations yet directed attention to what happened between God and the people rather than to either side of the partnership. But the term *meetings* is rather odd, and at the discussion of the document by the Conference it was suggested and agreed that the term *relationship* be used in its place. When this word had been suggested in our committee discussions, I had thought that it was so closely associated with an existentialist interpretation of Torah that it might seem a one-party usage. I was happy to be proven wrong and to learn here, as in a number of other matters, more of what my colleagues mean by the theological terms they use.

I believe there are four major liberal Jewish theories about the sort of relationship, between God and the people of Israel, which produces Torah. Since accepting one or another of these views—or some combination of them, though this is intellectually incoherent—has important consequences for our understanding of what we should and should not do as Jews, I want, most briefly, to set them out here.

THE POSITION OF HERMANN COHEN

The oldest of these positions, that of Hermann Cohen, is also the most radical; that is, its sense of Jewish duty is more distant from the Jewish tradition than any of the three views outlined below. Hermann Cohen, the dominant German Jewish intellectual in the four decades preceding World War I, was concerned with elucidating the essence of the Torah tradition. Cohen was not a rabbi but a university professor teaching philosophy. Following Kant, he considered it axiomatic that moderns should think for themselves, that nothing outside them, so to speak, had spiritual authority over them. Hence Torah had to come from something within the individual, not be given by an external God, no matter how powerful.

Being a philosopher, Cohen felt people got truth through their reason, and his analysis of human rationality led him to two conclusions important for our discussion. One was the necessity of being ethical. Any thinking person should know the call of duty and seek to respond to it in a rational way. The other conclusion was that every mind needed an idea of God to organize its understanding of the world and humanity properly. The idea of one God gave all other true ideas their ground and unity. Thus this God-idea was the basis of ethics. This ethical monotheism Cohen understood to be the essence of Judaism. We may say, therefore, that for Cohen, Torah comes from people using their minds with proper rationality. This Torah mandates ethical action and clear thinking about God.

Cohen also tried to find a way to encourage Jewish practice and community life. The most he could say for these is that they are often useful in promoting ethics and keeping the idea of ethical monotheism alive. Grossly put, such a theory divides Judaism into ethics and ceremonies, with the former rational and directly related to the idea of God but the latter only possibly useful human resources. Ethics are the essence and ceremonies only a social and historical accretion. For all Cohen's appealing intellectuality and the continuing validity of his ethical emphasis, I find his theory inadequate to the sense of duty I have in relation to nonrational, spiritual obligations like prayer and to nonethical Jewish duties like Zionism or, say, making *havdalah*.

THE POSITION OF LEO BAECK

Cohen had a disciple named Leo Baeck who suggested a revision of Cohen's view to deal with personal spiritual needs. As a device to separate the closely similar views of these thinkers it is useful to remember that while Cohen was a philosopher, Baeck was a rabbi. Baeck could therefore understand that religion (Torah) was more than the mind's thinking and that its duties went beyond ethics. Baeck pointed to human consciousness as the place where belief arises. This can be more than ideas, for though we may be conscious of something in only a vague and formless way, it may still seem true and deeply important to us. When we contemplate creation, for example, we often come to feel ourselves deeply dependent upon nature yet called upon to be creators ourselves. Such consciousness is the basis of the religious life. In recent times this has come to be called religious experience, though often that means only emotionally overwhelming events which, unchecked, could validate the grossest excesses of paganism. In

Judaism, Baeck argued, religious consciousness is always channeled by ethical rationality. Thus, against Cohen, Torah derives from both sides of being human, the feeling and the thinking, and keeps them in proper balance.

For Baeck the Jewish way of life includes not only ideas and ethics but the pious practice which grows out of our response to the mystery we sense around us. While this makes Judaism something very much more recognizably religious than Cohen's ideas, it remains a doctrine of Torah in which the Jewish people and its ethnic life are only of secondary interest. Baeck argued that the Jews had made ethical monotheism so much a part of their folk life over the centuries that they and this notion could no longer be separated. Jews now kept the idea alive and their distinctive practices helped them survive for its sake. But Baeck's Torah makes only ethical monotheism essential. The Jews and their observances are valuable but not necessary, a critical distinction when we ask what we must do.

THE POSITION OF MORDECAI KAPLAN

Where Cohen and Baeck looked to the individual for the creation of Torah, Mordecai Kaplan, the American Jewish thinker who began writing in the 1930s, saw it arising from the Jewish people as a whole. Kaplan argued that science, not abstract philosophy, should teach us about the nature of human affairs.

Building on the early sociologists, particularly Emile Durkheim, Kaplan explained religion as the result of the special feelings aroused by group contagion. It was thus not something God gave but what people felt. Society fostered religion, for religion provided the ultimate authority for society's way of life. Religion should thus be seen as but one more part of a people's culture, though the central part. All peoples have created cultures—Kaplan used the older term *civilization*—and we should now understand Torah as the culture the Jews created. As culture is multifaceted and not merely religious, so should be our contemporary Jewish life. That it is restricted to religion is the root of our ills. Our people, through its culture, needs to be restored to health—"reconstructed," in Kaplan's language.

Kaplan has only one external, absolute standard for a people's creativity: the need to be ethical. For him, ethics are somehow part of nature itself (an assertion that hardly seems scientific). While the Jews cannot now claim that God chose them (tradition) or that their essential idea is better than that of any other people (Cohen-Baeck), they can be proud to be a distinct group, for that is natural. They can also take satisfaction from the way Jews built ethical concerns into their civilization over the centuries. Because of this primary emphasis on peoplehood, Kaplan, as against Cohen and Baeck, makes Jewish folkways a primary ingredient of Torah. Through them Jews will naturally express the universal human urge to self-fulfillment.

I think it is true that many Jews use Judaism in the same way other people live out of the repertoire of acts and values their culture makes available to them. However, that is not the same as saying that Jews must or ought to do so. The key question to me in the restoration of a significant Jewish life is that of authority. Why should I do a Jewish act? Kaplan's Torah says, "Because it is your people's way." But I am not certain that just because my folk once did something or want to do something today, I ought to do it. I am a concerned and involved Jew, but I do not see why I should give my ethnic group the power to override my personal sense of what I should do. Besides, I live, as Kaplan puts it, in two civilizations, the American and the Jewish. I can as easily, probably more easily, express my universal human needs in American ways as in Jewish ones. A doctrine of Torah as little compelling as this one hardly seems to me an adequate basis upon which to rebuild Jewish life.

GOD'S SHARE IN TORAH

The emphasis on the human role in creating Torah, which I suggested above is the key to the liberal religion, is clear in these three thinkers. If anything, people have almost completely displaced God. In Kaplan, God is as good as reduced to a term used to describe our sense of trust that something in the world supports our hopes. For Cohen, God is "only" an idea, but God is a true idea and one that all minds should properly arrive at. Thus the idea of God exercises, so to speak, some independent sway over the individual. Baeck's God is somewhat more compelling than that. For him the mind cannot comprehend God in a concept but reaches out to God through a consciousness of living in mystery. Since we sense that there is something beyond us from which we take our being, God has some commanding power over us. That is as far as these rationalists can go in connecting God with Torah. Mostly it is our creation, and thus, since we make it, it can have only limited authority over us. Only in Rosenzweig and Buber does God's share in creating Torah become great enough to make a qualitative change in our relation to its precepts.

THE POSITIONS OF ROSENZWEIG AND BUBER

Both Franz Rosenzweig and Martin Buber believe God to be independent of us, that is, more than our idea or experience, yet accessible to us. Rosenzweig thinks that the history of philosophy, as contrasted to the reality of human existence, makes it necessary to posit this. Buber says we know God differently than we know things. In the latter case, analysis, objective and empirical proof, perhaps even a definition are important to establishing its reality and nature. Yet even with a person there is another way of getting acquainted, a more important, because truer, one. We establish a relationship and then only do we say we know who that person really is. The same, Buber points out, is true of God. We know God not as we might know a thing—that would necessarily be an idol. But, while it sounds odd, we know God in the same way as we truly get to know persons—and therefore God is just as real, as independent of us, yet as involved with us as is a good friend.

Both Rosenzweig and Buber understand Torah as arising from the relationship between this independent God and the Jewish people, the Covenant. (They do not deny that non-Jews and perhaps even other ethnic groups have had similar experiences, though they consider the consequences in the case of the Jews most singular.) They do not think God gives the Torah in the sense of speaking words or inspiring verbal messages, so they are not Orthodox. Rather they call our attention to the way any serious relationship engenders commandment and responsibility. The best example is love. If you love someone, there are things you feel you must do for them and other things that you may not now do. You don't even have to be told this, but you know yourself that this is required of you. If the relationship is important, you need to live in faithfulness to it and not violate its mutual trust.

Religion is most like a love affair with God, involving all one's heart, and soul, and might. Torah is the Jewish sense of duty and expectation arising from its love affair with God (a rather stormy one, according to the Bible). One might go further and say that the Jews and God got married at Sinai, the first five books of the Bible being their marriage contract, the rest of the Bible being their diary and love letters. All of Jewish life, then, is an effort to live up to the match we were so lucky to make.

Torah in Buber and Rosenzweig's view is created by people, but only in response to a real God who stands over against them. Their Jewish sense of what they know they must do comes from being involved with God, though they work out its details. And because we share our people's historical relationship with God, Torah may start with us individually, but cannot end until it includes our people and a concern for its tradition.

I find Buber's view the most appealing of our modern ideas of Torah and yet not fully satisfactory. It does explain a lot of what I believe. Since Torah here is based on a relationship with God, Buber's view shows why we must give Torah some sway over our lives. Since it understands that Jews are members of an ethnic group and not a church, it knows that the responsibilities of Torah are as much communal as individual. Yet it falters in integrating these two aspects of our being, our personal love of God and our sharing of our people's unique experience of God. Mostly, it tends to put the emphasis on what the individual feels is right, undercutting law and weakening the role of tradition in our lives. For all its sense of God, ethnicity, and revelation, this position does not move on to validate community standards in some fresh liberal way that would be more than ethics and less than Orthodox Halachah.

However, I consider this position more adequate than the others. Cohen, Baeck, and Kaplan have little sense of a real God, and thus verge on humanism, or, in Kaplan's case alone, so exalt the folk as almost to make an idol of ethnicity. My own solution to this problem, theoretical and practical, comes in ending the split between one's self and one's Jewishness. When one is no longer a person who also is a member of the people of Israel but is, at the core of one's being, an integrated Jew-human, then the gap between "what I personally must do" and "what the Jews need to do" falls away. That is not the same thing as saying that God gives us a law that all of us can know objectively. I do not believe God gives or has given such a Torah; I am not Orthodox. I believe Torah arises from the relationship between God and the Jewish people, the

Covenant, and that I and other Jews are the living bearers of that relationship. As we accept the reality of God and identify our inner, personal reality with the Jewish people (by no means, thereby, sacrificing our individuality), we share in the relationship which creates contemporary Torah. If enough Jews lived by their Covenant—that is, with God as part of the people of Israel—common patterns might arise which any Jew would have to take seriously. That would become our humanly created, divinely related, communally oriented Reform version of Jewish discipline, Torah.

CHAPTER FOURTEEN

If Torah Is Human, How Special Can It Be?

AN ACT OF REVERENCE

When the Bible was God's book and the Oral Torah had been given by God to Moses on Mount Sinai, there was no question why one should give them reverent attention. They were God's own communications and, in a time when there no longer was prophecy, the best way one could be in touch with the Divine. When Reform Judaism insisted that the various books of the Torah tradition were largely human creations, that had the advantage of allowing unprecedented innovation. It also devalued the old texts and made them less sacred.

A simple experience brought the point home to me tellingly. I was teaching a group together with Rabbi Norman Frimer, an Orthodox scholar. After reading a rabbinic passage to the group he put his book down on a desk, but so near the edge that it became unbalanced and fell off. He quickly retrieved it, kissed it, and put it more carefully on the desk, not stopping in the development of the theme he was presenting. Kissing books, particularly when they

133

have fallen, is a nice old Jewish custom which reflects very much more than respect for authors and publishers. It is related to our belief that our books derive ultimately from God—that in loving God one loves God's words, the Oral and the Written Torah. I wonder if liberal Jews with their sense of the humanity of our sacred literature could ever come to such regard for Torah that—leaving aside their sense of propriety—they could ever think of kissing one of its volumes.

CLARIFYING OUR OWN ATTITUDE

This sort of question is most significantly raised with regard to the liberal Jewish attitude toward the Bible. If it is taken as essentially the product of one unusual people in ancient Near Eastern civilization and reflective mainly of that particular social-historical situation, why should modern Jews, living under radically different circumstances, pay very much attention to it? On a simple level the question is liturgical: shall we really read the weekly Torah portions when, say, so much of Leviticus details sacrifices we have not offered in two thousand years and when Numbers transmits long lists and catalogs of no special discernible religious meaning? Or the question may be one of religious obligation: Are we still expected to study the Bible with a constancy and attention greater than we should give to major human writers like Shakespeare, Freud, or our most compelling contemporary teachers?

The problem is reflected, I think, not only in the general Reform neglect of Shabbat and festival morning services (where the Torah is read), but in Reform's indifference to adult Jewish education, personal or institutional. I do not think issuing the *Centenary Perspective* or elucidating its attitude toward Sacred Scripture will change things much. The evil urge being so strong, people who are told Torah is largely human will use that as a reason for paying little heed to it. Yet for Jews prepared to take their Reform Judaism seriously the *Centenary Perspective* says that there is good reason to consider the works of the Torah tradition, though human, different from all other human books we know.

THE BIBLE'S ETHNIC DIMENSION

The *Perspective* says simply, "The records of our earliest confrontations [between God and the Jewish people] are uniquely important to us." Three possible explanations of that last phrase suggest themselves. The first is directly ethnic. If one believes that being a Jew means belonging to a group and participating in its culture, as Mordecai Kaplan does, then nothing can take the place of our people's great, ancient saga. It tells us about our origins. It reflects our values and aspirations. It has been our greatest ethnic treasure. Its contents have kept us unified as a people and alive as human beings. It is no accident that in the State of Israel today, though the overwhelming majority of the citizenry considers itself formally areligious, the Bible is a national passion.

THE BIBLE'S PHILOSOPHICAL DIMENSION

Oddly enough, though from a different premise, the rationalists like Hermann Cohen agree that our special interest in the Bible stems from our being part of the Jewish people. They would glory in the fact that the books of the Bible, specifically the prophets, are humanity's earliest substantial understanding of the concept of ethical monotheism. The prophets not only spoke of it but tried to get the Jewish people to put it into effect in their society, often at great personal risk. We should not only be concerned with the origins of our ideas and be proud of our forebears' accomplishments, but benefit personally from their example. Any thoughtful comparison of the prophets with the Greek philosophers will reveal how much more we remain indebted to Hebraic rather than Hellenic thought.

Yet for all their appreciation of the Bible, I do not find convincing the position of either the rationalists or the ethnicists. As to the rational viewpoint, it is modern philosophy which has clarified and validated the true nature of ethical monotheism. That makes the Bible and other works of Jewish tradition old versions of a truth dimly perceived, hence learned better and more directly from modern writers. They retain antiquarian interest and nostalgic appeal, but that hardly gives them a central role in our lives. Putting the value of the Bible on a purely ethnic level, as Kaplan does, is to raise again the question of ethnicity's commanding power. Or, accepting that, one wonders why less demanding, more rewarding ethnic activities, like folk dancing or fund raising, do not more effectively raise our group consciousness, again relegating the Bible and traditional literature to the status of special or ceremonial concerns.

THE BIBLE'S SPIRITUAL DIMENSION

If one believes, with Leo Baeck, that religion is born in our consciousness of mystery, then one can add a special, qualitative dimension to the ethnic arguments given above. Now the Bible is not just our old basic Jewish Book but one in which much of humanity, certainly the majority of people in the Western world, has come to know what is meant by the presence of God. Our Bible is the supreme document of the dawning consciousness of God around us. Its very humanity, all the personal foibles and personality quirks we see in its pages, makes the spiritual greatness of its authors stand out in greater eminence. Such ordinary people gained so intimate a consciousness of God and set it down in words and images so compelling (for all their difficulty) that we, reading them, are often brought to a deeper, more illuminating sense of the mystery which leads to the Divine. This they linked closely with the need to serve God ethically—the prophetic motif reasserts itself—thus instructing us not to rest content with feeling but to direct this religious sensibility into a life of doing the good. Though some books in other cultures occasionally show this understanding, none brings us so closely in touch with people who sensed the Divine and its commands and wrote of them in ways which enable us to share their experience. Insofar as the rest of the Torah tradition is, so to speak, a commentary on and an extension of the Bible, we must attend to it if we are to know the standard by which our faith and lives ought to be measured.

THE BIBLE AS COVENANT

An even more compelling case for Jewish sacred literature may be made from the Rosenzweig-Buber position, for these thinkers see in it not merely the rise of human religious consciousness, a rather internal matter, but the record of true human relationship with the divine. From our own experience we know that certain events have had a lifelong influence on us and that some things have happened to other people with an intensity we apparently never know. Since Buber and Rosenzweig believe God is real and can be present to people, they can believe that as people met and came to know God some might have found these moments of intense personal relationship deeply affecting. The Bible is important, then, not because it records the first time people ever came into relationship with God; but it is the earliest record which testifies to a continuity of such experience with God and which discloses an unprecedented freshness of contact with God over centuries.

Then, too, the Bible narrates how a people transformed its ethnic existence because it established a relationship with God and undertook to serve God in history. We today who come into personal relationship with God are well schooled in the possibilities of religion (and skepticism), so that we are often screened off from a spontaneous sense of what God means to us or is "saying" to us. We occasionally get the feeling in the Bible or rabbinic literature that we are dealing with slogans or stereotypes. That should not surprise us. It only makes it more astonishing, then, when again and again we are brought into the personal experience of people who have come to know God with powerful immediacy and were decisively shaped by that experience.

If we can read the classic Jewish books staying open for whatever is being said in them, we too may find ourselves repeating the experience of great Jews of other ages, standing before the living God. Is that not what collections of love letters or souvenirs do for us—enable us to relive old, great moments in our lives? If a relationship with God is fundamental to our personal lives, no book can take the place of the Bible. If we share the people of Israel's historic Covenant with God, no other book can teach us what we have meant and continue to mean to one another. So, too, the tradition which derives from the Bible will speak to us as nothing else in human accomplishment.

"THE RECORDS OF OUR EARLIEST CONFRONTATIONS"

Whatever our interpretation of Torah, then, the *Centenary Perspective* insists the Bible is "uniquely important to us." I cannot now recall (and my sketchy notes are of no help in this regard) whether there was ever a conscious decision made by the drafting committee not to use the phrase "the Bible" and instead say "the records of our earliest confrontations." I think not, and, though it may be an after-the-fact rationalization, I think our present language is preferable. It allows for some Reform Jews not finding all of the Bible equally significant to us. It provides for the possibility that some archaeologist may find another early Jewish religious document which our people will come to venerate. But I am certain that "the records of our earliest confrontations" is not meant to be identified with the five books of the Torah scroll. Rather, the text immediately goes on to join together "lawgivers and prophets, historians and poets . . . . " No single section of the Bible is being specified as "the earliest," and the term is not meant in strictly historical fashion—the time of the Patriarchs, say—but in the figurative sense of those many, varied experiences which generated the Torah tradition. Whatever the historians or literary critics might understand the earliest historical traditions to be is probably acceptable to us.

Reform Jews will have no hesitation in accepting as "the records of our earliest confrontations with God" sections of the prophetic or historical books. The exact, scholarly decision must be left to the historians and literary critics. We are using the term *earliest* here in a more general way to acknowledge our special attachment to the Bible by contrast to all the later writings created by our people.

TWO DUTIES ARISING FROM TRADITION

Two major duties devolve upon those whose lives are joined to this religious tradition. One is common to all religions, though unusually emphasized here—namely, to live our faith. The Torah is full of commandments and guidance by which Jews are expected to mold their existence. It explicitly says that doing the right acts is the primary means of serving God. Hence to have and value Torah means a commitment to live it. That also stands to reason, for if one had direction from God as to how to live, one ought to follow it, for one could not get help from any better source.

The second duty which comes from having Torah is that of study. The Torah traditions are recorded—recorded, moreover, in language that, with but a little help, almost anyone can understand. Torah study is not by necessity an elitist activity. We are not certain how early there was study of Torah by all the people or how "you shall teach them diligently unto your children" was carried out. The rabbis traced the practice of reading from the Torah scroll in the synagogue (on Mondays, Thursdays, and Saturdays) to Ezra, the Fifth century B.C.E. scribe whose dramatic, public reading of the "book of the Torah of Moses" is described in the book of Nehemiah, chapter 8. That notion does not seem historically implausible. In any case, the regular reading of the sacred texts to the people (the Ezra story repeatedly says that the Levites explained it clearly to the whole community—men, women and children) is something of a religious revolution. When the people know what God has said to them, their priests and teachers no longer have a secret knowledge by which to claim special status or privilege. Any learned person can now discuss what God wants. Instead of hierarchy, a democratic principle rules and its basis is knowledge. The power structure of Jewish communities throughout the ages has been affected by this respect for learning, and thus religious and social factors have created an unusually heavy pressure among Jews for education.

One can also discern an inner impetus to study. The Jewish tradition sees a close link between knowing and doing. One ignorant of the Torah can hardly be expected to fulfill its precepts. As I read the earlier and later books of the Bible I see a shift with regard to motivating people to carry out the law. First one hears much about the rewards and punishments God metes out. In the prophets this not infrequently rises to the level of dire threat. Later a change is felt. I am not suggesting that the belief in God's judgment is given up, only that another way of motivating observance is utilized, namely, educating people. Education then becomes the primary Jewish strategy for getting people to do God's will. The Jewish commitment to study is thus directly related to the religion's major thrust, sanctified living, and so becomes a major religious duty, not a possible option for one's leisure. It is also primarily an adult activity, since the commandments devolve upon them, and only secondarily upon children who study to learn what to do as adults. The whole glorious Jewish tradition of learning thus begins in our sense of Torah. And I would argue that all our modern intellectuality derives from it. As we modernized we became secular. We did not give up our commitment to study. We merely turned away from the old Jewish books to the science and literature of contemporary culture. Giving ourselves to this new "Torah" with the old Jewish motivation produced the unbelievably heavy Jewish contribution to modern intellectual life of which our proportion of Nobel Prize winners is one clear testimony. The content of our study may have changed; our existential sense of what people ought to devote themselves to remains the same.

The rabbis debated whether doing or study has Jewish priority. Since the rabbis were themselves scholars and gained their status by learning, they tended toward the preeminence of study. (Pirke Avot, for example, is full of their exhortations about its value.) But the Torah, which was the focus of their scholarship, itself clearly placed the emphasis on doing. In one popular case a reconciliation was effected between the views of Rabbi Tarphon, who favored doing, and Rabbi Akiba, who favored study. The Talmud records the majority of sages siding with Akiba, but then gives as their reason "because study leads to practice." The *Centenary Perspective* may be said to follow in this rabbinic tradition by putting the two duties side by side when it says of Torah that its "study is a religious imperative and [its] practice is our chief means to holiness."

CHAPTER FIFTEEN

How Broad Is
Our Modern Sense of Torah?

Instead of speaking of the five books of the Torah, the *Centenary Perspective* refers more expansively to the records given us by "lawgivers and prophets, historians and poets." This broader sense of Torah is carried over into the Reform understanding of the tradition which derived from the Torah books proper. Traditional Jews, believing in the Oral Torah as well as the Written, consider rabbinic literature, the Talmud and Midrash and the works which derive from them, as Torah. (By association, the study of such works itself comes to be known as "Torah," perhaps as a shortening of the rabbinic phrase *talmud Torah*, the study of Torah.)

Reform Judaism, focusing on the human element in Torah, can see a spiritual quality in much other Jewish creativity as well. The *Perspective* thus goes beyond "rabbis and teachers" to include, first, "philosophers and mystics." This might be acceptable to traditional Jews, though it does begin to strain the older sense of what constitutes Torah. But the statement then goes on to add a much more inclusive phrase, "gifted Jews in every age." Few limits are placed here on those whom we might see as having "amplified the Torah tradition." Here the Reform attitude is quite explicit. For liberals who define revelation in terms of human discovery, whether it is their music or art, the folk tales they told or the proverbs they coined, the focus on "gifted Jews" is exactly right. They brought their gifts, intellectual and esthetic, personal and ethnic, to the creation of Torah. For those who feel that God as well as people are involved in the creation of Torah, the emphasis will be on "in every age." The relationship between God and this people was not a one-time event, at Mount Sinai, but a continuing one. Gifted Jews have continually arisen over the centuries who expressed the Covenant relationship in Torah forms appropriate to their social context. For both groups Jewish religious teaching is to be found in a far broader range of Jewish experience than rabbinic literature.

IDENTIFYING TORAH WITH ETHICS

The rationalist stream of Reformers, while not limiting Torah to classic Jewish texts, would, however, limit its content, wherever found. To them, only ethics are divine instruction, all other forms of Jewish lore being on a lesser qualitative level. Ethics are true because they are universal, a fundamental characteristic of all rational human beings. Likewise, they are the essence of Judaism. Until recent years the representatives of this view connected it with the idea of human progress. That is, they believed humanity, despite occasional setbacks, shows continual growth in spiritual understanding and ethical accomplishment. Normally, those who come later in a history see reality more clearly, in part because they build on what went before but mainly because history, so to speak, has a way of clarifying the truth. Thus later Jews are really in a better position to say what Torah truly is than were previous generations, a radical reversal of traditional Judaism with its heavy deference to the past and its strong dependence on precedent. Modern Jews, therefore, have a right, even a mandate, to follow their Torah even though it disagrees with that of earlier generations, as the Reform Jews did in their struggle to modernize Judaism. Because many of its adherents took the idea of progress quite literally, this concept went under the name "progressive revelation."

Yet in its prefatory historical paragraph the *Centenary Perspective* said that one of the things Reform Jews have learned in recent decades is that the idea of "inevitable progress" is largely untenable. This section on Torah seems explicitly to reject "progressive revelation" in the strict sense by calling the records of our earliest confrontations "uniquely" important. That implies that nothing since has been as significant, much less better. This does not mean the *Perspective* denies that revelation

is continual or that we today are obligated to
follow our sense of what God wants of us. The
Perspective explicitly talks about Torah continuing into our own time and makes this the
climax of this section. This rejection of inevitable progress in Torah should also not be
taken to imply that Reform Jews should no
longer see ethics as the core of Torah. Those
who define human spirituality in terms of universal moral obligation will not find their sense
of Reform violated by this paragraph on Torah
unless they are such rationalists that they do
not concede that Jewish "mystics" amplified
the Torah tradition. It is not ethics, but steady
progress, which no longer seems believable.

GOING BEYOND THE ETHICAL

I do, however, think that most Reform Jews,
would no longer want to identify Torah only
with ethics. The objection is not to saying that
Torah is fundamentally ethical, rather, some
have understood that to mean that whatever is
not an ethical teaching is not part of what God
truly wants of us for all its educational or folk
value. Our understanding of Torah has changed
because our sense of what it is to be a person
and a Jew has changed. A person is at least
someone who thinks clearly and does the right,
but also very much more than that. When we
are most fully human—choosing, loving,
willing—it is not merely our minds or
consciences that are at work but all of us at

once. That must include, without overemphasizing them, our emotions—more, that full integration of mind and emotion and unfathomable individuality we call a self. If we live out of the mystery that leads to God or out of a relationship with God it must be with more than our reason and our ethical sense. God must be be giving us Torah for the whole person, Torah which is thus more than ethics.

In the same way, a Jew is more than a rational individual born into this odd ethnic group. For many of us, Jewishness is no secondary, almost accidental matter but a primary part of who and what we are. In good measure we live our individuality as one of the people of Israel. Hence our Torah must be more than a universal ethic with an ethnic coloration. It must be an instruction directed to the sanctification of the Jewish people as a whole, beginning with each individual Jew. In this instance it makes no difference whether we think our people created culture-Torah or that God and the people create it out of their relationship. In both cases the corporate dimension, the particularly Jewish aspect, is emphasized. As against the older Reform Judaism's rationalism, so concerned with individual autonomy and universal ethics, Reform now sees individuality as having greater dimension and focuses much of its attention on Jewish peoplehood. This paragraph on Torah then reflects the themes which run through the *Centenary Perspective* as a whole. (These emphases are basic to section IV, religious duties, discussed below in *Reform Judaism Today: How We Live*, Part II.)

LIMITS TO WHAT IS TORAH

For myself, I find it important to specify certain limits to what should be regarded as Torah. There is a danger in saying that people or the Jewish folk play a major role in creating Torah. One can easily exaggerate that thesis so that almost every personal or Jewish activity is given the high significance of Torah. Perhaps I can best indicate my desire for some restriction of the idea by exaggerating its possible negative consequences. On the individual level, one often hears great people in our time referred to as prophets, and I would agree that one might have heard a transcendent call in some of the addresses of Stephen Wise or Martin Luther King, Jr. This makes us call them modern prophets. But I doubt that their words, or even their deeds, will continue to exalt us for very long. Already their teaching begins to fade and some of it seems quite dated.

I am, of course, suggesting that significant truth has a way of lasting generations or centuries. Much of our Torah tradition has been around for millennia. I do not think I underestimate the value of an utterance which speaks God's word to a given moment, but I feel that a good deal of what passes for great truth in our time, for our equivalent of Torah, is quite fleeting, more a matter of moral fashion than of lasting insight. With our modern temptation to see worth only in the novel, we expect spiritual breakthroughs to come with some degree of regularity. I am saying that not everything that is intriguing should be considered Torah and treated with its appropriate dignity. I think that caution might be uttered by humanist interpreters of Torah. Those of us who take God's role in revelation seriously (though we do not think God says words or dictates details) will regularly want to know, for all the difficulty involved in finding it out, whether we hear God speaking to us, from some contemporary effort. I think I have found my relationship with God stimulated or enriched by some modern writing or painting, for example, and hence my sense of what might be Torah is fairly comprehensive. But trying to attend to God as well as to human creativity, I do not see or hear very much that deserves to be called Torah.

I find the same applies on the folk level. Not every act of ethnic invention is modern Torah. Again let me exaggerate. One of the greatest folk creations of American Judaism, I would contend, is our variety of *oneg shabbat*. The modern use of the term stems from Chaim Nachman Bialik, the great poet and literateur of the early part of this century. He conceived of the idea of having literary afternoons on Shabbat at his Tel Aviv home, thus giving special content to the day's secular observance. The term was taken up in the United States to denote the synagogue activities following the late Friday evening service (themselves an American innovation, attributed to Issac Mayer Wise). Despite the effort to introduce into this period some singing, discussion, or other cultural activity, the American *oneg shabbat* remains mainly a time for eating and drinking—almost universally coffee or tea with cake and cookies, not infrequently those with eastern European Jewish ethnic overtones as transformed by our affluence. Besides eating and drinking, the major activity of our *oneg shabbat* is *schmoosing*—greetings are exchanged, news transmitted, gossip passed, temple and community affairs attended to, all in a happy buzz of in-group familiarity. In the American *oneg shabbat* culture is dispensable, the food and talk are not. It is not what Bialik had in mind, but it meets our situation: in the synagogue, not at a home; in connection with services, not as a secular activity; with devotion to chit-chat, not culture. Yet nowhere in our community does the simple folk nature of the Jew appear as clearly as in this weekly gathering of the clan and renewal of our ethnic ties. By contrast, the service does little for most Jews, either in moving them personally or bonding them to their people. At the *oneg shabbat* they are involved, animated, caring, and ethnic in ways that only rarely have analogues in the sanctuary.

If, then, our people creates Torah, we should have less service and more *oneg shabbat,* for it truly expresses and enhances our peoplehood. Yet the proposal to do away with the service altogether and, after some delay to let us get over dinner, to spend our time together in Jewish talk is too radical, even for humanistic interpreters of Torah. Somehow they know that the Jewish people ought to aspire to more than *schmoos* and that to turn the Sabbath essentially into what the folk most want is wrong. Even for them, I am arguing, modern Torah has to be as much an ideal as what Jews will readily do. For those who think God has a share in Torah it is clear why the *oneg shabbat* cannot replace services, though Jews today prefer talking to one another than to God. Ethnicity without simultaneous devotion to divinity should not be considered Torah. I concede that in Judaism the line between "pure" ethnicity and responsiveness to God is difficult to draw and is probably fictitious. But it is a useful analytic tool in our time when secularity has such a hold on Jews. The emphasis on ethnicity easily becomes an excuse for ignoring God, and we prefer a Torah of folk activities, so we need not attend much to religious obligations. In sum, not everything that passes for *Yiddishkeit* should be part of our sense of Torah.

In our present Jewish mood, I cannot judge whether the danger of equating Torah with tribalism is greater than that of equating it with individual creativity. As with so many of the problems this the *Centenary Perspective* addresses, it is the balance among the beliefs which is critical. Reform Judaism is committed to individualism, peoplehood, and the service of God. Undue emphasis on any one of those beliefs leads to a skewed doctrine of Torah.

"THE CREATION OF TORAH HAS NOT CEASED"

One further theme requires elaboration, though here the century or more of Reform Jewish teaching has been successful enough that it can be put briefly. "The creation of Torah has not ceased and Jewish creativity in our time is adding to the chain of tradition." That has become so much a part of modern Judaism that many an Orthodox spokesman would find the sentence acceptable. The great scholars of our age, they would say, like the great scholars of every age, add to Oral Torah. Yet that was not always so acceptable a belief. For much of the nineteenth century in Europe and in some pockets of world Jewry today, it is unthinkable to call innovations Torah. One great Orthodox figure of the last century, a rigorist to be sure, the *Hatam Sofer* in Hungary, said bluntly, "Anything new is forbidden by the Written Torah." Modern Orthodox leaders and Reform Jews would likely disagree over what is meant by the *Centenary Perspective*'s inclusion in Torah of "Jewish creativity in our time." The

Reform Jewish construction would likely be quite broad indeed, going far beyond the work of Jewish legal authorities to include artistic, cultural, and institutional creations of our people. Even though I have said we need some limits to our liberal reading of what is Torah, we would still see significant religious value in areas which traditional Jews would consider essentially profane.

The *Perspective* does not often resort to traditional terms, for our committee felt people would be more likely to think about what was being said if they heard it in reasonably fresh language. Yet here an old, highly charged phrase is utilized; "the chain of tradition." Though it was limited, to be sure, there was a sense in the classic Jewish understanding of Torah that succeeding generations added to what had gone on before. Reform Jews, for all their broadening of what should be considered Torah, believe they are restating that old Jewish truth. Indeed, they would insist that the dynamic way they conceive of the development of Torah is far truer to what in fact happened than any other interpretation—that, therefore the Reform view of Torah is today the authentic one. It, like other "Jewish creativity in our time," is not a break with the past but the proper continuation of it, and hence another link in "the chain of tradition." And seeing Reform Judaism itself as an extension of the Torah tradition, the *Perspective* uses a traditional phrase to describe its teaching.

SUPPLEMENT

How a Document
Came to Be Written

I. THE SITUATION WHICH CALLED FOR THIS STATEMENT

Reform Judaism: A Centenary Perspective was adopted by the Central Conference of American Rabbis at its meeting in San Francisco on June 24, 1976. This was the first time since 1937 that the Conference, the organization of the Reform rabbis of the United States, Canada, and some other countries, had formally articulated its sense of "the spiritual state of Reform Judaism." Since such religious declarations are rather rare, they merit close study, and that is the purpose of this commentary. As chairman of the committee which produced the document and as one who has taught modern Jewish thought to Reform rabbinical students for nearly twenty years, I hope I can add some special insight to those who wish to read this statement with some care. I think it best, as the inclusion of this supplement indicates, to describe the context in which the *Centenary Perspective* came into being. We can divide our consideration between the surface, relatively positive factors which

159

occasioned it and the deeper, relatively negative forces which also were at work (the latter hinted at in the document's phrase "our sense of the unity of our movement today").

A Century of Existence: The Reform movement approached the year 1973 with special anticipation, for it would be the hundredth year since Isaac Mayer Wise founded the Union of American Hebrew Congregations (the "Union") and thus laid the foundation for the other national institutions of American Reform Judaism. Previous attempts to found a rabbinical school in the United States had failed, but once Wise had a group of congregations behind him, support for his Hebrew Union College (the "College"), founded in 1875, was relatively assured. In turn, the graduates of the college provided the basis for the establishment of the Central Conference of American Rabbis in 1889.

In 1973, then, Reform Judaism would celebrate a century of nationally organized existence, itself a good reason for celebration. But the event had more than internal significance. Because of the special characteristics of Jewish history in the United States, Reform Judaism is the oldest nationally organized form of Jewish religious life in this country, and its tripartite structure—congregational, rabbinical, and rabbinical school—has largely become the model for other Jewish religious movements in this country, for their central institutions were founded after those of Reform Judaism. So the centenary of the Union would say a good deal about American Jewry as a whole.

The Work of the Commission: The committees planning the Union's celebration did not want merely to rejoice over past accomplishments, but thought this a good time to look to the future as well. A number of groups of lay people and rabbis was appointed to try to project the directions Reform Judaism should be taking as it moved toward the year 2000. A key consideration was the nature of Reform Jewish belief. A commission of eminent scholars and rabbis with some lay members and a host of consultants was appointed by the Union, the College, and the Conference jointly to prepare a new platform for the movement. Taking its mandate seriously, the commission discovered that the number of problems of great seriousness Reform now faced was overwhelming. Thus at one of its meetings it listed as needing treatment twenty-seven separate themes, such as the nature of God today; who is a Jew?; intermarriage; and biomedical ethics. The commission concluded that the challenges of the time were too great to be met with the sort of short statements ("platforms") which had been issued by a group of Reform rabbis in Pittsburgh in 1885 or by the Conference in Columbus, Ohio, in 1937. Something very much more substantial was required, and some commission members suggested that the sort of small library statements issued by the Second Vatican Council might be an appropriate model. With such a task before it, the commission found its work barely begun by the time of the Union centennial convention in 1973. Unfortunately, the hope that something might be made ready by the time of the College's celebration in 1975 was also frustrated. The commission had by then lost its momentum and seemed, for various reasons, effectively to have ceased operating. (Its records were in due course made available to the Conference committee which wrote the *Centenary Perspective.* They are now available at the American Jewish Archives at the College's Cincinnati campus.)

The Continuing Need: Perhaps the impulse to produce a new statement about Reform Jewish belief might have died then had it not been for a number of other, essentially negative factors that kept the idea alive. Since the late 1960s a number of thoughtful Reform Jews had been concerned that their movement no longer had a clear sense of direction, that it was not responding directly to the challenges posed by our unsettled times. Many people had become skeptical about our heavy reliance on the ideas of Western civilization generally and felt that our religion should now be giving us a more positive sense of human values. They also held the opinion—hardly separately from the previous one—that what had happened to the Jewish people in the past few decades demanded changes in the way we thought of ourselves as Jews and expressed it in our lives. Perhaps individuals had found ways to meet this experience of cultural discontinuity. The movement as a whole had not confronted it. Nearly forty years had passed since the Columbus Platform. This spiritual discontent merited a response.

This mood was exacerbated by a debate on intermarriage which broke out in the Reform rabbinate and threatened to split the movement as a whole into two groups, those championing freedom and those calling for greater adherence to tradition. I have reviewed this controversy in Book I to provide a proper background for understanding the section of the document dealing with Reform Judaism's diversity. Here I think it important to note only that the general concern about the direction of Reform had, through the polarization which developed around the intermarriage issue, been channeled into such antagonistic positions that schism seemed possible. This led Robert Kahn, who devoted most of his *President's Report* to the 1975 meeting of the Conference to the problem of the divisions within Jewry, to approach those in Reform Judaism with the following climactic suggestions:

There is still one more area in which we can find reconciliation. We need, it seems to me, to find a definition of our movement which can pull together its disparate factions. When white light is viewed through a prism, it is broken down into a spectrum of colors. Would it not be possible to bring the prismatic divisions into which the light of Reform has been broken into unity again? This was attempted in Pittsburgh; it was revised in Columbus; perhaps the process should begin again in Cincinnati as we celebrate the one hundredth anniversary of our movement.

I should like to offer, for your thought, the beginnings of such an affirmation of the principles of Reform Judaism.

I.

Reform Judaism is an interpretation of the Jewish faith. We claim the same right of interpretation and re-interpretation which was claimed by the prophets, by the Pharisees, by the Kabbalists, by the Chassidim. We base our interpretation upon a free and non-authoritative exploration of our sacred literature, liturgy and life-story. We are open to the discoveries of modern science. We seek to apply and to live by Judaism's abiding truths in a democratic and pluralistic society.

In so doing, we do not reject any body of Jews (not even those who reject us), but extend to our fellow-Jews of differing interpretation our loving fellowship in the service of our people and our God.

II.

When we say that we believe in God, no matter how we define that term, we affirm the Jewish conviction that the universe makes sense, that this world is not chaos (tohu va-vohu), a blind and purposeless succession of physical-chemical events, but a cosmos, an orderly, intelligible and purposeful process.

Even though we may not be able to grasp that process in its entirety, we are aware of the continual working of a creative power. And even though the order of nature seems impersonal (which accounts for much of human suffering), at the same time we recognize within it a progressive evolution toward ever higher forms of life, reaching their climax in the flowering of human personality.

III.

When we say that human beings are created in the divine image, we affirm the existence within us of spiritual qualities which rise above the natural order; vision, compassion, a sense of the holy, a realization of our infinity and, above all, a knowledge of good and evil, and the freedom to choose between them. In that freedom, human beings can sink to the level of the animal and cause great suffering to their fellows, or rise to their full stature as children of the Eternal.

IV.

When we say that God has given us Torah, we affirm our faith that morality is not the invention of man, but written into the structure of the universe. The apprehension of ethical principles, like the comprehension of physical laws of nature, is a process of progressive revelation in which our people have played a primary role throughout the centuries. In Torah, both the revelation of the eternal moral order which comes down to us from the past, and the word of God still waiting to be heard, we recognize the demand for response by men and women equally to the highest values of Judaism.

V.

When we Reform Jews pray, and when we gather for public worship, we affirm the need of the human soul for spiritual companionship, and the outreach of the heart toward the spiritual power residing in the universe. We look upon the traditional pieties, the order of worship, the holy days and sacred symbols of our tradition as having a myriad meaning and endless possibilities for inspiration, identifying us with our past, uniting us with our people, pointing toward our purpose. As Reform Jews, while not regarding these traditions as binding upon us, we think of them as options and opportunities for the ever-renewed hallowing of our lives.

VI.

When we speak of the mission of Israel, we share the special vision of our ancestors, who conceived of themselves as set apart both by promise and by hope toward the goal of perfecting the world under the kingdom of God. Thus we affirm the meaningfulness of history, not as the endless rise and fall of the tides of power, but the working out of moral truth in the laboratory of space and time. Our survival is testimony to that vision. Our role in history has been multiple; suffering servant, surviving witness, faithful teacher, holy nation, whose constant aim has been the righting of wrong, and bringing ever nearer the Messianic goal of a just and peaceful world.

In the Diaspora, our mission is to share these goals with our neighbors and to work with them toward their fulfillment, as a light unto all peoples.

In Israel, our mission is to help make it possible for those in physical need or spiritual hunger to be gathered into the land, and to aid them in the building of a State in which the principles of Judaism can be applied to every aspect of human life, so that Israel shall be like a pilot light unto the nations.

VII.

We pledge ourselves to the survival of the Jewish

people. We will share the responsibility for that survival with all our hearts, and all our might. We affirm the priority of every Jewish need. In the absence, however, of sufficient human and financial resources to fulfill them all at once, we will seek, by thoughtful and democratic processes, to respond to the most pressing without neglecting the rest.

VIII.

In accordance with our faith in progressive revelation, we affirm the right of Rabbis and congregations to continue the process of interpreting the Jewish faith by the varied responses of intellect, emotion and temperament which characterize all human life, and to continue to search as individuals and as congregations for more light and more love, seeking, not in mutually exclusive nor competitive ways, but with mutual respect, to foster the growing values of our faith.

I present this brief affirmation in the hope that it may help to lead us in binding together the many colors of the Reform spectrum into a single rainbow of promise and of hope.

This was the immediate background for the centenary statement we now have before us.

II. THE COMMITTEE'S SENSE OF ITS TASK

The Committee and Its Members: The members of the Conference agreed with Kahn that "We need . . . to find a definition of our movement which can pull together its disparate factions." They voted that a committee be appointed which, on the basis of his effort, would bring in such a statement for consideration at the Conference's June 1976 meeting. In November, after the Fall Conference Executive Board meeting, the new president, Arthur Lelyveld, appointed an ad hoc President's Message Committee to deal with this matter. It consisted of the following rabbis (school of ordination—C=Cincinnati, NY=New York—and date of ordination in parentheses): Gerald Goldman, Plainfield, N.J. (NY '64), Robert Kahn, Houston, Texas (C '35), Daniel Polish, Washington, D.C. (C '68), Elliot Rosenstock, South Bend, Ind. (C '61), Robert Rothman, Rye, N.Y. (C '57), Samuel Sandmel, Cincinnati, Ohio (C '37), Ronald Sobel, New York, N.Y. (C '62), Jack Stern, Jr., Scarsdale, N.Y. (C'52), Alfred Wolf, Los Angeles, Calif. (C '41), Sheldon Zimmerman, New York, N.Y. (NY '72), and, as chairman, Eugene B. Borowitz, Port Washington, N.Y. (C '48).

The committee met for the first time January 12-14, 1976, but its work had already begun in the preceding weeks. Since its mandate called for it to begin by considering the Kahn statement, this had been sent to the committee members and their reactions requested in writing. These were then circulated for the members' deliberation prior to the meeting. Thus our first session began with a mature discussion of Kahn's "platform." Our work in this respect was greatly facilitated by Kahn's generosity. He opened the meeting by saying that he had thought of his statement primarily as a means of getting this project started. He urged the committee to feel free to follow its own direction, using his words only when they appeared to suit the committee's needs. This was not an empty act, for Kahn never insisted on trying to get his June 1975 version into one or another part of the committee's document but regularly lent his hand to drafts and revisions which went in somewhat different directions (see below). The praise bestowed upon Kahn for this at the June 1976 meeting of the Conference by Alfred Wolf, senior member of the committee present, was thus not the routine fulfillment of an organizational propriety but the honest expression of what our committee felt. To me, Kahn's selflessness in sacrificing his text (as it turned out) for what his colleagues deemed to be more useful set a model for the work of the committee. No one was ever asked to sacrifice his principles, but once we did not confuse ego with conscience it became much easier to work at finding out what people of different views could jointly affirm.

Principles and Procedures: In the account of our work which follows I have divided the general principles our committee established from the procedures it followed. This is somewhat deceptive. In a number of ways the two were intimately joined, and they made sense in terms of one another. Besides, some of our committee guidelines emerged as our work was proceeding, and I may inadvertently give the impression that they were all established at the very first meeting. Despite those difficulties, I believe I can more easily explain what we tried to do if I may separate our aims from our process, and I have therefore organized this narrative accordingly.

I think it also important to note that in much of what follows I have relied upon my memory. The committee did not take minutes of its proceedings, only of the substantive decisions with regard to the text of the document itself. I regret this, since I have only occasionally been able to recall who was responsible for a given interesting idea or valuable phrase, and I wish it were possible to give my colleagues all the credit they deserve. Moreover, the committee felt that our experience together, the give and take of suggestion and rejection, of proposal and its improvement, was uniquely rewarding to us. It would be interesting now to retrace that procedure and relive the emergence of our collective text. But such details are now beyond recall. We were all so intensively involved in the deliberations that none of us wished to withdraw from them to take notes, and we felt we would be inhibited by a tape recorder. Let me therefore apologize here to my colleagues for not giving them, by name and instance, proper recognition for their input to our document. When I am reasonably certain that the committee took formal action on a given matter, I speak, in what follows, of "the committee." When I merely describe what went on or what was involved in a given statement, I am recording what I believe was our consensus, or, to put it differently, this is what remained with me as I recollect the committee's discussions. But each member of the committee may have understood what we were doing in a somewhat different way. Fortunately the reader is now free to reach an independent judgment about this because the members of the committee—themselves writing some months after the document had been accepted—produced a commentary to the *Centenary Perspective*, each one speaking for himself on a given paragraph. This was published by the Conference in the *CCAR Journal*'s spring 1977 issue. Where I believe that what I want to say in these books about the document is quite personal to me and may only incidentally have been in the mind of one or another of the committee members, I use the first person singular.

These qualifications having been stated, I believe it possible to delineate seven concerns which early came to guide the committee in its work. I present them here in something of a logical order and would find it difficult to say at just what point the committee, or I as its executive officer, became conscious of some of them.

The Pressures of Time: First, we were sensitive to the pressure of time. We had been directed to bring in a report by June 1976. Appointed only in November 1975 and meeting for the first time in January 1976, wanting to leave some time for the Conference members to consider our work (see below), we felt caught in quite a squeeze. While the possibility of asking for a year's delay did come up several times, almost all of us believed it would be better to try to get the job done in the time available or, if we could not, report why we found the task set us impractical. As it turned out, by mid-March the response of our colleagues indicated that an acceptable, useful document could be written and that, with some good fortune, the schedule could be met. Yet I think it fair to add that the failure of the Union-College-Conference Platform Commission to produce a document despite several years of work, some professional staff, and a modern budget to work with weighed on the minds of the committee members. People had so long awaited a statement on Reform Judaism that it seemed better not to produce one than to ask for new postponements. Equally, we agreed that it would be better to submit no statement to the Conference than to advance one which met the deadline but did not speak positively to the real situation of contemporary Reform Judaism.

Limitations of Scope and Claim: Second, the committee early recognized that if it was to accomplish anything it would have to be limited in scope and in claim. Again, with the image of the Platform Commission before it, the committee was quite satisfied, as Kahn had been in his document, to produce a statement of limited size. While there are special problems involved in trying to speak briefly about important matters, the committee felt that the only thing it could responsibly undertake was the creation of a relatively short text which it could intensively review and revise. The precedents of Pittsburgh and Columbus gave us some confidence in taking this approach.

Brevity was, however, early linked with the committee's recognition of the special situation in which it had come into being. The previous statements had largely been proclamations of new thrusts for Judaism or Reform Judaism. They spoke for a new consensus which had gathered and which now sought formal articulation. But the committee working in 1976 had been appointed to overcome polarization. Amid the controversy that was troubling our movement, its function was to discover and verbalize whatever significant unity remained. Since its task was somewhat different from that of previous platform writers, and specifically more limited than that of the Platform Commission, the committee agreed, informally, I think, to eschew the term *platform* in referring to its work. It did not want to make too many claims for what it was doing, and it was quite satisfied to let people call its statement whatever they considered appropriate. I endorse that understanding and follow it.

If I may call it that, this humility about our document also arose from a profound respect for the autonomy of the individual members of the Conference. The right to follow one's conscience had been the theological crux of the debate over intermarriage. By extension our committee knew that their colleagues would be outraged if our document made any pretense of setting the standard of what all Reform Jews must now believe. There never was any question of this on the committee. No one suggested that we try to create or consider what we had written a dogma or creed which would supersede the right of individual Reform Jews to think for themselves. Our introduction to our statement makes plain what we consider it to be: "The Central Conference of American Rabbis . . . [describing] the spiritual state of Reform Judaism." We give our "sense"—no more—"of the unity of our movement," not forever, but "today." And this is followed three paragraphs later by an unprecedented discussion of the role of freedom in Reform Judaism.

I think it typical of the document as a whole—and a critical factor in its acceptability to the Conference—that it is scrupulously attentive to individual autonomy. Yet it is also and equally characteristic of it that this concern for freedom is balanced by the limits, small and few though they be, set by our being Reform Jews. And I think that this balancing of freedom with the Reform Jewish claims upon us was an equal factor in the overwhelming support the document received in San Francisco. Again and again in its work the committee dealt with views that had become polarized and needed now to be seen in their proper tension with one another. Restoring the balance of the two poles, without losing their opposition, or, to shift metaphors, hearing the harmony as well as the distinct tones, became the major concern of this document.

For example, though implicit recognition is taken of individual freedom, some demands upon it are also advanced. The organized Reform rabbinate is saying what it thinks Reform Judaism is about today. It does not do so very often. That an overwhelming majority supported this document in this divisive time gives its words special weight. These factors alone should give the individual Reform Jew a good deal to consider while pursuing a personal interpretation of our faith. Should it turn out that our movement as a whole reacts well to the statement and finds it expressive of its present religious condition, that will make the *Centenary Perspective* all the more authoritative, though not giving it an authoritarian claim upon us.

Practically, the committee approached this issue via an intriguing quantitative question. No serious document could gain the unanimous approval of the twelve-hundred-odd listed members of the Conference. The question was then put to the committee: How large a majority would our statement need to win before our committee could feel it had given a sense of "the unity of our movement"? No one would have felt comfortable with a bare majority; few would have been satisfied with the support of two-thirds of the Conference members, as difficult as that is to achieve on controversial matters. Yet the more we discussed this issue the more it seemed evident to us that the extremists of either the freedom or the tradition camp were a relatively small percentage of the Conference. For all the polarization of our membership, we believed that a very large proportion of our colleagues affirmed something of their opponents' position while vigorously upholding their own. Making playful estimates on the first day of our January meeting, we reached a consensus that perhaps 5 or 7 percent of the Conference at either pole of the debate might be so fanatic about their view that they could not accommodate it in any significant way to that of their opponents. If so, then there was a chance that while we might not be able to speak for 90 percent of the Conference, then we might do so for 85 percent of our colleagues. The

possibility that there might be that much agreement in the Conference was startling. For
safety's sake we agreed, since we still considered it a utopian goal, to adopt an unofficial
criterion of 80 percent of the Conference as
the group whose views we would seek to articulate. Thus it was our rule of thumb that anything we felt more than 20 percent of the
Conference might disagree with could not be
included in the document. (The two substantive miscalculations the committee made in
using this standard are discussed in Book III. I
believe it was Ronald Sobel who, at this discussion, raised the possibility (perhaps as
devil's advocate) of our not producing any
document, as we could not speak for any
sizeable group of rabbis. But the 80 percent
figure seemed a worthy goal for us to strive for,
and he then enthusiastically joined in our
effort to see what we might accomplish in
terms of it. Though 80 percent is an extraordinary majority in most democractic bodies, 20
percent is a sizeable minority. We were conscious of whom we might not be speaking for
and made every effort to try to find space for
them within what we felt we had to say for our
majority. We therefore made an effort to avoid
overstatement.

To round out this numerical discussion, let
me record here that the final vote on our statement at the 1976 San Francisco meeting of the
Conference, while not numerically tallied,

supported it in overwhelming numbers. Some of those who voted against it did so because they felt that there had not been sufficient discussion, not because they had some major substantive objection to it. In any case, a number of observers judged—the committee members not being objective in this matter!—that there was at least a 4-to-1 majority in favor, the 80 percent or more which all along had been the committee's goal.

Seeking a Strong Statement: The third concern of the committee was to produce as strong and positive a statement as would gain the 80 percent majority we sought. Obviously the danger of trying to speak for so many people was that, in the effort to offend no one, the resulting statement would be bland to the point of being contentless. Some thoughtful critics of the working draft (the version sent to the Conference in early March 1976, on which see below) felt that it was just that. Bernard Bamberger, a past president of the Conference and a much-respected scholar and thinker, found the document so empty that he suggested that we withdraw it from consideration. Alan Sokobin, of Toledo, Ohio, gave a strong indictment of the document for failing to give us new directions for the future, and while he said he would not vote against it, he considered the adoption of so innocuous a statement of little significance to our movement. The committee considered their criticism and that of others at its April meeting in terms of the widespread positive response to its draft and on the basis of its own, admittedly subjective, evaluation of what it had accomplished. It felt its document needed refinement and editing by a competent stylist, but it did not think it should withdraw the statement or that it could make it any stronger within the situation in which it was operating. Whether that judgment was correct perhaps some future historian will clarify for us, but we should be able to see in the next few years whether our statement has had any significant effect upon the Reform movement.

Dealing with Major Problems: Fourth, though seeking to speak as strongly as possible, the committee was determined to try to face directly the major problems of Reform Judaism. These, it was quickly agreed, were the nature and extent of Reform religious observance, our relation to the State of Israel, and how we are to balance our duties to our people and to humanity. Two more problems were then suggested and became part of the committee's working agenda: how to live with diversity in the Reform movement and how to find hope in a world largely despairing and cynical. This decision to face the controversial issues head on marks the major difference between the committee document and Kahn's original proposal. He had felt that division could be overcome by calling attention to those matters where there was no serious difference of opinion. The committee believed that the cause of unity would better be served by showing where, in the areas of our deepest division, we still had major agreement among us. This approach, we thought, should also help us avoid the problem of saying nothing or of restating the obvious.

Seeing with a Century's Perspective: Fifth, though the problems were to be the major focus of the document, the specific occasion which brought our statement into being was the centenaries of our national organizations. Our document therefore had to have a historical base, and while one might just as well ask in one's ninety-ninth or hundred-and-first year just where one had come, the achievement of a centennial seemed a particularly appropriate time for such a glance backward. We were unanimous that this should include not only a section on what Reform Judaism had given all modern Jews but also one on what it had itself learned with the passage of time. Ironically enough, it was not the notion that Reform Jews had been required to change some of their old ideas that stirred some dissatisfaction with the document but the apparent self-glorification some readers found in the description of Reform as a teacher of contemporary Jewry.

Stating Theological Positions: The committee also had some discussion over whether it should include paragraphs on the basic Jewish beliefs, that is, on God, the people of Israel, and Torah. I confess it was I who urged the committee to consider leaving out sections on these topics. By omitting all statements on these beliefs I thought we might show that we did not think anyone could say very much about them in a few sentences. My hope was that people would then realize that if they did not want to consider these matters with some seriousness they should not claim to know what these matters involved. My colleagues, to a man, were opposed to my stand on pragmatic and substantive grounds. To leave these matters out of the document would not motivate deeper search, they suggested, but make it appear to our people that these matters were irrelevant or marginal to Reform Judaism. The document was supposed to serve as a starting point for an understanding of Reform Judaism today, and it therefore required some statement concerning our fundamental theological affirmations. Besides, while not much can be said in a few sentences, some fundamental directions can be indicated, and, considering the low state of belief and affirmation in our time, even to provide this stimulus to further search would be to make a contribution to the education of our people. I was persuaded by the committee and, in retrospect, think they were correct.

However, I know that I am largely influenced in that judgment by the fact that the committee has gone on to supplement the document with its own commentary, and I have in these pages taken the opportunity to suggest further intellectual directions inherent in our few words.

A Concern with Our Own Procedure: Seventh and finally. I had felt from the moment the possibility of my being appointed chairman of this committee was discussed with me that whatever success the committee might have in its efforts would be directly linked to its exemplifying in operation what it wrote on paper. Since we were going to tell others how to live in unity despite intellectual diversity, the committee itself ought to show how this is done. Thus, I had suggested—to already equally determined hearers—that such a committee represent our Conference's religious variety, our geographical spread, and our different age groups. As the list above indicates, this was done and, quite appropriately, without any consultation with me. For my part, I tried to clarify early to the committee, by action rather than by word, that we would operate with scrupulous concern for democracy. Thus before our first meeting I made special efforts to get responses to the Kahn document from all the committee members and circulated them as received. It was a minor matter, to be sure, but it was an early indication that the chairman did not intend to dominate the committee or to screen what came before it. I wanted complete openness to all views and serious attention to their substance to be the hallmark of the committee's deliberations. All members, whether in attendance at meetings or not, received all documents. On several occasions the work of the committee was delayed, despite the tight schedule, so that we might have the benefit of the input of members who had been unable to reach a decision or to submit it to us. The committee members appreciated this attitude and responded by applying it to our relationship to the Conference as a whole. They happily accepted my suggestion that we not carry our work through to completion but submit a working draft, though a responsible one, to the members of the Conference. Quite early, then, they could tell us whether we were moving in the direction they desired and what changes of course seemed appropriate to them. They received the draft in early March, and when we met in early April we studied all the substantive changes submitted about which more than a single colleague was concerned. We did so in the language of those who submitted the suggestions but without the committee knowing who had offered it. We thus exposed ourselves as fully as we could to the diversity in our midst and out of it, while respecting our differences, sought to make as strong a statement as possible of our unity. Having already touched on the description of the process we went through, let me turn directly to it.

III. HOW DO DIVIDED LIBERALS CREATE A POLICY DOCUMENT?

What follows is an account of the steps we went through in creating the *Centenary Perspective*. Reading it, I think, will be as dull as going through it often was tedious, frustrating, and demanding. I shall not at all feel bad if readers who are interested in the content of the document choose to skim or skip this section, and for this reason it has been presented as a supplement to the work as a whole. Yet the commitment to democracy means nothing if it is not worked out detail by detail. Since much of what is said later about living with diversity is to be seen in the actual work of the committee, it deserves recording here. I only regret that I cannot fully convey the tone of what we did. It was carried on wholeheartedly, by people who believed in what we were doing and the way we were doing it, even if that should not have yielded a proposed document or a document the Conference would endorse. I am certain that commitment to the task and to our colleagues had something to do with the unusually positive reception of our work.

The First Communiqué: The committee was formally appointed in November 1975. A first letter asking members of the committee to indicate which dates in late December or January they had available for a meeting, and requesting responses to the Kahn document to circulate before that first meeting, went out in late November. Some weeks later it became clear, from the lack of replies, that something had gone wrong. On checking it was discovered that the list of committee members in the Conference office was incorrect. Additional letters were mailed and the late December meeting dates withdrawn from consideration. To determine a date for the committee meeting, calls had to be made to various committee members, and this made it possible to put some pressure on the committee for written responses to the Kahn document.

The First Meeting: The first meeting of the committee was January 12-14, 1976, copies of the responses to the Kahn document having been mailed in advance. The meetings were held at the College building in New York, Monday afternoon and evening, Tuesday morning and afternoon, Wednesday morning and afternoon. In attendance at most of the sessions, variously, were Goldman, Kahn, Polish, Rosenstock, Sobel, Stern, and the chairman. By Monday evening many of the general issues discussed in the previous section of this account had been decided upon, and the committee proceeded to the discussion of what should be included in each section. Notes were taken by the chairman as well as others on what we agreed should be treated in them. Eventually each theme to be treated in the document received such detailed consideration. Already on Monday night several people (I specifically remember Kahn and Sobel being involved) were asked to report the following morning with quick drafts of various sections, occasionally several drafts being requested for a given topic. Though everyone did drafts and revisions as we worked along, the main responsibility for initial versions eventually fell to the chairman and most of the bulk of the original draft completed by the committee at this meeting was from his hand. The committee turned to reviewing the drafts only after it had discussed its intentions for each section of the entire document. It did so by subjecting the draft or drafts to meticulous, word-by-word scrutiny. There were additions, deletions, substitutions, wholesale revisions, and demands for substantial recasting. The committee was somewhat content to do a rough job at this point because the process went very much better than anyone had anticipated and because it was clear there would be further circulation and discussion of what was done before even a working draft was approved for release to the Conference. The meeting ended with a document, substantially in the same general shape of the eventual one, except that the final paragraph had not been completed and the chairman was instructed to prepare this in accord with the will of the committee.

This rough draft was sent to all the members of the committee on January 22 asking for responses and reworkings. It had been hoped that much of our revising might proceed via a telephone conference call of the entire committee. The many revisions suggested made that impractical. In addition, one of the members who had been unable to attend the meeting but wanted to respond to the rough document was prevented from doing so beyond the deadline set. Finally, on February 20, three complete reworkings of the document plus a composite of four sets of emendations were submitted to the members of the committee to be considered at a meeting on February 26. Before that meeting the material of the tardy member was received, and it became another document before the revision session.

The Second Working Session: The second thoughts of the committee, both those who had been present and those who had only seen the resulting rough draft, were essentially linguistic. That is, there were many opinions as to how matters might best be expressed and some difference of opinion as to what should be stressed. Yet the revision meeting of February

26 could be entered with the feeling that the
committee itself felt it was on the right track.
Despite their diversity, none of the committee
members had taken strong objection to any
topic that had been treated or to any significant opinion in the document. No one seemed
to feel that some major topic had been left out
or that any essential aspect relative to a given
theme had been omitted. The February 26
meeting therefore was devoted essentially to
literary revisions of the rough text. Rosenstock, Sobel, Stern, and Zimmerman as well as
the chairman were present at Temple Emanu El
in New York for this session. In one grueling
day a word-by-word revision of the rough
document was completed. Since five did not
constitute a majority of the committee, the
new document was then circulated to all the
members to see if what had been produced was
objected to by any substantial minority of the
committee. The committee's goal at this stage
was to produce a responsible working draft
which could be mailed in early March to the
members of the Conference. Then, on April 7
and 8 the committee was to meet to review
their response and, if possible, produce a final
version to be submitted to the Conference.
There were no objections by the members of
the committee to the working draft completed
on February 26 being sent to the Conference
members for their suggestions. The Conference
office mailed it to them, with a covering letter

introducing the document (the committee had also discussed its contents) and soliciting their response by March 31. (The Conference office, normally quite efficient, had inadvertently dropped the section on "The People Israel" from the working draft our committee had submitted to it. As a result, it sent a second mailing, March 16, to the members of the Conference with the missing paragraph.) In addition, each member of our committee was asked to discuss the working draft with at least one colleague and also with various lay people so as to be able to bring to the April 7 meeting a personal report on the draft's merits and failings.

A Telephone Survey: Impersonal mail solicitations of responses from a large group generally draw few answers. Since I felt that it was important to have a good sample of the reactions of the Conference and also to find out from people what they felt about the document but might not want to put on paper, I asked the Conference to authorize me to make a phone survey. They provided me with a list of approximately every twentieth name on the Conference membership list and defrayed the expenses of my calls. I also contacted every past president of the Conference. The calls were invaluable in giving me a feel of the range of response the document was receiving. In all I phoned or was in personal contact with sixty-five colleagues, including Richard Hirsch who phoned me from Jerusalem when the mail response from our Israeli colleagues (which I had particularly written to request) was, for various reasons, going to be delayed. I also received one hundred eighty-seven letters in answer to our Conference mailing, some because I had called the person who had at that time not yet responded to the document. (Another twenty-one arrived after our deadline but before our meeting, and additional mail continued to arrive until shortly before the San Francisco meeting.) We thus came to the April 7 meeting with good feedback. In addition, since the completion of the working draft, I had studied it one Shabbat afternoon with the Board of Trustees of Shaare Emeth Congregation, St. Louis, a class of the Hebrew Union College School of Education, and the Executive Board of the Central Conference itself. This enabled me and a number of other members of the committee to deal with suggestions for the revision of the working draft in terms of some personal experience with it as well as with the written responses.

The Third Meeting: The April 7-8 meeting began with a discussion of some general questions I thought the responses had raised, and these were sent to the committee members so they could give them thought prior to our sessions. In addition, wherever there were several substantive objections to our text, these were photocopied, identified only by number, and collated by theme so that on the master sheets provided the committee could at once see the range of response to a given topic in the language of the person making it.

The major decision of the April meeting may well have been that none of us was to serve as the committee's ultimate authority on matters of English style or usage. We agreed to turn over all such questions to a writer of established reputation whose work on the text would be subject to the guidance of the chairman and review by mail to the committee. This was our response to the large number of complaints by our colleagues—with which we often agreed—that much in the working draft was clumsy, imprecise, and repetitious and that the whole was too long. With the literary questions assigned to an outside expert the committee spent its time on substantive issues. Though there were many suggestions for change here and there, there was a general acceptance of the document by our colleagues that was astonishing to us. There was no substantial outcry against its treatment of freedom or tradition. A number of people considered significant partisans of the antagonistic groups wrote that they found the document at least acceptable and, in some cases, even nicely expressive of their views. There was no complaint that an important topic had been left out (at San

Francisco the lack of direct treatment of social action was mentioned) or included which did violence to a sizeable group in the Conference. The document's structure, specific themes, and overall tone seemed acceptable to most of the respondents, even though they suggested changes for one spot or another. Far more expressions of enthusiasm than of dislike for the document were received. The committee was thus in the happy position of dealing with specific suggestions for change within a framework of a broad-scale acceptance of what they had written. Aside from altering or reaffirming the text in a number of specific instances, the committee decided to explain the statement's purposes by a brief introduction; to have an additional opening sentence about the relation of Reform Judaism to North American democracy; to provide rubrics at the sides of each section; and to give the document the title *Reform Judaism: A Centenary Perspective*.

Present at this session were Goldman, Kahn, Polish, Rosenstock, Sobel, Stern, Wolf, Zimmerman, and the chairman. The resulting text, which was to be submitted to a writer for styling, was then mailed to all members.

Guidance in Style and Usage: Hugh Nissenson, the short story writer and novelist, was good enough to lend his talents to the Conference for the rather unpleasant chore of reviewing and revising a draft which had resulted from these many hands, opinions, and previous revisions. In going over his recommendations with him, I found him to be supremely sensitive to our intentions as well as to the English in which we might best express them. I was not always able to accept his suggestions, as occasionally a given wording seemed required by a committee decision and he and I could find no reasonable substitute for them. On May 10 the Nissenson revision, a much-pruned-and-polished version of our April 8 revision, was circulated to the members of the committee.

While awaiting their responses, due May 25, I had the pleasure of being invited to discuss the April 8 draft with the members of the Union Board of Trustees. It was a most enlightening and enjoyable occasion. That session, as well as a discussion with a class of students in the rabbinical school of the HUC-JIR in New York, indicated to me that the price of our brevity was that even informed readers missed much of what we had condensed into a few words. My concern with our need to follow up this document with additional educational resources may, I think, be traced to these experiences—and my discussions of the statement with groups since it was given its final form has confirmed that impression.

Several committee members suggested some changes in the Nissenson revision, and since these involved only a return to our April 8 version they were acceptable without complete committee consideration. As a result, the altered, Nissenson revision was mailed by the Conference office to all members some weeks in advance of the June meeting in San Francisco.

Prior to the Conference meeting I received a request from some of our Israeli colleagues that a slight change in wording be introduced into our sentence on Jewish survival and that a sentence on *aliyah*, immigration, be added to the section on the State of Israel. I circulated their letter to the members of the committee present in San Francisco, indicating that I thought the former matter was within the committee's intentions. The *aliyah* question had already been posed at the April 8 meeting and the committee felt that 80 percent of the Conference would not support it, so it had not included such a sentence. Believing we should honor the request of the Israeli colleagues, I put it before the Conference, where it was overwhelmingly accepted. (Further details are given in *Reform Judaism Today: How We Live*.)

Presenting the Document: The *Centenary Perspective* came before the Conference late Thursday morning, June 24. It was a somewhat uncomfortable situation for the discussion of a statement of principle proposed by a committee which had been deeply concerned about democratic procedure. Thursday was the last day of the Conference which was to continue only through the afternoon. But, as often happens, the business of the Conference on previous days had begun to back up and, as the Conference had put an overabundance of rich programs on its schedule, there was too much for the organization to do that day and too little time to do it. The members, to whom this had happened before, were relatively tolerant of the situation, though there were occasional ripples of annoyance in the assembled group. Unfortunately, too, we had lost the use of the ballroom where our previous sessions had been held and were now rather cramped in a somewhat smaller hall. Add to this the fact that the best nonstop flight to New York was due to leave early in the afternoon and that a number of the East Coast colleagues were straining to make it and one gets something of the mood in which the discussion of the document began.

Robert Kahn first indicated how the document came to be and moved its acceptance. Alfred Wolf then discussed the process by which it had been produced and seconded the motion. As chairman, I then indicated some of the major concerns we had in mind writing it. We were quite brief, perhaps ten minutes for the three of us. I had thought that there was a relatively good mood about the document from all the feedback we had received. I was not prepared for the immediate will of the body to adopt it and get on to the next item of business. No sooner had our opening statements been made and the question of the *aliyah* sentence put to the Conference then a motion was made to end discussion and proceed to a vote. A standing tally indicated that while the two-thirds vote necessary to end discussion had not been attained, a large number approved of the document and were ready, apparently, to vote for it. (If I recall correctly, the CCAR transcript of the proceedings giving no tally, there were about one hundred twenty rabbis favoring an end to discussion and seventy-odd for keeping it open. Apparently some 60 percent of the membership were already in favor of the document.

The Conference Discussion: The discussion which then ensued first centered around our proposed statement on Torah which, in the Nissenson version, had been cut to two sentences. The Conference objected to this more as a matter of emphasis than of doctrine and suggested that this section be amplified. Since in the working draft it had been much longer, the chairman accepted the suggestion and it was agreed that he would expand this paragraph on the basis of the Conference discussion. A motion to remove the word *mystery* in the paragraph on God and substitute *reality* was roundly defeated. Some questions of wording, of the emphasis on social justice in the document, and on the adequacy of the Conference's discussion then ensued. On several occasions the chairman indicated that suggestions for improving the language would gladly be received for some weeks yet. Another motion to end discussion was then easily carried and after some parliamentary jousting the matter was put to the Conference for a vote. President Lelyveld then said, "The document *Reform Judaism; A Centenary Perspective* is overwhelmingly approved by this body." There was loud applause from the floor and Bob Kahn and I and then Alfred Wolf and I spontaneously embraced one another at this extraordinary outcome to an enterprise we had all entered with such doubt and hesitation some six months or so previously.

In retrospect it is easy for me to say that I wish there had been more time for discussion so that no colleague would have left the meeting with a sense that he had been denied a proper chance to discuss this document. Nonetheless, I know that no major statement has ever come before the Conference with as much prior involvement of the membership as did this one. Moreover, for whatever such a statistic is worth, we had received more comments on the document in the course of its composition than there were rabbis sitting in the room at the time it was voted on. I would have preferred that the acceptance of the document be as free and as participatory as the process which brought it into being. But considering the realities in which we must operate, I believe that whatever failings there may have been in connection with its final acceptance, the will of the overwhelming majority of members was done.

Completing the Task: The committee may have accomplished its goal, but it had not yet finished its task. On the basis of the suggestions made at the Conference meeting and some that were sent me later, I suggested to the committee by mail that five changes be made in the document, ranging from two that were largely verbal to the requested reworking of the paragraph on Torah. This was sent to the committee on July 13 asking for a response by August 13. A number of the members of the committee replied, and some further changes were made in accord with their suggestions. The final version was then prepared, the original of which was sent to the Conference office and a copy to each member of the committee.

Technically that might have finished the committee's assignment, but the various sessions I had conducted based on the document had indicated to me that it could benefit with a commentary. I therefore suggested to the Conference leadership that I would be willing to do such a volume if the Conference was interested in its publication. The Executive Board of the Conference suggested instead that we utilize a series of articles to appear periodically in the

CCAR Journal for some such project. Since that seemed not to supply the space for the substantial treatment I thought the document required, I suggested to Bernard Martin, editor of the *CCAR Journal*, that our committee might produce a commentary to the *Centenary Perspective* for one of its issues. He made some helpful suggestions as to how this best might be carried out, and the result may be seen in the spring 1977 issue of the *Journal*. I was particularly pleased that each member of the committee had a chance there to show how he reads a section of our statement. Obviously, each rabbi approaches Judaism with special concerns of his own, and this comes through clearly in their comments. Yet it was out of such a combination of different approaches that the *Centenary Perspective* came into being. I hope that people reading their interpretations will not only learn something directly from them but will come away from the variety of interests represented with a fresh sense of the unity in diversity which the document calls "the hallmark of Reform."

The committee's commentary should encourage people to study the *Centenary Perspective* to see what it says to them. Only when Reform Jews have had a chance to consider its contents in such depth will we know how useful our committee effort has been. If the document turns out only to have stated what tied us together in 1976, a time of great disunity in our movement, that already will have been an accomplishment. But I believe that what we said went far beyond the understanding most Reform Jews had of their movement and its message. When one sees what is hidden in the few pages of our statement, the things left unsaid, the choices made, and the alternatives rejected, when one recognizes where ambiguity has consciously been resorted to and what content might fill it in, when one sees the ways in which polar faiths have been balanced one against the other, when one recognizes the many strong positive assertions of faith contained here, one comes away with a fresh sense of the power and majesty of the Reform approach to Judaism. At least I do, and that is why, so to speak as a continuation of my work for the committee, I have set down here something of what I see in this document.

My Own Commentary: I have offered at length my views on the *Perspective* because by profession and position I feel I am in a unique position to open up what the document contains. For nearly two decades now I have had the privilege of teaching rabbinical students, and for most of that time I have been writing in the field of modern Jewish thought. I have lived professionally and personally for a long time with the questions raised in this document. I have written my commentary not as an academic exercise but as one of explanation.

However, had I not been a specialist in theology, much that I have strenuously labored to make plain in these pages would not have occurred to me. And I have lived with this document more closely than anyone else. I nursed it through every stage of its long and difficult development; I have been over every one of its words many times with many people under many circumstances. I never had any illusion about its being "my" document, for I know that it does not express my personal understanding of Judaism. It is the Conference's statement, and to that extent Reform Judaism's. It is the document of my movement and I respect it as such. It is the work of a committee I headed and I am proud of it. I hope that by opening up its layers of meaning I may help others catch something of the greatness I see in the Reform movement and the riches I believe are contained in the Conference's centenary statement. Regardless of my official positions, then, I know I speak in these pages only for myself, and yet in doing so I hope I articulate the contemporary spirit of Reform Judaism as a whole.

REFORM
JUDAISM TODAY

Book Three
HOW WE LIVE

Book Three

HOW
WE
LIVE

REFORM JUDAISM TODAY

Eugene B. Borowitz

BEHRMAN HOUSE, INC. New York

Library of Congress Cataloging in Publication Data

Borowitz, Eugene B.
  Reform Judaism Today.

  CONTENTS: Book 1. Reform in the process of change. Book 2. What we believe. Book 3. How we live.
  1. Central Conference of American Rabbis. Reform Judaism, a centenary perspective. 2. Reform Judaism—United States. I. Title.
BM197.B67   296.8'346   78-24676

Published by Behrman House, Inc.
1261 Broadway, New York, New York 10001

Produced in the U.S. of America

CONTENTS

PART I

An Introduction to the Obligations

Each of the three major statements created by Reform Judaism in America has spoken to another need. The Pittsburgh Platform of 1885 proclaimed a new program of change for Judaism. The Columbus Platform of 1937 called for a fresh openness among Reform Jews to ritual and the restoration of the Jewish homeland. The most recent statement, the Central Conference of American Rabbis' *Reform Judaism: A Centenary Perspective* (adopted 1976) sought to address the serious problems confronting the movement after 100 years of national organization.

The committee which prepared the drafts of the *Centenary Perspective* had no difficulty identifying the three issues Reform Jews were finding most troublesome[1]: One was the question of religious duties: just what must a Reform Jew do? The second focused on our involvement with the State of Israel and how this related to our local responsibilities. The third dealt with

---

[1] For a full description of the work of the drafting committee, see "How a Document Came to Be Written," the *Supplement* to *Reform Judaism Today: What We Believe.*

the tensions now often felt between our duties to the Jewish people and those to humanity as a whole. These are all questions of what Jews should do, not questions of philosophy or proper belief. We all knew that our colleagues were most concerned about what Reform Jews ought to be doing, not what sort of theology might currently be most acceptable. This attitude will occasion no surprise to those who know Reform Judaism is a modern creative form of classic Judaism.

Considering the tension which surrounded the issues—Halachah versus freedom, Zionism versus local loyalties, ethnicity versus universal duty—our working draft of these paragraphs met with an extraordinarily positive reception. Despite the breadth of opinion elicited, there was no major substantive objection to the positions we had taken on these three supposedly explosive issues. There were complaints about the wording, a sensible suggestion (from Rabbi H. P. Uriel Smith), that we change the order of the paragraphs, and some specific objections as to emphasis, particularly with regard to the section on the State of Israel (discussed below in Part III), but that was all. To our delight and astonishment, no bloc in the Central Conference of American Rabbis (CCAR) seemed to feel that its position had been violated or that something dear to it had been omitted from the draft.

FORMULATING A STATEMENT

One explanation of the committee's success in dealing with these controversies is that it did not attempt to say very much. By limiting itself to what it knew the overwhelming majority of rabbis would accept, it might be said that a minimalist statement was produced. While personally I would have liked a far more positive and directing statement, I think this charge is largely untrue. For one, the committee's mandate was to state the unity underlying our movement. Mostly we could not have said very much in a more substantive way and achieved that goal. Again, I think careful study of the *Centenary Perspective,* as is undertaken in these pages, will show how rich in content and guidance it is. Many of our colleagues indicated that it had gone farther than they ever thought it could and put into words notions about Reform Jewish obligation they had felt but had not themselves been able to articulate.

Another explanation for the phenomenal reception of the committee's working draft is that the Reform rabbinate's unity was far greater than it had appeared to be and our committee through skill or good fortune had been able to intuit and express this. This matter of what had, in fact, unified us despite our arguments merits further comment.

THE QUESTION OF
REFORM JEWISH PRACTICE

The most explosive of the three issues we dealt with was that related to Reform religious duty. For twenty years or more there had been great agitation for Reform Judaism to produce a guide to religious practice. Even though proponents of this plan carefully distinguished it from a code of required practice, every suggestion or tactical maneuver which sought to further it was hotly attacked and voted down. The advocates of spelling out Reform Jewish obligation used many lines of argument. They wanted to end anarchy in the movement and to restore Judaism's interest in detailed instruction for action, i.e., Halachah. They suggested that we adopt some stipulations of traditional Jewish law to make Reform Jews an integral part of the Jewish religious community and acceptable to the religious establishment of the State of Israel.

Each notion provoked anguished outcries from other rabbis. Some made freedom of choice the only dogma of their faith; others variously insisted on full respect for individual autonomy or denounced spineless concessions to the Orthodox or nostalgic returns to tradition. The notion that Reform Jews might somehow revive Halachah was particularly outrageous, for it suggested not only standards of action but sanctions against those who did not obey them. These fears reached a climax in the CCAR vote of 1973 asking colleagues to refrain from performing intermarriages. Those who had been voted down saw the condemnation as the opening wedge for the advocates of a Reform return to Halachah. They were fearful lest the CCAR now move into other realms of practice, such as Sabbath observance or keeping kosher, overriding individual autonomy, and, in this instance, the autonomy of rabbis to do what seemed right to them.

Since it bears on each of the three areas of "our obligations," it is important to keep in focus the major issue of the controversy: by what right did any group of Reform Jews tell any other group of Reform Jews what they ought to do? Note that in the 1950s and 1960s there had been intense suspicion of any form of official "guidance," that is, of any Reform body suggesting certain practices as desirable. The fear was often expressed that what would begin as recommended options would quickly turn into expected norms of behavior. Yet something had apparently changed by the early 1970s, of which the CCAR's *Shabbat Manual* is the chief testimony. It is a book which makes suggestions for Reform Jewish Sabbath observance and it was adopted by the Conference without much objection. In recent years, then, the members of the CCAR had apparently come to accept the distinction between guidance and prescription. Those who favored strong CCAR stands on issues of practice and believed the rabbinate had too long abdicated its leadership in matters of Jewish duty had finally found a theme and a format which their colleagues, for all their concern about autonomy, were willing to accept. Perhaps the old antagonist of a "guide" had come to see that in a time of spiritual confusion and search, what Reform Jews needed more than an emphasis on their freedom was some counsel as to what their leaders thought they ought to be doing with it to live their Judaism. A more cynical interpretation is that, by contrast to the intermarriage question which decisively touches Jewish lives, the question of Reform Sabbath observance was of interest only to a pious minority. Historians will have to judge the relationship of this event to the analogous phenomenon of the publication and overwhelming reception of *The Jewish Catalog* which did the same task for much of Jewish life in a more sprightly though traditional fashion.

A BASIC SENSE OF UNITY

Hindsight also gives further insight into the unsensed unity in the movement when one thinks back to the debate on the theoretical question of Halachah versus freedom at the 1975 meeting of the CCAR in Cincinnati. Despite much anticipation, it is now intellectually clear why the widely expected ideological split of the Reform rabbis did not take place. The protagonist of Halachah had no intention of suggesting that the right of individual decision be curtailed.

He only called upon his colleagues, when thinking about issues of practice, to give full weight to the sensitiveness of the rest of the Jewish community and serious respect to the major thrusts of Jewish tradition. The advocate of personal autonomy made clear that he did not think Judaism could exist without structure. He conceded that Reform Jews needed some continuity with Jewish tradition and concern for the Jewish people but felt this must not override the voice of conscience. Therefore, Reform Jewish institutions like the CCAR should not set general standards for action, but individual rabbis should work out their own set of norms with their community. There was, then, no radical difference of opinion. Rabbi Jack Stern, Jr. may well have been speaking for the majority when he said that while he did want to make up his own mind it was useful and important for him to know where most of his colleagues, that is, the CCAR, stood on a given issue.

Perhaps, then, as our committee began its work, we should have realized that the contentious wings in our movement had more in common than separated them. Surely the decline in ideological tension among rabbis is so palpable to me even a few months after the passage of the *Centenary Perspective* that it makes the turmoil of 1973-75 seem highly overblown and unsubstantial.

Perhaps too we should have guessed that our very articulation of the underlying unity among

Reform Jews on the issue of Reform Jewish practice would assuage some of the traumas of the intermarriage resolution of the CCAR and momentarily, at least, ease the tensions between the Halachic and freedom factions in the movement. Nonetheless, though the drafting committee felt it had composed a fair, occasionally creative description of the theory of Reform Jewish obligation as it applied to three troublesome areas, it circulated its working draft in March 1976 with a good deal of apprehension. We had no way of knowing then whether the document itself might not provoke new civil strife as either or both sides of the practice issue felt its sense of the mandates of Reform Judaism had been violated.

CREATING A REPRESENTATIVE STANCE

We were sensitive lest what we said in one section of the document lead to discontent with what we said in other sections. This problem is most readily seen with regard to our understanding of just "what Reform Jews had learned" in recent years. To one group in the CCAR, "Jewish survival" meant richer Jewish observance, strong concern for the State of Israel, the primacy of the interests of the Jewish people in the face of universal human concerns. The other group identified survival with personal choice, diaspora independence and a substantial involvement in the affairs of humankind. I think it fair to say that we believed both groups, aside from some small percentage of extremists, shared the concerns of their antagonists. The particularists were not chauvinists, unmindful of general human concerns. The universalists were not Unitarians, uninvolved in the ethnic dimension of Jewish existence. But each group was concerned that its position be properly represented or, more threatening to the possibility of our agreeing on a statement, that its priorities in this clash of commitments not be upset. There thus existed the possibility that writing an acceptable statement in one of the three sections on Reform Jewish obligation might be offset by a perceived failure in another section. This might then precipitate a debate on the general issue of Halachah and freedom or of particularism versus universalism, thus bringing all three paragraphs under fire. When this did not materialize in the responses to the draft or in the public debate, it first began to dawn on us that perhaps we had been able to intuit and speak for the overwhelming majority of the CCAR in this area.

In studying the *Centenary Perspective* in its various versions with different groups, I learned that one reason rabbis could accept it was that they tended not to come to it with false expectations. Thus its three sections on Reform Jewish obligation do not spell out the detail of our religious practice, our duties to the State of Israel or local communities, or our responsibilities to our people and humanity. The

Centenary Perspective should not be confused with a guide to Reform Jewish practice. It was not intended to describe what the CCAR thinks are useful suggestions as to what Reform Jews might choose to do. I believe there is great need for a literature of detailed guidance, but our brief statement could only lay down the general principles which might serve as the basis for such instruction.

The results of the committee's desire to be as positive as possible were quite different in each of the three sections. Working backward, we found not much could be said about the tensions between our particular and universal duties other than to note how our historical situation differs from that of our forebears and resolutely to maintain both sorts of commitments, though they occasionally seem to clash. Our section on the State of Israel and Diaspora communities is, as I indicate below, rather specific in its suggestions. Surprisingly enough, the paragraph on religious commitment, the most contentious issue, is, in my opinion, the most concrete and detailed of the three.

Finally, for all its concern with principle, the *Centenary Perspective* ought not to be confused with a theology, a rigorous intellectual examination of what Reform Jews believe, in this case, about their duties. It is too brief and too much concerned with representing the several currents of our movement for that. Yet, despite its shortcomings, the fact that the *Centenary Perspective* could be created, considering the state that Reform Judaism seemed to be in, was no small accomplishment. And that it was brought into being and achieved widespread acceptance in less than three months seems, even in retrospect, a small miracle.

PART II

The Religious Duties of a Reform Jew

Judaism emphasizes action rather than creed as the primary expression of a religious life, the means by which we strive to achieve universal justice and peace. Reform Judaism shares this emphasis on duty and obligation. Our founders stressed that the Jew's ethical responsibilities, personal and social, are enjoined by God. The past century has taught us that the claims made upon us may begin with our ethical obligations but they extend to many other aspects of Jewish living, including: creating a Jewish home centered on family devotion; life-long study; private prayer and public worship; daily religious observance; keeping the Sabbath and the holy days; celebrating the major events of life; involvement with the synagogue and community; and other activities which promote the survival of the Jewish people and enhance its existence. Within each area of Jewish observance Reform Jews are called upon to confront the claims of Jewish tradition, however differently perceived, and to exercise their individual autonomy, choosing and creating on the basis of commitment and knowledge.

From the Centenary Perspective

15

CHAPTER ONE

A Religion of Obligation

Jews not associated with Reform Judaism often think of it as a religion of convenience, in which one is free to do whatever pleases one. By contrast to the demanding law traditional Jews should follow, Reform Jews seem free to do whatever they find comfortable for them. So goes the common perception, which is not without its polemic aspects. There is some truth to the charge. Some, perhaps many, have taken Reform Judaism's concern with personal freedom to mean that choosing for oneself was good no matter what standards one used in one's choice. Particularly since we are immersed in a gentile and secular environment, the temptation to do little, to be Reform by one's omission of Jewish duties, is very strong. That we sophisticates should be pious or work at keeping a touch of holiness in our lives seems inappropriate if not laughable. And the evil urge is real. Most people prefer self-indulgence to self-discipline.

Thus Reform Jews, for so many decades involved in changing traditional practice to give it modern form, have often been most visible by what in Jewish law they no longer did rather than by what they still do or have created for Jews now to do. Since Jews often crudely identify "religion" with observance, this has given rise to the vulgar notion that Orthodox Jews are the most religious, Conservative Jews less religious, and Reform Jews the least religious of all.

Such misconceptions are the background for the *Centenary Perspective*'s flat assertion that Reform Judaism understands itself fully to continue traditional Judaism's emphasis on action—not merely on faith or freedom—and is itself a religion of "duty and obligation." What one must do as a Reform Jew may differ from traditional Judaism. Our nonsegregated social context is bound to make it less all-embracing than what was expected of Jews in self-isolated or ghetto communities. Yet the primacy of demand and its life-pervading quality remain substantially the same. Reform Jews have duties. They are obligated to live in the service of God as members of the Jewish people which has a special involvement with God. There is no difference between Reform and traditional Jews when it comes to the priority of duty over, say, thinking or meditating.

EARLY PRIORITIES

Early Reform concentrated its attention on a Jew's ethical obligations. This had not been highly elaborated in previous Jewish teaching, but now the Jew's radically changed social situation demanded that Jews make explicit their sense of responsibility to humankind. Jews found themselves regularly thrown into unanticipated circumstances of involvement with non-Jews and general social problems. They needed to know that aspect of Judaism which helped one gain a sense of what was right and what an ethical person ought to do. Some Jewish literature of the middle ages was of immediate help. Not the Halachah, for the law was mainly devoted to a Jew's obligations to other Jews, and its few mandates concerning duties to non-Jews were naturally based on a distinction between who stood within this legal community and those who were outside it. The *musar* books (the medieval ethical writings) however, beginning with Bahya's *Duties of the Heart,* went beyond law to general spiritual and moral responsibility. The virtues described there and the acute sense of the pitfalls awaiting the person who wishes to be good, were not limited to intercourse with Jews alone. Their spirit was transferrable to the world of Emancipation. Yet their guidance is largely devoted to developing a proper inner spiritual life, much of it related to the medieval anxiety that the physical body is a person's major difficulty and society is, on the whole, a great impediment to moral development. The founders of Reform had the intellectual task of drawing forth the general ethical assumptions of traditional Judaism and developing them so that they addressed a Jewry avidly participating in the full range of general social enterprises.

Ethics was not their only interest in Jewish duty. Much of their attention was given to the creation of a modern liturgy, so prayer must be considered a major constituent of their sense of obligation. And study, for here too they re-shaped the old patterns of Jewish observance. As most men were occupied with the demanding schedule of an industrial world (especially in these early days before the five-day, forty-hour work week), retaining the yeshivah or the daily study circle was largely impractical. Instead, they brought the sermon back into the Sabbath service—in pre-radio and television days, these were often extended lectures of an hour or more, hardly what we would call a convenience. They had a somewhat similar sense for other religious observances, particularly the Sabbath. When Saturday work was almost unavoidable, they ingeniously invented a mid-Friday evening Sabbath service so that even those who worked late on Friday could get a taste of Shabbat in the synagogue.

With all that, they "stressed" ethical duty. This was clearly their major challenge. For some decades they could take it for granted that most Jews lived in a social context in which Jewish observance was expected and that they largely knew what tradition expected of them. Assuming this, they did not much discuss it, but we need to keep these assumptions in mind today as we try to understand them.

ETHICS AS LAW

The terms in which they talked about ethics disclose a good deal about their sense of Judaism. They regularly talked about moral law—and they meant law, not "values" or "standards" or "guidelines." Most of their thinking in this regard derives from Immanuel Kant's pathbreaking work in ethics around the end of the eighteenth century. Kant argued that ethics, like nature, had a rational structure. As nature can be described by science in terms of laws, so a rational person would recognize that the truly ethical takes the form of a law. He described it more explicitly as a "categorical imperative." Conscience does not operate by asking, wheedling, or suggesting. Its behests come as an imperative: "Do!" or "Don't do!" They are categorical, that is, without cosy qualifications like "when the other person is Christian," or "of your social class," or "whom you like," or "whom you owe a favor anyway." There is nothing soft or mealy-mouthed about Kant's sense of ethics. It emphasizes doing one's duty as a rational being. It has nothing to do with convenience. That Kant's ethics long dominated Reform Jewish thinking testifies to the seriousness with which they took their Reform definition of Jewish duty.

Much of their insistence upon ethics as law came from their need to deny the attractiveness of Christianity. The desire for an alternative to conversion was a major impetus to the creation of Reform Judaism, and the threat of identifying modernity with Christianity remained in the minds of the Reformers long after the movement was well established. There was great social pressure for Jews to convert. No vast secular middle-ground between the faiths, such as we see today, then existed. Sophisticates did not take their Christianity very seriously, but one still needed to be a member of the church to be accepted in various callings and social circles. Hence, Christianity was an immediate threat to the continuity of Jewish life. Reform refuted one of Christianity's appeals by showing that one could leave the ghetto, modernize, and still be a Jew. It countered another by taking a strong stand on the issue of ethics as law. Christianity claimed that, as a matter of content, it was a superior religion for it was a religion of love while Judaism was only a religion of law. The Reform Jews countered with the Kantian argument that every rational person will see ethics as a matter of law. Love can easily become sentimental and irrational but moral law preserves the supremacy of reason and thus of responsibility in our lives. Love does not lead to the regular and repeated action we need if our lives are to have stability. One cannot run a society on the basis of affection; one can hardly run it without people sharing a high sense of duty. The Reform thinkers argued that Halachah, Jewish law, was essentially concerned with the transmission of moral law, in a communal and religious sense to be sure. This sort of argument vindicated Judaism as a religion of law and the Reform Jews therefore had an additional, though polemical, reason to take the imperative connotations of moral law seriously.

JUDAISM AS AN ETHICAL RELIGION

This entire argument rests on a deep-lying assumption which should be faced; namely, that modern Jewish obligation, ethics, though apparently different from the Judaism of earlier ages, had always been the essence of Judaism. Neither the Bible nor the Talmud know the word *ethics,* and one can argue that they do not have an abstract concept analogous to it. Instead they tell how God gave the Torah, Written and Oral, to the people of Israel, and they take it for granted, therefore, that the Jews are obligated to follow it. Jewish duty has classically meant fulfilling the commandments God gave in the Torah, and these cover a whole range of activities, a significant number of which we cannot reasonably call ethics.

The founders of Reform rejected this idea of Torah, and this constituted their major break with Jewish tradition. They did not believe all of Jewish law as they received it was God's commandment. They differed as to the content of what God wanted done but they did not reject the root Jewish religious intuition, one shared by few other of the world's religions, that God revealed commands and that religion was living in response to them. They largely limited their sense of what was commanded to moral law, but they did not differ with the basic Jewish experience of what God asked of them. They transformed Oral Law into moral law, but they remained believers in law.

This fresh teaching about Judaism was widely accepted. First Reform Jews and then other Jews, as noted above, adopted the idea that ethics are a primary indicator of Jewish faithfulness. Recently our widespread adherence to this standard was seen in the general response of the Jewish community to the case of Bernard Bergman, the nursing home operator who pleaded guilty to defrauding the government of great sums, after initially defiantly proclaiming his innocence. Most people assume—though this has not been proven or acknowledged—that Bergman had similarly cheated on giving proper care to the aged and infirm in his charge. Thus he is an admitted thief and public liar who probably also stole from the weak and powerless, sins heinous enough for anyone. But Bergman is an ordained rabbi, was one of the heads of an international Jewish religious body which makes a point of its piety, and a man whose deportment connotes punctilious religiosity. Since the Enlightenment, the corrupt member of the clergy has been a stock character in our cultural world and a continuing reason for skepticism toward religion. Yet the contrast between Bergman's outward show of meticulous observance and his despicable ethical behavior affected many Jews emotionally because they had come to believe that ethics toward all people should have priority over other forms of Jewish observance. No committed Jew can take satisfaction from any nonobservance or agree to an easy split between ethics and other duties the Torah prescribes. Still the Bergman case shows how the Reform Jewish sense of ethics as law, not convenience, has become the working standard of most Jews.

THE MORAL RECORD

To some extent one can argue that our Reform Jewish forebears not only spoke of morals as required of them, but lived it. Our perceptions in this regard are somewhat obscured by the 1960s' emphasis on activism. Then living one's ethics meant organizing, protesting, shaking, and reshaping institutional structure. Previously, people had largely gone about things much more sedately and often more ineffectually, for which reason the brand of activism of the '60s came into being. If then we ask what participatory mass activities Reform Jews carried out in earlier decades, we will find little. Social improvement in a quieter, more naive time meant speaking up, associating with humanitarian efforts, giving one's energy, money, and vote for proper causes. Personally it meant doing the right and merciful thing. On both scores I think Reform Jews come off reasonably well. In most cities they were disproportionately engaged in activities for social reform or human betterment. Personally the devout among them were characterized by high human decency. Neither form of Jewish observance was a major concern of traditional Jewish law, yet both could clearly be traced back to it.

In rebuttal, one may say that all this was due more to their adoption of middle class standards than a religious response to what God was now demanding of Jews. There is much truth in this observation. Social realities regularly have more influence on most people than does religion. But one's beliefs are not without significant effect. I think any effort to reduce what the early Reformers did to mere social adjustment is unfair to the normal mix of human motives. Since they were middle class, their sense of morality was applied to that situation. And much of what is loosely called "middle class morality" is not simply social convention but, in a philosophical sense, an ethic. Besides, the Jews have not merely followed their socioeconomic norms. They have always demonstrated significant statistical deviations from others in their class and these skewed statistics—on drinking, violence, education, social betterment and the like—are a continuing testimony to a morality which transcends both personal convenience and social situation.

CHAPTER TWO

A Changing Sense of Duties

The ethical focus of a previous generation was intellectually based on its certainty that morality was mandated in a way that little else religious was. In the spirit of Kant, they considered it self-evident that being rational meant accepting the reign of moral law. No special experience or act of faith was involved. To have a mind and use it entailed the command to be ethical. No other religious activity was as surely founded. Study could be commended as giving one insight into how other generations had used their minds. Liturgy might sensitize one to one's deepest reality and help one project it outward in terms of one's personal and social ideals. Ceremony awakened the esthetic side of one's being and linked one with the history of one's people and thus gave one a context for action. With God no longer commanding them, with human nature the source of authority, they were all, at best, auxiliary activities. They were aids to being ethical but not themselves commanded by human reason. The early Reformers were largely unconcerned that most people are not very rational and that they might want to approach

God rather directly through their feelings. They insisted that a mature person, though sharing the need for some esthetic and emotional expression in life, would accept only moral imperatives as having ultimate authority.

A SENSE OF ETHNICITY

As long as that remained the basic Reform Jewish sense of commandment—of Torah for modern Jews—Reform Jewish obligation would not have changed very much. And for some Reform Jews it still follows that outline. Yet even a slight familiarity with contemporary Reform Judaism indicates that the tone as well as the content of its practice has undergone substantial alteration. Many social explanations have been given for this, and while the *Centenary Perspective* indicates the general historic context in which this change in observance has taken place, nowhere does it mention that in recent decades there was a major shift in the ethnic base of Reform Judaism. What was in the 1920s still largely a German Jewish movement became, after World War II, largely populated by the children of East European immigrant families, thus reflecting the makeup of American Jewry as a whole. This demographic shift from within substantially affected what was desirable in the Reform synagogue and family, while from without American society began to appreciate the virtues of group difference. While the idea can easily be overstated, much of the recent

Reform turn to ethnicity can be linked to a difference in style between German and East European Jews. Generally speaking, the groups brought a somewhat different Jewish experience to this continent. Germany was relatively more modernized than was the Russian-Polish heartland from which the later immigrants came. German Jews were relatively more integrated into their society than were their East European peers. Even when the latter came from modern cities rather than the backward shtetls of Sholom Aleichem fame, they were accustomed to a more separatistic, ethnic way of living than were the Germans. Their Judaism had a far richer folk character than did that of the German Jews, so much so that we often forgot that the German Jews had their own distinctive Jewish ethnic style. By the time the East European Jews flooded into this country and began their adjustment to America early in the century, the German Jews, who had been here for some decades, were already well adapted to America, having modified their German-Jewish style in terms of the relatively pale Americanism fostered by the melting-pot theory enthusiasts. I have been able to trace German-Jewish Reform calls for a richer form of religious practice as far back as the late 1920s. This inner development accelerated as the traumas of the mid-twentieth century were felt and the population of the movement itself became largely East European.

A NEW SENSE OF AUTHORITY

Against this social background a new sense of
authority developed in Reform Judaism. On the
simplest level it stemmed from a greater commitment to Jewish peoplehood. The older, Kantian,
ethical teaching was essentially individualistic.
Humanity plays a role in it, but that is because
reason is not just one person's way of thinking
but everyone's way of thinking. But ethnic
groups have no direct place in such a scheme. A
people does not have a collective mind and a
conscience—though some thinkers, trying to link
rationalism to nationalism, have tried to endow
groups with the attributes of personality. Some
early Reform Jews sometimes utilized such folk
psychology to explain Jewish distinctiveness,
but with personal autonomy so dear to them,
they could not find a way to say we had duties to
our people which were as important as those to
our rational selves. The most they could say for
our peoplehood was that it was important as the
means of carrying the idea of ethical monotheism through history.

With events making many of the theses of
Zionism incontrovertible, and in response to
thinkers like Mordecai Kaplan who have argued
that the Jews are as much an ethnic as a religious
group, Reform Jews have come to see that the
old rationalism talked about us in terms that
were too isolated and individualistic. On a practical level the world forces Jewishness on us. Or,

more positively, we often feel within us a stirring of Jewish pride and identification, a knowledge that in our inmost being we are part of the people of Israel. More specifically, what Jews do—or what is done to Jews in the State of Israel, the Soviet Union, or Argentina affects our lives. We not only have a sense of obligation to them but of mutual aspiration with them, though if we met face to face we might not be able to speak to one another. There is also a historical dimension to our being. Much of what we believe, and therefore of what we are, is as Jewish as it is modern. It did not begin with us and, in its significance, ought not to end with us. We are, more than we are likely to acknowledge in this individualistic world, largely the product of the Jewish past and of the Jewish community. If our values have any sweep to them and go beyond us and our families, then their future working out depends upon the Jewish people and transcends what we or our children alone can do.

If our membership in the Jewish people is so much a part of our being, then it legitimately may make claims on us. Our basic Reform principle of personal autonomy now has another premise with which to share power in our lives: Jewish responsibility. Let us take some obvious examples. We owe fellow Jews charity and political support though that may not be personally appealing. When we are moved to celebration and rejoicing, say of a birth or a wedding, it seems reasonable to do so in the presence of our community and in our people's way. Though Wednesday may be the day we do not have to work, our community observes Friday night to Saturday night as Shabbat, and what we personally do or do not do on Wednesday simply cannot substitute for the Jew's special day. How strong the claims of what other Jews do and think will be upon us depends on how much being part of the Jewish people means to us. The balance between autonomy and ethnicity cannot be given one proper, correct formulation. Indeed, I think that in many Jewish lives it is a dynamic thing with now this side and now the other demanding priority. In any case, compared to the individualism of a previous generation, most Reform Jews today have a far greater communal and historic sense of authority.

GOD-CONCEPTS

God, too, occupies a greater role in the religious consciousness of many Reform Jews today than for many of our forebears. For them God often was obscured by the overwhelming experience of the ethical. The presence of God was replaced by the immediacy of conscience. They were most comfortable speaking of God as an idea or a concept. For some, God was little more than a word used to give religious legitimacy to an ethical philosophy of life. For others, God was the intellectual term used to integrate the diverse realms of human activity, most significantly science, ethics, and esthetics. At best God was some sort of spiritual reality of which people could be conscious, and thus some measure of religious experience was basic to any properly rounded human life. Yet even at the fullest, God commanded only the ethical and thus God's commanding presence was quickly assimilated to human conscience. So our founders "stressed that the Jew's ethical responsibilities . . . are enjoined by God" but little more than that.

In varying ways some Reform Jews apprehend God more directly today and thus with greater effect on their lives. As we have learned to trust reason less, we have become more available to the direct experience of the holy. As what conscience once mandated categorically now comes to us trailing questions, we have recognized the need to sensitize our intuition to what, in an often irrational world, may be a proper standard of right and goodness. We have come to think of people as more than their minds and their conscience, but rather as persons who sense more than they can clearly know or say. So too we have become open to the possibility that God must be more than an ethical idea and that God touches our lives in many of its dimensions, not only with regard to our duty to other people. As our sense of the reality of God has grown so has our sense of responsibility to God expanded. Taking God more seriously, we must not trifle with the mandates which arise from so close a relationship. This is, I think, our contemporary, non-Orthodox sense of God "commanding" us. I know a few rare Reform Jews for whom this has led to an acceptance of

God as giver of the Written and Oral Laws and who thus autonomously choose to live by Orthodox law. I suggest that, paradoxically enough, they are Orthodox for Reform reasons.

Most of us sharing this riper sense of God's reality still do not believe that God gives verbal commands or detailed instructions. This is where humanity comes in. We respond to God's reality with a sense that we must reflect it in our lives, but then we alone fill in the details of what we must do. We thus create religion, its institutions, and its practice. For all their human quality, they will be very much more comprehensive and authoritative than they were to previous generations of liberals, for God is directly involved in them. Such a stronger role for God in the Reform religious life yields a sense of duty more intense and more inclusive than that of moral law. If this fuller sense of God is added to a personal identification with the Jewish people, if one now sees the Jewish folk intimately involved with God, if one sees one's personal relation to God as part of the Jewish people's historic Covenant relationship with God, a more richly traditional sense of authority emerges. The highly individualistic sense of duty of early Reform now takes on extensive corporate and sacred dimensions. All this lies behind the *Centenary Perspective*'s statement, "The past century has taught us that the claims made upon us may begin with our ethical obligations but they extend to many other aspects of Jewish living."

OUTWARD SIGNS / INWARD COMMITMENT

This sort of changed social religious consciousness has given rise to a turn in Reform Jewish
practice which outsiders call "a return to Orthodoxy." Judging by externals—some *yarmulkes*
here and a bit of *kashrut* there—it may seem so,
and all such evidence makes some traditionalist
critics of Reform happy and self-justified. Since
what underlies such changes is likely to be a
heightened sense of peoplehood and God, they
should give every Jew some satisfaction. But
they should not be confused with an acceptance
of Orthodoxy or a commitment to traditional
Jewish law, Halachah. The autonomy of the
individual is still being exercised here, and
though it now often chooses to do acts of a more
recognizable ethnic and religious content, such a
principle of authority is clearly in the stream of
Reform, not traditional, Jewish teaching. What
has happened is that the relative isolation of
individual reason in early Reform has now been
breached. Where personal autonomy once found
its fulfillment only in the dictates of reason,
Reform Jews now see the individual Jew fulfilled
as well in membership in the Jewish people and
in a personal relationship with God. Reforming
in keeping with the needs of a changing historical
situation, the movement has come to something
of a fuller traditional Jewish religious balance of
motives to action but without sacrificing its
basic innovative stance.

CHAPTER THREE

Major Categories of Reform Jewish Responsibility

THE PRIMACY OF THE ETHICAL

Nine specific areas of a Reform Jew's religious obligations are specified in the *Centenary Perspective*. These, it says, "begin with our ethical obligations." The continuing emphasis on the ethical should elicit no special surprise. For all the evolution which has gone on in Reform Jewish practice, the primacy of the ethical remains. This is true at least for a historical reason, that it has been the pattern among Reform Jews for some time now and will thus naturally be the first thing they think of when it comes to religious duties. Many, however, will insist that for all the extension of our sense of Jewish religious obligation, none of its consequences remains so well founded as is our responsibility to be ethical. People may be more than rational beings, but they surely cannot be unethical and still remain human. As long as Reform Judaism remains committed to individual autonomy, it will insist that we all have a profound personal sense of right and wrong and should act on it. For all that we are now also personally involved with God and people, the

duty which derives from them is hardly likely to
be as clear and manifest as is that which is felt
from the religiously sensitized conscience. Thus
the commitment to ethics remains basic to contemporary Reform Judaism, an additional indication that the *Centenary Perspective* continues
classic Reform Jewish teaching though it sets it
within something of a new context and thus
revives its old priorities.

Over this century, however, it has become
abundantly clear that Reform Judaism is far
from being a movement for ethical culture.
Thus, though "The claims made upon us may
begin with our ethical obligations . . . they extend to many other aspects of Jewish
living . . . ." Before going on to list eight realms
of such duty, the *Centenary Perspective*
modestly says, "including." No intimation is
given that these eight are the only ones or officially regarded as the most important ones.
While they seem central and quickly come to
mind, the wording does not exclude those who
feel that some other aspect of Jewish living is
critical.

CREATING A JEWISH HOME

The area of duty first specified is "creating a
Jewish home centered on family devotion."
That was not listed first, nor given in those
terms, in the working draft circulated to the
rabbis. In response a number of them wanted us

to bear in mind that they considered the contemporary challenges to the Jewish standards of married life and the Jewish ideal of the home the greatest single threat facing Jewish life today. That theme, like so many others, is too complex to receive anything like adequate treatment in a document of this small size. The committee, acknowledging the seriousness of the issue, sought to respond to it by expanding the few words of its working draft to what is now stated here, and by moving this topic to the first position in the list. I think it fair to say that for all their willingness to accept social change and to encourage experimentation with new forms, the Reform rabbinate is socially conservative when it comes to home and family. They believe that modern Judaism remains based on the family; thus, creating a Jewish family remains a primary Jewish duty. Almost everyone assumed, I am sure, that this meant marriage and children and not merely living together, refusing to propagate in marriage, or insisting on some new social form to substitute for the family. Much else of importance could not be touched. How marriage is to be conducted in a day of woman's equality, consistently with the belief that marriage should contribute to each partner's personal growth, is left for other documents. That Jews more frequently accept divorce as a legitimate option, as the recent experience of rabbis themselves shows, is, I assume, taken for granted in line with the traditional Jewish acceptance of divorce.

How many children to have or how to rear them with good standards while fostering their sense of personal choice is not specified.

Yet, though so much is left unsaid here, I find these few words contain an implicit rejection of the present-day speculation that we should radically alter what previous generations evolved as a proper structure for the relations of a man and a woman and the rearing of another generation. I cannot help but see the experience of the people as a whole as a model for our individual lives. Through our relationship with God over the centuries, we have gained a rich sense of what faithfulness can mean to partners and, from the centuries we have been involved with the Divine, we have learned how not just the present but endurance through time enriches and strengthens the reality of a relationship. Constancy and continuity are critical to us as Jews; marriage and the family will be a major, though not the only, means of carrying on Judaism.

STUDYING THE JEWISH HERITAGE

"Life-long study" is listed next. For Reform Jews as for all Jews, education is in theory, but unfortunately not in practice, primarily an adult responsibility. One educates children so that they can participate in the community and be prepared for proper study of Judaism. Our religion is focused on adults, and it takes an adult mind and many years of human experience to appreciate it. The more life and experience, the more one is in a position to appreciate and comprehend Judaism. Since ours is a religion of history and one which has recorded much of its accumulated wisdom in books, study remains a major duty to us. And since we live in relation to God in continuity of our predecessors' relationship with God, it is a special means of bringing us in touch with the holy.

PRIVATE AND PUBLIC DEVOTION

The private and public aspects of worship, next, are mentioned jointly, to avoid the implication that one obviates the other. When Reform Jews were highly individualistic, one might have argued that attendance at synagogue worship was not important in a modern Jewish life. As soon as one recognizes that one is part of the Jewish people, praying alone cannot be finally satisfactory. One needs to join one's folk in their corporate, public celebration and affirmation of their Covenant with God. One might become so ethnic about one's Jewishness that one recognizes the need to gather with one's people but ignores the reality of each individual's personal relationship with God. This private prayer expresses and enriches. Since we are single selves as well as devoted Jews, the *Centenary Perspective* calls both types of prayer an integral part of Reform Jewish living.

DAILY RELIGIOUS OBSERVANCE

Daily religious observance, aside from ethics, has not always been associated with Reform Jewish practice. Rabbis have tried to get people to say blessings and carry out ritual practices which would sanctify the everyday, but secularization has made this seem old-fashioned and many people have assumed that Reform Judaism was something one did in the synagogue on the weekend. As ethics may not be restricted to a certain time and place, so one may not similarly circumscribe a relationship with God and the Jewish people. If anything, considering how our secularized life-style has tended to rob us of our humanity, we desperately need to bring some religious practice into our everyday activities to make unassailable our consciousness of our inalienable dignity founded in our being children of God. Surely the current American concern with all sorts of mysticism testifies to this religious need in a time when rationalism no longer seems adequate to the human situation. The *Centenary Perspective* passes no judgment on what sort of regular effort to maintain contact with the Divine is appropriate to all of us, but it does say that this is an aspect of Jewish piety which rightly lays a claim upon us.

OBSERVING THE HOLY DAYS

There has never been much question that

Reform Jews should observe the traditional Jewish calendar with its special days and weekly Sabbath. Yet if our obligations as Jews were primarily ethical, then one could easily substitute other times and activities for our customary Jewish observance. However, when God is basic to your life and, further, you live as part of the Jewish people, then its calendar and customs take on fresh importance. The holy days and festivals mark critical moments in the life of our people and its relation to God. They accent the passage of our years with their reminders of what history is all about. They give us a weekly and seasonal rhythm that commercial and social time does not know. The Jewish calendar does impose special burdens upon us, but as Sunday is no longer the compulsory day of rest, and as we are able to exercise more personal control over our schedules, the religious challenge of the Jewish calendar becomes increasingly real. No Reform Jew can legitimately avoid it.

CELEBRATING THE JEWISH LIFE CYCLE

One should think that moderns, with their feel for the importance of emotion, would not casually pass by birth, coming of age, marriage, death, and the like. Yet for all our understanding that we are celebrative animals, for all our love of a good party or our recognition that it is healthy to share grief with others, we often still ignore the rich wisdom our people has accumulated over centuries. We know that life is too social to be faced in isolation, that its great moments affect us too deeply to be passed without rite and community sharing. Of course, the old Jewish sense that food and wine and people are an intimate part of happy occasions can lead to excesses. But even a modicum of vulgarity is worth risking to affirm that we are not so refined as to be beyond emotion and not so individual that we do not gain by communal sharing. For a Jew, simhahs are enriched and *tzorus* made more bearable when shared with our people. God and peoplehood give the private events of our lives their true cosmic and social context.

SYNAGOGUE AND COMMUNITY LIFE

Through our synagogues and community life we reach out together to God and our people. At one time, the two institutions may have been so closely identified, that the terms were practically synonymous. In modern times ethnicity and religiosity have tended to go separate ways, so we must list them as if they were quite separate entities. That difference is easily exaggerated. Believers come to the synagogue to find their people and join in their common Covenant with God. The community in its apparently secular concern with fund raising and politics still reflects our people's historical involvement with God. If we are related intimately both to God and to our people, our duties include participation in both of these institutions in their various manifestations.

ACTIVITIES TO PROMOTE OUR SURVIVAL

We cannot say in our time with its continual succession of unexpected twists and turns just what activities will "promote the survival of the Jewish people and enhance its existence." Some years ago we could not have dreamed that Soviet Jews would reassert their Jewishness and call for us to help them in their incredibly courageous struggle to emigrate. We are somewhat better equipped to deal with the persecutions of Jews, as in Syria and Iraq recently. But the presently unanticipated possibilities may well turn out to be local, as in the opportunity in recent years to establish chairs of Jewish studies in universities in our locale. We cannot now know what we will shortly be called upon to do or may find ourselves newly capable of doing. But "what we have learned" in our time is that Jewish survival is central to our contemporary Reform Jewish sense of obligation. Therefore the *Centenary Perspective* summarizes and climaxes its outline of Reform Jewish obligation by reiterating this major theme and directing our attention to its broad and open entailments.

CHAPTER FOUR

Autonomy and Its Limits

Having specified in unusual detail what sorts of observance are incumbent upon Reform Jews, the *Centenary Perspective* then reverses its thrust and explicitly reaffirms a classic Reform notion. It calls upon Reform Jews "to exercise their individual autonomy." It goes so far as to specify four separate ways in which autonomy might well be utilized.[2]

CONFRONTING AND PERCEIVING TRADITION

Reform Jews are called upon "to confront" the claims of Jewish tradition. At first, that might

[2]The issue of congregational autonomy is not mentioned here, but is taken for granted. By the simple extension of individual freedom, it has long been conceded that each congregation has the right to make its own decisions as to proper Jewish practice and belief. The Union of American Hebrew Congregations (UAHC) is organized on the basis of this reservation of rights to the individual congregation, though the UAHC is authorized to speak on behalf of the movement as a whole when the biennial convention of congregational delegates so votes.

not seem an endorsement of personal freedom, but contrast this position with that of traditional Judaism, which calls on one to "accept" or "obey" the Torah. *Confront* means more than paying attention, but less than compliance. It implies serious concern, but also the right to stand back from and, if necessary, dissent from what is before one. These days, a *confrontation* is often a meeting centering on a sharp disagreement. The *Centenary Perspective* is not suggesting either that Reform Jews respond to our heritage with negativism or that they always do what it says. Rather, while asserting that the Jewish tradition properly makes claims on us that we ought to face, it seeks to protect the rights of the individual to freely engage our sacred lore. It then acknowledges that these claims are often "differently perceived." There is more involved in this comment than the simple truism that different people will interpret the same text in a variety of ways. The Jewish heritage is incredibly varied. Over the centuries it has been created to meet the broad diversity of human needs in a great variety of social circumstances. Multiply its many facets by our individuality, and a nearly infinite reading of the past seems possible. Some Jews are bound to get excited about putting up their own *Sukkah* or staying up all night to study on *Shavuot,* while other Jews will insist our first priority must go to daily Jewish practices like study or keeping kosher. Thus, the tradition is not seen as having the right to settle what we must do; instead, the predilections of the individual Jew are legitimated here.

CHOOSING AND CREATING TRADITIONS

Specifically, the Jew is encouraged to "choose" from the tradition. Nothing could be more Reform Jewish or non-Orthodox. A traditional Jew stands under the authority of Jewish law. Free will is exercised only in terms of obeying or sinning against the commandments. There is no personal freedom as to what constitutes Torah— though the leading interpreters occasionally differ on some points of law, these are generally small differences in which some choice is permitted. The traditional Jew may not choose which commandments are still important and which may be neglected. In actuality, of course, there are many American Jews who call themselves "traditional" but also insist upon their right to determine Jewish practice for themselves, even against explicit statements of the Torah or the sages. These Jews may be traditional by dint of their synagogue affiliation, but they are Reform in their principle of authority. The notion of personal choice with regard to practice was at the heart of the Reform revolution, and this section on religious practice reasserts it in plain and unmistakable language.

Choosing implies that the alternatives are already before one and one only needs to make a selection. That is too static a notion and does not do proper credit to the dynamic nature of personal life and human history. Things change, sometimes radically, and the past often did not adequately anticipate our problems or our opportunity. Thus, there are simply not sufficient traditional possibilities to satisfy our modern Jewish belief that women should have full equality in Judaism. Or, to give another example, our circumstances of work and leisure, our scattered communities and dependence on the automobile require some new sense of synagogue life, not only on Shabbat but at other times of the week.

We need to create new forms of Jewish life. If our eyes are only directed to the past, a stance not required by tradition but associated with it, we will not meet the challenges and opportunities of the movement. Moreover, creativity is not limited here to great halachic authorities. Everyone is encouraged to exercise it, personally and together with other Jews in synagogue or community. One person may pass the drudgery of the daily jog by reciting psalms. Another may insist that the best bottle of wine served each week be reserved for Shabbat. Neither suggestion is anti-traditional, but one will not easily find either of them in older Jewish literature. And where creativity does require a break with the past, then it is not stigmatized. Rather, Reform Jews encourage creativity, for it makes Judaism meaningful in modern lives and thus helps to guarantee Jewish survival.

PRECONDITIONS

I believe this fourfold amplification of personal autonomy in the realm of practice is a continuation of Reform Judaism's classic view of authority. I think this is why, seeing their position so vigorously stated, the anti-halachists in the Reform movement supported this document.

This is, however, only half the story. Had the *Centenary Perspective* put it in so bald a fashion, without any conditions, it would have made autonomy a religion in itself. "Reform" the adjective would have become a noun. There are some in our movement who hold such a view, but it is rejected by the overwhelming majority of rabbis, including most of those who steadfastly oppose any Reform Jewish halachah/ "halachah." For all their passionate espousal of freedom, they believe that there are certain preconditions for the responsible Reform Jewish exercise of freedom. This the *Centenary Perspective* also articulates, setting the context in which Reform autonomy ought to operate in terms of four standards.[3]

---

[3]The similar number is an accident of composition. The committee made no effort to give the exact same weight to the affirmation of autonomy or to the setting of limits upon the process. If anything, I would judge that the weight of this section as a whole leans toward the conditions of properly utilized autonomy, for it, not the principle itself, is the major problem we face. This final sentence, however, speaks mainly of our autonomy.

The initial three preconditions hardly require comment. The first has already been noted, that the Reform Jew needs to confront the claims of tradition. If one heavily accented the last three words, this might sound terribly oppressive. Yet it merely acknowledges that, for all our Reform creativity, we did not start Judaism, and in living it today we should seriously consider whether the way previous generations lived their faith should not be our way as well. The section on Torah in the *Centenary Perspective* has already said that the early generations of Jews, those of Bible times particularly, but also the rabbis, shaped Judaism in patterns which remain basic to our existence as Jews. Perhaps this is only a repetition of the old Reform Jewish belief that we need to study and to listen to the classic Jewish texts before we utilize our autonomy. Thus, our choosing and creating, the document then says, should be done on the basis of "commitment and knowledge." These preconditions seem self-evident. We are talking about religion, not a pastime, hence decisions need to be made seriously and on the basis of such depth of belief as a person can muster. Convenience and ease are, in this context, minor considerations. Our criterion in every choice is: *As one who shares the Jewish people's relationship with God, what constitutes my proper response to God?* Our faith must guide our freedom. So too, if we derive from the Jewish tradition and propose to choose from it, we ought to know it.

Autonomy exercised in ignorance is foolish freedom, a great human gift exercised in a self-negating way. For Jews to determine what they will do to live Judaism knowing little about it, and that remembered from their pre-adolescent days as now filtered through the emotional screen we call memory, is a disaster. A religion sophisticated enough to insist three thousand years or more ago that God was so great as to be invisible yet more real than anything one can see, has a right to demand that we know it well before we make decisions concerning it. All this, I think, repeats in other words what was said in the section on diversity as to the limits of Reform Jewish freedom.

FINDING ACCEPTABLE JEWISH LIMITATIONS

The fourth precondition, however, to the best of my knowledge, is radically new in Reform Jewish thought and in the movement's discussions of what a Reform Jew must do. Note the problem. We refuse to compromise on personal freedom. It is too dear to our Reform faith. We insist that people ought to be free to choose what they personally think is right for them as Jews, yet we feel that this liberty ought to operate within some Jewish context and result in some way of life that is recognizably Jewish. Two ways of providing acceptable Jewish limits quickly commend themselves. The one is descriptive, that is to point out that, in practice, most Reform Jews have chosen to act in certain ways and that these patterns of behavior are now the accepted norms for our movement. Perhaps if one did not push such patterns as laws, one might be able to get Reform Jews, for the sake of being part of their community, to bend their personal freedom to some measure of general conformity. This is a social process we all know from our families, work, or other social activities.

Something of that sort of general consensus seems to have operated in an earlier, more settled time. For some years there was a Reform Jewish style, which was satisfactory for the German Jewish immigrants who created it in adaptation to a relatively stable American melting-pot environment. But one cannot suggest such a descriptive solution today. If anything, it is because there is so little consensus today as to what might be a satisfactory Reform Jewish style—Jewish life and the American culture are continually changing—that some Reform Jews keep seeking guidance concerning Reform religious practice. Besides much of the ferment in the Reform community has come from a feeling that what many people were doing was not sufficiently related to God and the Jewish people. Hence, the committee could not satisfactorily channel our freedom by giving its sense of what is now going on.

Another, older possibility would be to specify just what it is that directs us in the exercise of our autonomy. For a previous generation of Reform Jews, that was quite clear: our conscience or our reason, understood in a Kantian way. That created a problem for later generations because countless Jews spoke and acted as if ethics were all that really counted in Judaism, with the result that the rest of Jewish obligation atrophied. Most of us today know we need some richer sense of Jewish authority than that, for we feel our lives should more directly reflect our love of the Jewish people and of God. But while a number of theories exist describing such a Jewish use of personal freedom, none is widely accepted. The committee could not then speak to the nature or source of our freedom as a means of setting its Jewish direction.

This dilemma was resolved by Rabbi Jack Stern, Jr. who suggested an approach, which the committee, upon analysis, agreed met our needs. He argued that while we might disagree about the way in which we are commanded to live (authority) or the details of our observance (content), almost all of us would agree that there are certain broad areas of Jewish life in which a Jew ought to be doing something—or, at the extreme, about which a Jew must think seriously before deciding to do nothing. It was an elegant solution to a problem which, when our deliberations began, appeared to be insoluble. As we thought about it we could not believe that there were very many rabbis who would deny that Reform Jews have some significant responsibilities in the realms of prayer, study, family life, Sabbath and holy day observance, and the like. What they did in these areas remained for them to decide. We did not presume to dictate the specifics of their Jewish duty, and their autonomy was given full scope. But being a Jew, we felt, lays certain broad dimensions of responsibility upon one, and the exercise of one's freedom ought to take place within them. This means that Reform Jews who never ask what they ought to be doing about "life-long study" or "daily religious observance" have a poor sense of a Reform Jew's religious obligation. They have their freedom but they are misusing it as Jews. The statement directly says that we believe autonomy has its limits, that with regard to practice it needs to be exercised "Within each area of Jewish observance . . . ."

AFFIRMING FREEDOM AND TRADITION

I take it that this specification of realms of obligation made it possible for the "halachists" in our movement to support the *Centenary Perspective*. No other official Reform Jewish statement has ever laid such claims upon the individual Reform Jew and none has spoken in terms of duty and obligation as is done here. For all its strength, this decision was typical of the way almost all the other problems of the movement were met in this document: by rejecting the extremes and stating a reasonable balance between what are the partially contradictory faiths which the movement affirms Thus the section rejects the notion that Reform Judaism is committed only to freedom or that Reform Judaism can be a religion of required discipline, of halachah. Rather, it insists that we affirm both freedom and tradition, gives a sense of how these may be balanced, and suggests that our freedom is therefore properly utilized within certain domains of Jewish living. I consider it a most ingenious suggestion, and I await with great interest the practical reception of the idea by rabbis and the Reform Jewish laity.

If Reform Jews are now to "choose and create" wisely in the various areas specified, the CCAR needs to provide them with appropriate guidance. This section of the *Centenary Perspective* requires fulfillment by the creation of a literature which alone will make its suggestion practical. The CCAR's *Shabbat Manual* is a good start in this direction, and the areas specified in this section of the *Centenary Perspective* practically lay out a publication program.

All this, let it be noted, though it is specific Jewish religious practice, is connected with the goal of Jewish living, our messianic aim of achieving "universal justice and peace." The particular acts of Jewish living are again understood in terms of the embracing Jewish hope for humanity.

PART III

The State of Israel and the Diaspora

We are privileged to live in an extraordinary time, one in which a third Jewish commonwealth has been established in our people's ancient homeland.

V. Our Obligations: The State of Israel and the Diaspora

We are bound to that land and to the newly reborn State of Israel by innumerable religious and ethnic ties. We have been enriched by its culture and ennobled by its indomitable spirit. We see it providing unique opportunities for Jewish self-expression. We have both a stake and a responsibility in building the State of Israel, assuring its security and defining its Jewish character. We encourage *aliyah* for those who wish to find maximum personal fulfillment in the cause of Zion. We demand that Reform Judaism be unconditionally legitimized in the State of Israel.

At the same time that we consider the State of Israel vital to the welfare of Judaism everywhere, we reaffirm the mandate of our tradition to create strong Jewish communities wherever we live. A genuine Jewish life is possible in any land, each community developing its own particular character and determining its Jewish responsibilities. The foundation of Jewish community life is the synagogue. It leads us beyond itself to cooperate with other Jews, to share their concerns, and to assume leadership in communal

57

affairs. We are therefore committed to the full democratization of the Jewish community and to its hallowing in terms of Jewish values.

The State of Israel and the Diaspora, in fruitful dialogue, can show how a people transcends nationalism even as it affirms it, thereby setting an example for humanity which remains largely concerned with dangerously parochial goals.

From the Centenary Perspective

CHAPTER FIVE

What the State of Israel Means to Us

One would expect that a group that believed in God would, as the previous section indicates, have a concern for acts of piety, prayer, ritual, ethics, and the like. But in this second section on "our obligations," the folk side of being a Jew comes decisively to the fore. Here, by contrast to anything a "religion" would be interested in, a political entity, the State of Israel, and its geographic base, the land of Israel, are the focus of our duty. Since section II of the principles, "The people, Israel," has made it plain that we consider ourselves a people and not a church, our special, that is, un-Christian, involvement with politics and geography is appropriate for us as it would be for any ethnic group. Yet because our people has a religious as well as an ethnic character, our involvement with the land and State of Israel takes on uncommon form, as we shall see below.

THE PRIVILEGES OF AN EXTRAORDINARY TIME

Having already indicated that one thing Reform Judaism learned in recent years was the virtue of

establishing a Jewish state, the document now
moves on to describe our obligations to it.
Because the State of Israel exists, this is an
"extraordinary time" in Jewish history and we
who see it before us are "privileged." If anything, these are understatements. Time alone
would make the reestablishment of the State of
Israel exceptional. Eighteen hundred seventy-
eight years passed between the end of Jewish
self-rule in 70 C.E. and the founding of the third
Jewish commonwealth in 1948. (The *Centenary
Perspective*, following common usage, ignores
the three years of Bar Kochbah's revolutionary
restoration of independence, 133-135.) In
assessing the accomplishment of recreating a
Jewish state, one needs to keep in mind the dark,
resigned mood of the pre-emancipation centuries. They were among the most difficult in
Jewish history. The ghetto meant more than
physical segregation. It symbolized the many
social degradations visited upon the Jews. The
offer of freedom came to a people unaccus-
tomed to self-assertion and broad horizons. Yet
the new opportunity was met with an outpour-
ing of Jewish energy, adaptiveness, and accomplishment. As a simple human phenomenon,
that would have been a cause for wonder. Yet,
before too long, some Jews refused to concede
that adjusting to other people's society was
freedom. For the Zionists the new equality had
to be social as well as individual; the Jews like all
other peoples had to have their own home on

their own land. Their early efforts produced scanty results.

When the Jewish people saw a third of its members murdered by Hitler, that should have put an end to Jewish hope and endeavor. It didn't. Rather, out of the worst of times came the will and the courage of the Jewish people, almost as a whole, to establish and maintain the State of Israel. To many Jews today this was, and is, a wonder, an event which speaks to us of transcendent reality. Living in the presence of the State of Israel, we gain intimations of what humanity might yet accomplish and what great things God sometimes aids us to do. Both can deeply affect the soul of believing Jews.

THE LAND AND THE STATE

The opening lines of this section take care to distinguish between the land of Israel and the State of Israel. In theory, an attachment to the "homeland" does not mean one insists on having one's own government there. One might be content with some sort of political arrangement which allowed one's folk to be ethnically autonomous and substantially self-governing yet not a full nation-state. Something of that sort seems to have been the situation in the sixth and fifth centuries B.C.E. when, after the return of the Babylonian exiles to Judea, they had ethnic self-determination but were politically part of the Persian Empire. One might extend that line of reasoning further by noting that the Bible talks of God's freely granting the Jews a land while the permission to have a king and thus a central government seems rather reluctantly given (at the time of Saul). The land of Israel, and Jerusalem as the center of Jewish religious life, play a large part in post-biblical Judaism. There the notion of a Jewish state appears in connection with the memories of the kings of the Davidic dynasty and the aspirations for its restoration. In rabbinic times, this was a genuine political hope, as Akiba's proclamation of Bar Kochbah as the king-messiah shows. To some extent it was always that, but in later centuries the coming of the messiah was thought of in terms of the end of days, and thus in increasingly nonpolitical, nonhistorical terms. For intellectual precision, then, one ought to keep the Jewish devotion to the land of Israel separate from the Jewish need for a state on that land.

The political and human realities of our time, however, have made this logical distinction relatively unimportant; thus, though Martin Buber, a lifelong Zionist, thought that the Jews should try to form a binational state with the Arabs, most Israelis considered the idea naive and, indeed, few Arabs could be found who supported the notion. More recent experience with the civil war in Lebanon, the one bireligious nation in the Middle East, has cast doubt on all the proposals for joint sovereignty in so disputed an area. In a world where ethnic rivalries are great, apparently reaching intense hatred in the Middle East, having a state of one's own seems the only way to assure having a society and culture of one's own, perhaps even to survive. The Jewish experience with having other people grant them rights, most traumatically the right to enter a country in the 1930s, has been calamitous. So Jews came to feel there must be one place where Jews control the immigration of Jews—every Jew has the right to enter the State of Israel—as well as the social controls which make it possible to create a Jewish culture. Statehood is today the indispensable medium of Jewish ethnic survival and development in the land of Israel. Hence, the worldwide involvement of the Jewish people with its land inevitably means that it is directly concerned about the political entity which makes Jewish life there possible; namely, the State of Israel.

THE LAND AND THE COVENANT

The ties we have to the land/state must not be seen in only this ethnic context. The Jewish relationship to divinity, as pointed out in section I of the *Centenary Perspective*, "God," is not merely that of individual persons and their God. Rather, the single Jew is part of a people and its rich historic relationship with God. Jews thus have corporate as well as individual religious responsibilities to fulfill. The people as a whole must live up to the divine demands; creating a righteous society is central to Jewish religious obligation as the Bible understands it. The best way of doing that is as a self-determining group living on its own land. The Bible considers the gift of the land essential to God's Covenant with the Jewish people and the working out of the divine purposes. On their own land they will be able to create the sanctified sort of corporate existence God asks of the covenanted people. There is, then, a special religious reason for Zionism: fully to live out the social responsibilities of a Jew. When the *Centenary Perspective* says, "We see it providing unique opportunities for Jewish self-expression," it has this corporate dimension in mind. The word "unique" is not too strong a term to use in this connection. Jews may live by the Jewish calendar in other parts of the world, but they do so only by conscious, often sacrificial effort, necessarily wrenching themselves out of the calendar of the society in which they live. The same may be said about learning Hebrew, being familiar with Jewish history and literature, praying with a minyan, and much more. There is only one place where one lives naturally as a Jew, where one's environment cooperates with one's Jewishness, where there is no difference between one's civic and one's Jewish duties. Even casual visitors to the State of Israel feel the unique Jewish quality of life there. No Jewish neighborhood, no self-created ghetto, no isolation of one's Jewishness within one's observant institution can compare to it.

ISRAEL AS A CULTURAL CENTER

To hold up to world Jewry such a model of free Jewishness would already be a major accomplishment of the State of Israel and a substantial reason for Jews to care about it. Yet the Israelis have done far more for us. Though in existence only thirty years, they have enriched our sense of Jewish culture and strengthened our Jewish morale. We have, for example, created few, if any, American Jewish folk songs, and no American Jewish folk dances. We rely on the Israelis for both. We increasingly read their authors, buy their printings of classic Hebrew texts, and attend to the findings of their scholars of Judaica. As we know more Hebrew and their culture develops its native voice, we shall benefit even more profoundly from their creativity.

So much we had expected of a Jewish state. What was largely unanticipated has been the inspiration we have received from the nobility the Israelis have shown in meeting the brutish realities in which they have found themselves. They have taken an arid soil and made it produce agricultural surpluses. They ignored their poverty and personal needs to take in Jewish refugees from around the world. They have cared for the social welfare of their citizenry while trying, with few natural resources, to develop their economy. They have treated their minorities with concern and understanding. They have refused to be intimidated by terrorists and have been restrained in retaliation. They have waged war with intelligence, even brilliance, and have largely avoided the loss of morality so often associated with warfare. They have stood before a hostile world with high dignity. They have remained a democracy. With all their faults and failures, they remain recognizably the people of the Bible, serving transcendent ends in a perilous historical situation. They have made world Jewry proud of them and happy to be Jews; our feeling for the State of Israel is as simple and grand as that.

OUR INVOLVEMENT WITH THE STATE OF ISRAEL

All this has made us Diaspora Jews believe that our lives are intertwined with the State of Israel and profoundly associated with its destiny. What happens to the Israelis affects us as Jews. Hence the *Centenary Perspective* terms our involvement with the State of Israel "a stake and a responsibility." The former term is passive, indicating that we have much invested in them and so we view events in the State of Israel, vicariously, as part of our lives as Jews. The latter term, "responsibility," is active and seems peculiar since it is clear that we are not citizens of the State of Israel and have no political duties toward it. Yet, being Jews, we have responsibilities to our people, and especially to this central expression of Jewish existence. The paragraph before us specifies three of these:

"building the State of Israel, assuring its security and defining its Jewish character." The first would cause little difficulty to any American ethnic group. The Irish and the Italians have for years been involved in trying to do things to help their mother countries. Among Jews, even non-Zionists have often felt they wanted to build up the one country which welcomes Jews no other country would have. "Assuring its security" necessarily involves taking political action on behalf of the Israelis—but here, too, there has been consensus among most American Jews. Some people do not understand why, though we are essentially a "religion," we lobby for arms for the State of Israel or are aroused when American support for it seems to waver. Though we are a religion, we are also an ethnic group and we know that the defense of the Jewish people is our responsibility before anyone else's. Hence, when the security of the State of Israel is involved, American Jews, for all their fractiousness, have shown themselves remarkably united.

The statement, however, goes beyond economic and political assistance to sound a quite uncommon note when it speaks of our role in "defining its Jewish character." This sounds almost as if Jews living elsewhere should tell those living in the country what to do with it—a peculiar, even unethical notion. Here again the odd nature of Judaism sets an uncommon mission for us. The State of Israel, in its founding document, describes itself as a "Jewish state."

No one is quite certain what that means, yet without some such assertion the whole of Zionism is meaningless and the relation of the State of Israel to the Jewish people and the Jewish heritage is thrown in doubt. Yet if the State of Israel aspires to be a "Jewish state," then not only Israeli citizens but Jews everywhere have a stake in "defining its Jewish character." To be sure, noncitizens will do so by discussion, suggestion, criticism, and the fostering of special projects—not by any sort of political interference—all in terms of what they believe Jews should be and do, which thus sets the standards for a "Jewish state." Israeli citizens will themselves have to make the decisions and bear the consequences. But though those who take the risks have a unique and primary responsibility for determining the destiny of the Jewish state, the attitudes of other Jews must play some role in their thinking. As long as the state claims to represent a worldwide tradition, Diaspora Jewry must be involved in determining its Jewish character. And while this is an obligation and opportunity for all Jews, the *Centenary Perspective* makes it clear that Reform Jews see themselves along with all other Jews as having this duty.

ALIYAH

A sentence on *aliyah*, immigration to the State of Israel, then follows.

Other than the word Torah, which, one might

say, is practically part of our English vocabulary, this is the only Hebrew term used in the document. The committee early decided to forego the use of Hebrew words because it felt that the problems associated with them generally outweighed the gains their rich associations might add to the text. One problem with the Hebrew words is that they very often are not understood in the way that they are meant. In a document which sought to be as clear and unforbidding as possible, this was a serious drawback. Another problem is that many of the Hebrew words used in contemporary Jewish rhetoric have been politicized. Terms like halachah (law) or *talmud torah* (study) have highly charged emotional overtones to those who employ them and are taken to say a good deal more than their simple translation indicates. In my experience, this is often due to people's wanting the authority of tradition behind an activity but being unable to give a modern equivalent for it. They unconsciously think that by using the classic Hebrew term for a practice, they will be able to carry over something of its old sense of being commanded. This unstated expectation then makes for great difficulty in discussion with those who use the same term but clearly interpret it in an autonomous way. One can imagine the communications static this sort of modern, unspoken demand sets up with those who are sensitive to any attempt to reintroduce traditional categories of authority into Reform

Judaism. Whether my explanation of the problem is correct or not, the committee felt it best
to avoid the use of Hebrew terms, particularly
those which, while dear to some members of
the CCAR, incited others to do battle. The
result was that the working draft had no
Hebrew terms other than the word Torah.

In drafting its statement on the State of
Israel, the committee had felt it most important to be in close touch with the Reform
rabbis now serving and residing there. Much of
the wording of this paragraph resulted from
such Israeli reactions to an early committee
draft. But these colleagues also asked that a
sentence on *aliyah* be added to extend the
open-ended suggestion that the State of Israel
provided "unique opportunities for Jewish self-
expression." When the committee met to consider the various proposals for revising the
document, it gave special attention to this suggestion. None of us voiced any objection to the
principle of including a statement on *aliyah* as
long as it was clear that this was a matter of
free, personal decision. The CCAR had some
time before passed a resolution encouraging
aliyah for those who saw it as an appealing way
of living as a Jew. Yet, for political reasons, the
committee decided unanimously not to include
the *aliyah* sentence in the document it would
present to the CCAR at the San Francisco meeting. The committee had set its goal as writing the
strongest statement that would win the support

of an overwhelming majority of CCAR members. It judged that a sentence on *aliyah* could not win the votes of eighty percent of the membership, and it feared that this issue might become so divisive it could be a basis for rallying support to reject the *Centenary Perspective* as a whole. The committee's assessment of the situation was utterly incorrect. When the *Centenary Perspective* formally came before the CCAR plenum, the decision of the committee not to include a sentence on *aliyah* was called to the body's attention with a request that they indicate whether they desired such a statement. The reaction was strong, positive, and almost unanimous. They wanted *aliyah* mentioned, and the *Centenary Perspective* now does so, including the Hebrew word whose connotations the Reform rabbis have no difficulty accepting as long as it is not presented as anything other than another personal option.

What the sentence says is simple enough. Reform Jews encourage immigration to the State of Israel and they do so in terms of the slogan-word which has come to have high emotional overtones in contemporary Zionist rhetoric. The use of the word *aliyah,* despite the qualifications which here are set on it, would have caused a furor some years back. Then Reform Jews, like most American Jews—other than our Zionist officials who needed to establish their credentials with their Israeli counterparts—shied away from open encouragement of *aliyah.* In those days, it somehow seemed a derogation of the United States and Canada as well as an extreme rather than a normal form of support for the State of Israel. I can still recall how embarrassed American Jewish leaders were when David Ben-Gurion visited this country in the 1960s and publicly called for the *aliyah* of 10,000 American Jews a year. Even worse, Ben-Gurion explicitly identified Zionism with a commitment to emigration, thus immediately reading almost all North American "Zionists" out of the movement. Since then our mood has changed, though not to the point of agreeing with Ben-Gurion.

For a few years after the Six Day War of 1967, there was a sharp rise in American migration to the State of Israel. Since then, the numbers have fallen, apparently back to the pre-1967 low levels. Economic factors and the assessment of the relative quality of life in America and the State of Israel are largely significant in this regard. In any case, Reform Jews now feel sufficiently secure in their relations to their countries and the State of Israel to be able to call for *aliyah.*

Two conditions are given, however, and these may explain the relatively unanimous support registered for the statement. *Aliyah* is encouraged "for those who wish" it. It is an option, not a duty the rabbis think every Jew has. Among the things a Reform Jew might do in creating an appropriate Jewish existence is to immigrate to the State of Israel. Moreover, it is commended to those who are seeking "maximum personal fulfillment in the cause of Zion." The latter phrase, "cause of Zion," was suggested by our Israeli colleagues. I found this wording quite appealing. It seemed to me a good way of avoiding the difficulty of commending *aliyah* only to those who considered themselves Zionists. It also made provision for those who cannot identify themselves with that organizational label but love the land of Israel and might seek personal fulfillment in its Jewish society. Besides, "Zion" has appealing messianic overtones and to call people to immigrate for so great a reason seemed to me appropriately Jewish. Immigration is recommended for those who want "maximum personal fulfillment in the cause of Zion." While partial satisfaction can surely be gained from various Diaspora activities on behalf of the State of Israel, the fullest gains can only come from going to live as an Israeli.

DEMANDS UPON THE STATE

For all this admiration of the State of Israel, the paragraph closes with a jarring shift of tone and with uncharacteristically harsh language, "We demand that Reform Judaism be unconditionally legitimized in the State of Israel." The problem of Reform Judaism there can easily be exaggerated. Reform Jews are not prevented from organizing congregations, conducting services, teaching their view of Judaism, or living their own style of religious life. The major problems of Reform legitimization are that Reform rabbis in the State of Israel do not have the right to perform marriages, and that Reform conversions carried out anywhere are not considered valid. This official discrimination is symbolic of a host of unofficial problems. With Orthodoxy—largely of a modernized, though European sort—the established Jewish religion in the State of Israel, many forms of quiet community discrimination against Reform Judaism exist. To picture these difficulties as a major Israeli denial of freedom of religion seems to me a distortion of reality. This does not make them any the less objectively repugnant and, in view of the service, energy, and money Reform Jews have given to the State of Israel over decades, utterly unreasonable.

The committee, cognizant of the pain our problem caused, but recognizing that many of our American and Israeli colleagues did not wish to embarrass the State of Israel in any way, originally formulated its statement on this matter somewhat delicately. It said only, "We hope . . . ." This formulation turned out to be too timid for a good number of colleagues, and to our surprise, I would guess, this was also the position of our rabbis in the State of Israel. Though anxious to present our movement's positive concern for the State of Israel in the strongest possible terms, they urged us to adopt a much stronger stance and suggested the verb

which now opens the sentence, "We demand . . . ." The committee concurred, but this
wording caused some concern when the document was discussed at the CCAR conference.
One member pointed out that this imperative
tone was never used elsewhere in the *Centenary
Perspective* and urged us to utilize more mod-
erate language. But when it was explained that
the softer language of the working draft had
evoked some strong objections and that it was
our Israeli colleagues who asked for the harsher
language, the rabbis assembled seemed to accept
the present wording, and no motion was made to
amend it.

Twice, then, the committee had misgauged
the mood of the CCAR. In both cases, it took a
weak stand where the CCAR wished to be
strong. The rabbis wanted an affirmation of
aliyah for those who chose it, and they wanted
sharp language used with the Israelis on the issue
of Reform Jewish rights. One might see this as an
inconsistency on the part of the CCAR—supporting the State of Israel strongly on the one
hand and, by implication, criticizing it on the
other. I see it, rather, as typical of the balance of
commitments which runs through the *Centenary
Perspective*. Because we care so much about the
State of Israel, we insist upon being granted full
rights there. We will encourage our people to go
live there, but will not ask them to keep quiet
about the rights which are being denied their
movement. In this case, speaking for the over-

whelming majority and balancing beliefs one against the other did not result in blandness of content, but in two vigorous assertions of Reform Jewish concern.

CHAPTER SIX

Are We Too Zionistic?

ZIONISM AND THE
CENTENARY PERSPECTIVE

The *Centenary Perspective* sums up its treatment of the State of Israel by saying it "is vital to the welfare of Judaism everywhere." That is strong language—enough, I think, for some people to consider our document fully Zionistic. With the folk aspect of Jewishness so much in evidence, with the State of Israel mentioned in the opening and closing paragraphs and here dominating the second section on Jewish obligation, it almost seems as if Reform Judaism has rejected its religious orientation and become another Jewish nationalist movement. Such a distorted reading of this document could only come from a fanatic refusal to see what is in front of one and a need to see only that which one wants to see. True, the *Centenary Perspective* is pervaded by a sense of Jewish peoplehood and focuses specifically in several places on the State of Israel. More, it relates to the Jewish state in highly positive terms, going so far as to urge *aliyah* upon Reform Jews who wish it, and talks of Jewish community life elsewhere within the context of the existence of the State of Israel. If that is secular nationalism, then the *Centenary Perspective* would mark the end of the Reform movement rather than its continuance and evolution. Or, less dramatically, if Reform Judaism had to be in 1976 what it was in 1926 or 1876, then this Zionized document is the epitaph of Jewish liberalism. But just as the Reform of 1876 claimed a right to move on from the beliefs and practices of a previous time, so our Reform Judaism must speak to our situation: Can we claim to be concerned Jews and ignore the deep appreciation of the Jews as a people and the rich affection for the State of Israel which are so widely felt among us? Had the *Centenary Perspective* made these two realities marginal to its interpretation of Judaism, could we have at all considered it relevant? The critical question we must ask is not whether matters which Reform Jews once felt were marginal or even unacceptable have here been made central, but whether these affirmations are made "in the spirit of Reform Jewish beliefs." Has the document's emphasis upon folkhood and the Jewish state altered the assumption that Reform Judaism is primarily a religion, one intended to be lived by Jews in the Diaspora?

THE CONTEXT OF THE DOCUMENT

We can best answer such questions by putting the affirmations concerning the State of Israel in their context. In this respect the *Centenary*

Perspective is quite logical. The statement on God precedes that on the people of Israel; the document discusses our peoplehood in terms of our relationship to God. The paragraph on religious obligations comes before that on the State of Israel; thus our general duties to God as part of the people of Israel set the framework within which we talk about our obligations to and concerns for the State of Israel. Most important, the discussion of the State of Israel is included within a section which discusses Jewish life worldwide, in the Diaspora. For all the forthright acceptance of the place of the State of Israel in our lives, strong limits are unequivocally placed upon it by the paragraph which follows in this section.

ISRAEL AND DIASPORA

Here too the tension of the affirmations—in this instance, the Diaspora against the State of Israel—yields a strong and compelling sense of obligation, not a neutrality whose moral weakness is gained by playing off one concern against the other so that neither can make demands upon us.

Let us begin by noting that while the State of Israel is termed "vital" to the welfare of Judaism everywhere, some colleagues would have liked us to call it "indispensable" or "necessary" to our Jewish well-being. The *Centenary Perspective* tries to describe fairly the great importance the State of Israel has to world Jewry. It is called "vital" for it is life-giving and soul-sustaining. It succors and supports us. To the overwhelming majority of Reform rabbis that seems fact, not theological assertion. Yet this same group will not go so far as to declare that there can be no Judaism without the State of Israel. They do not believe, as some do today, that were the State of Israel to come to an end, it would mean the death of the Jewish people and Judaism. For all that they consider the State of Israel admirable, even awe-inspiring, they would not say that the Jews are so identified with it, that its existence is so central to their being, that they can no longer live without it. The careless or fanatic reader who notes how much is said by the word "vital" will likely miss how much more might have been said that has consciously been avoided. Even in its praise, then, the *Centenary Perspective* carefully implies that though the State of Israel is a great Jewish good, it is not the greatest Jewish good. This is one of several explicit differences made here between Reform Judaism and classic Zionism. (If some humor may be permitted in a matter which is deadly serious to some, if Reformers are Zionists then they are as Reform in their Zionism as they are in their Judaism.)

The second paragraph of this section goes on to reaffirm "the mandate of our tradition to create strong Jewish communities wherever we live." Diaspora Jewish life and its authenticity are not bemoaned as "exile" or some other such unfortunate circumstance. Jewish life outside the land of Israel exists as the result of a traditional "mandate"—obviously one which derives from our serving God who is everywhere and who, therefore, may be served wherever Jews find themselves. The power of this affirmation of Diaspora life is heightened by its introductory words, "At the same time as we consider the State of Israel vital . . . ." The extraordinary significance of the Jewish state is here balanced by the value seen in Jewish life outside the land. I assume that the statement of equivalence, "At the same time . . . ." is meant to be taken figuratively, for I think most rabbis would prefer not to have to place a precise weight on the worth of one form of Jewish existence as against another. Nonetheless, while I do not see this as a claim that our life in the Diaspora has fully equivalent status to that in the State of Israel, the committee intended to indicate that the Diaspora has full Jewish authenticity.

A GENUINE JEWISH LIFE

There are no ambiguities in the following sentence, whose theoretical affirmation and practical consequence will disturb traditional Zionists. The document boldly asserts that, "A genuine Jewish life is possible in any land . . . ." The word "genuine" jarred some readers of the working draft. They took it to mean "a full Jewish life" is possible anywhere and pointed out that this is untrue for Jews who live under oppression, as do the Jews of Russia or Iraq. The committee pondered this problem and decided that the distinction between "genuine" and "full" was normally quite clear. Theologically, "genuine" is the appropriate word. Jewish law does not require one to do the impossible. Almost everyone knows that under conditions of duress, a Jew may break all Jewish laws except those concerning idolatry, murder, and sexual sin and still be considered a proper Jew. The Torah's expectations operate within the realm of what can be done.

Many a Jewish law begins with the accommodation, "But if . . ." you are on a desert island, or have lost track of the calendar, or have no wine for *kiddush*, or there is no water with which to wash your hands—for these and many other special human circumstances, the Torah makes provision. Under odd circumstances one can still be a genuine Jew. Being in the Diaspora is, however, far from so uncommon a situation for Jews. Of course we cannot carry out the laws of the Sabbatical year or other such agricultural commandments, for these are binding only in the land of Israel. There are a few other such Diaspora Jewish disabilities, but this does not destroy or diminish the authenticity of Jewish life off the land. Living in the State of Israel provides unique opportunities to be a Jew and part of a Jewish community pleasing in God's sight; but it is not the only place one can achieve that status.

Thus, the *Centenary Perspective* rejects the notion that Jewish life as lived in the State of Israel today is the only genuine form of Jewish life we know. It denies the idea that the State of Israel sets the standard by which the authenticity of Jewish life elsewhere may be measured. It dismisses the contention that Israeli Jewish culture is necessarily central to Jewish existence everywhere else in the world. It spurns the claim that Jews living outside the State of Israel are, by that fact, inferior as Jews to Israeli Jews.

FORMULATING UNIQUE JEWISH COMMUNITIES

Some critical consequences of this positive attitude to the Diaspora are unhesitatingly spelled out. The *Centenary Perspective* talks of "each community developing its own particular character and determining its own Jewish responsibilities." Canadian, Chilean, British, or Greek Jews have a right to be true to their cultural environment in developing their expression of Judaism. They do not have to imitate the State of Israel as if all they could hope to be was its cultural satellite. As generations of Jews have done before, they need to respond to their specific social situation out of Jewish faith and learn to build what alone can be their authentic Jewish life-style. More, only they can know and judge what, ultimately, it is important for their community to do. If the State of Israel is as important as the *Centenary Perspective* has made it out to be, much of their energy will be directed toward it. But the critical agenda for their communal life cannot be set in Jerusalem or essentially determined by what is best for the State of Israel. So our simple sentence may be seen as a declaration of Diaspora independence. Taken seriously, any effort by the Israelis to dominate world Jewish life or to use it essentially for their purposes will be vigorously resisted. On this reading, the *Centenary Perspective* may be charged with being a resurrection of Reform anti-Zionism. We deny the classic Zionist notion that there can be no significant Jewish life in the Diaspora. We insist that the Jews are not merely a secular people, but one related to God. We oppose making *aliyah* a Jewish necessity or subordinating legitimate Diaspora needs to the interest of the State of Israel. We believe in independent Diaspora communities making up their own minds about what they consider to be the most significant priorities for their Jewish life. Many Zionists will be troubled by our refusal to accept their cherished ideological concerns, but I do not believe that thinking for ourselves should win us the label anti-Zionist.

CONFRONTING THE PARADOX

Obviously some strange transformation has overtaken this discussion. After reading one paragraph of this section, it seemed as if Zionism had overwhelmed Reform Judaism. After reading a few more sentences, the same group can be called anti-Zionist. Even for a statement characterized by balancing extremes this seems a bit much. Yet the *Centenary Perspective* was written specifically to clarify the dialectic which characterizes our belief today. And we see no inherent contradiction in the position we have enunciated. Reform Jews are no longer, if they ever were, a "church" in the sense that it has no relation to a land and a state. We are also not simple nationalists who think one can only be at home and normal when one is on the ancestral ground. Since our religion has an ethnic social ground, we are intimately involved with the State of Israel. But since our concerns with land and state are religiously based, they are neither the central, nor the dominating, nor the indispensable basis of our Jewish life. Reform Jews, loving God and the Jewish people, live in the tension between a service not limited by geography and an ethnic life which has one special place for its unique unfolding. Those who affirm only one of these premises will find this paradoxical mix of affirmations disturbing and press for an impossible either/or. Reform Jews living in the both/and will know their twofold obligations are certain if not always easy to live with.

CHAPTER SEVEN

Affirming the Diaspora, Are We Anti-Zionist?

THE FOUNDATION OF JEWISH COMMUNAL LIFE

The dual affirmation, religious-peoplehood, is now applied to Diaspora community life beginning with the thesis that "The foundation of Jewish community life is the synagogue." Those who radically insist that the Jews are an ethnic group like all other ethnic groups will disagree. They will say that some Jews will probably want to be religious as people are in any culture but, particularly in modern times, many other Jews will not want to and do not need to be religious. For such secularists or ethnic interpreters of Judaism, the synagogue is, at best, another institution contributing to healthy group interaction, but surely not "the foundation" of our community existence. I doubt that this theoretical matter ever appears in normal community life in as naked a form as I have given it. In America many ethnic Jews give at least lip-service to the synagogue. Yet the facts of Jewish life, how we spend our time and how our communities spend our money, show that many Jews act as if something other

86

than Jewish belief and practice were the basis of our community. Fund-raising, anti-defamation, socializing, and a host of other activities are given priority over the synagogue. The document categorically rejects such a hierarchy of Jewish values whether put into words or merely lived in day-to-day Jewish affairs. Consistently, despite their affirmation of peoplehood, Reform Jews remain convinced that religion is the ground of our ethnic existence or so closely intertwined with it that the two cannot fundamentally be separated. (So section II, The People Israel, on which see *Reform Judaism Today: What We Believe*, Part III.)

A BROAD DEFINITION

The term "the synagogue" should not, however, be read in the narrow sense of a given building or a certain organization. While Jewish life is corporate and naturally takes institutional form, complete with roles and rules and practices, "the synagogue" is a compact way of speaking of all of Jewish religious life. Jewish faith should obviously permeate one's family life, one's business dealings, and one's social activities. The "foundation" of our community is, in truth, the religious living of individual Jews. When individual Jews believe in Judaism enough to want to apply it to their lives, that supplies the ground from which all other Jewish activities spring. Charity, lobbying for Soviet Jews or Israeli interests, supplying the needs of the local poor or powerless, naturally come from Jewish devotion. But since the Emancipation has split religious groups and ethnic groups, Jews must be specially organized for religious as contrasted to communal matters; this is the synagogue as we know it in our time.

The greatest trouble we face in our communities today is the loss of Jewish commitment as the basis of Jewish life. People may be proud to be Jewish but they don't take it very seriously or propose to do very much about it. Most of the weakness of American Jewish life derives from this with the consequence that the synagogue and rabbinate have had to step in to try to remedy the situation. Where in the past, believing Jews wanted a synagogue in which to express their Jewish belief, in our day Jews who aren't certain how Jewish they still are, use the synagogue to try to strengthen their sparse Jewish roots. Jews once made synagogues; today synagogues exist to make Jews. So the major difference between our rabbinate and that of most other times is that we have quietly made our rabbi responsible for getting us to be more Jewish than we are. Thus in our situation the synagogue and its staff have become the custodians of authentic Jewish living and it is from them that our community might hope to gain its foundation.

Too steady a focus on reality can lead us to a distorted sense of our importance. The big givers or community manipulators are by now stock figures of American Jewish satire. So, too, to everyone else, is the ludicrous rabbinic type who identifies Judaism with self—my synagogue and thus my ideas and myself. With so few people caring, it is easy for rabbis to begin to think that the Jewish future hangs on their preaching or their projects. The document gives little aid and comfort to rabbinic self-aggrandizement. Though written by rabbis, it makes no claim that the rabbinate is the foundation of Jewish community life. Practically, no one doubts that though individual rabbis come and go—some after lengthy tenures—synagogues go on much beyond them. Organized Jewish religious life, for all its weakness, is much more enduring than individual rabbinic influence. Yet this much special pleading must be acknowledged: if the synagogue is basic to our communities then rabbis, whose knowledge and exemplification of Jewish tradition entitle them to lead synagogues, will have a central role in our community life.

THE OPERATION OF A JEWISH COMMUNITY

The synagogue is not singled out here in order to restrict the ethnic nature of our community life. Again the theory should be kept in mind: the Jews are not a church but a folk. Our religiosity grounds our social existence, which is ethnic, and thus Jewish life must include the realms of culture, social welfare, and even political concern which seem inappropriate in other "religions." Here Reform Jews are called upon, because of the beliefs enunciated in this statement, to participate in the full range of community activities our heritage suggests and our historical situation mandates. This specifically does not mean cooperating only with other religious Jews or limiting our activities only to those which are identifiably religious. Our faith makes us part of the Jewish people as a whole and, therefore, we reach out to all Jews no matter in what terms they identify themselves as Jews. Wherever we can we should lend help or exert leadership in our people's affairs.

This view of community life is far more pluralistic and democratic than one would have found in the pre-Emancipation Jewish community. Our understanding of how a community can function despite diversity has come from the American experience of many different people working together for the common good. Jewish communities of some time back regularly had quarrels which quickly turned into recriminations and mutual excommunication. Such absolutism in the face of difference seems unreasonable, even immoral to those who know from years of American communal activity what benefits may accrue to us all when we learn to work with people with whom we have something, though not everything, in common. Reform Jews, who emphasize human learning more than divine disclosure, make only small claims of what is certain and are particularly receptive to the appeal for a democratic Jewish community. Some would like to turn this will to cooperate into an excuse for denying differences, thereby requiring us to subordinate all our individual Jewish standards for what seems to be the common community good. As Orthodox Jews were once quietly told to sacrifice being kosher so the community could have well-catered meals, so Reform Jews now sometimes hear that they ought to be more accommodating about having the community live up to high ethical standards. But surely democracy does not imply the surrender of our values, only the cultivation of the skills of finding and acting on areas of common concern.

ASSIGNING A COMMUNITY AGENDA

The committee considered specifying at this point some of the projects our communities should be involved in. Some rabbis were disturbed by the working draft because it failed to mention the need to act in support of Soviet Jewry or to protest the oppression of the Jews of Syria and Iraq; however, the committee felt that once it began listing items on our community agenda, it could not easily limit what was included. Primarily for the sake of brevity, the decision was made to speak of our obligations only in general terms, to wit, "to cooperate with other Jews, to share their concerns, and to assume leadership in communal affairs." This was, in essence, a reiteration of what had been said in section II of the *Centenary Perspective*, on religious practice, that among Reform Jewish duties was "involvement with the synagogue and community; and other activities which promote the survival of the Jewish people and enhance its existence." These rubrics, it was felt, should cover the desired range of community activities. Both assertions exemplify the way in which the *Centenary Perspective* seeks to apply what we have learned about the importance of peoplehood and to set forth its consequences for Reform Jewish obligation.

FUND-RAISING AND JEWISH VALUES

What the committee agreed could not be omitted was some sense of disquiet at the actual practice of our communities and the need of Reform Jews to do something about this. This unease was converted into a positive call for "the full democratization of the Jewish community and to its hallowing in terms of Jewish values." This might seem merely a consequence of saying that the Jews are a people living in a democratic society whose roots are religious, and it is that. But it also needs to be understood as a criticism of what we often see happening in our midst. Our community is not very democratic despite some progress toward greater sharing of information and participation in decision-making.

Insofar as we have a structure for our community, it is generally built around our fund-raising apparatus and this sets our problem. A community organized to raise funds has somewhat different concerns from one set up to reach democratic decisions. The problem is aggravated by arithmetic: in most communities ten percent of the givers give ninety percent of the money. Since the success of our fund-raising depends on this minority, it exercises a substantial influence on community funding for local activities and therefore of much community programming.

Internationally, the situation is more troublesome. Local communities get no detailed accounting of how their funds were disbursed by the Jewish Agency (Israeli affairs) and the Joint Distribution Committee (other overseas aid), the major beneficiaries of the United Jewish Appeal. And the Agency and Joint boards are not subject to local Jewish election and thus scrutiny.

On a simpler level, the accepted standards of much of our community life must trouble a believing Jew. Becoming a Jewish leader means spending one's life with questions of quantity of money or members or attendees. It also normally involves one in personal politics of a petty sort that clash jarringly with the great goals for which Judaism supposedly stands. Much that we do is vulgar, showing little feel for esthetics or sensitivity. One finds people accepting amorality, or even immorality, for the sake of the greater good of the Jewish people. One sees energy, talent, devotion, and accomplishment but little learning, piety, or saintliness. In sum, though our tradition says we are a holy people and we claim that our folk is intimately involved with God, our communities give little testimony to it. To some extent this has always been true, as the Bible testifies. Yet the power of American materialism and the lack of countervailing Jewish commitment make our situation particularly distressing. Again avoiding the negative, the *Centenary Perspective* summons us to the "hallowing (of our community) in terms of Jewish values." For all the restraint in these few words, they should be read as a strong prophetic plea. The perennial Jewish task of sanctifying the social as well as the private dimension of existence is being taken up here in terms of the special challenges of our contemporary situation. For all its emphasis on peoplehood, this statement will not let us forget that we are meant to be a "kingdom of priests and a holy nation."

CHAPTER EIGHT

World Jewry in Dialogue

THE SEARCH FOR DIALOGUE

This section of the *Centenary Perspective* concludes with a plea for proper exchange between the State of Israel and the Diaspora. No effort is made to clarify what constitutes "fruitful dialogue." Despite all that has been written on this topic in the general Jewish press, it necessarily remains elusive. We have some idea of what might set the context for good Israel-Diaspora discussions, and it has already been provided for in the preceding two paragraphs of the document. A dialogue begins by affirming the worth and independence of one's dialogue partner. At the same time one needs to be sufficiently respectful of oneself that one is ready to make one's own contribution to the exchange and thus not let it degenerate into a monologue. These conditions are fulfilled here in affirming the unique meaning of the State of Israel to all Jewry, while simultaneously asserting the autonomy and worth of Diaspora Jewish life.

Yet the reality of recent years has been that, for all the promise of fruitful intercourse between the two communities, little progress has been made in achieving it. Mostly this has been due to the constant emergencies into which the Israelis have been plunged. War and the political pressures which have followed it have regularly made the security of the State of Israel the overriding consideration in our relationship. Rather than speaking freely, Diaspora Jews have largely had to accommodate themselves to Israeli needs.

Related to this has been the problem of finding a common language. Most Israelis identify the Jewish people with the Jewish state. David Ben-Gurion insisted on giving the Jewish state the name Israel rather than the older political term Judea in order to cement this identification. Since Israel is the name of the Jewish people as a whole (as in "Hear, O Israel . . ."), to call this state "Israel" is to purposefully blur the distinctions between world Jewry and the political entity situated at the eastern end of the Mediterranean. Ben-Gurion took the classic Zionist position which identifies the two, thus making the Jews like, say, the Scottish or the Norwegians, people from a certain country—in these cases, Scotland or Norway. Most Israelis today adhere to this notion. They think of being Jewish as essentially a national matter. Their Jewishness, therefore, has mainly to do with living in the State of Israel or intending to do so. Leaving the State of Israel to reside elsewhere or insisting on the possibilities of living a "genuine" Jewish life elsewhere, seems to them, consequently, a contradiction of Jewish identity. By contrast, American Jews, for all their recent affirmation of ethnicity, tend to see a religious factor involved in being Jewish. This makes it possible for them as it was for most Jews in the past two thousand years to conceive of being a "genuine" Jew anywhere. This religious dimension to Jewish identity may then lead Diaspora Jews to raise questions about the nature and quality of Jewish life in the State of Israel. Obviously, with such a major disagreement about the basic terms of the discussion, very little substantive headway can result. Until the Israelis are able to have some domestic tranquility—may the time come speedily!—progress in this direction will be slow if at all forthcoming.

NATIONALISM AND BEYOND

The American rabbis do, however, set forth something of their goal for future interchange. They hope it "will show how a people transcends nationalism even as it affirms it." The affirmation of nationalism is evident, for those who are engaged in discussion are members of one people. What is not so clear is how this demonstrates a transcendence of nationalism. Yet if there is something to being a Jew which allows the Diaspora communities to speak to the motherland with equality, and thus a measure of independence, we have moved beyond simple nationalism. Normally the moth-erland watches over the ethnic interests of its children around the world. They are not equal, as the metaphor of parent and child indi-cates. Ordinary nationalism implies the ethnic superiority and centrality of the ancestral soil; Scotland and Norway give, and the Scottish and Norwegians abroad receive, in an ethnic exchange that is not reversible. Jewish people-hood is spoken of in this statement in a differ-ent key and thus its homeland-Diaspora rela-tions sound another tone. Jewish ethnicity is admittedly most powerfully expressed in the State of Israel, but it is genuinely to be found in the Diaspora, as its functioning for two thousand years away from its soil demon-strates. We hold together as a Jewish people in a way that celebrates the State of Israel yet cannot simply be identified with it. We see Diaspora Jewry having as much right to speak about and on behalf of the people of Israel as does the State of Israel. While, therefore, we look to our homeland, we do not restrict our ethnic horizons to it. When we Diaspora Jews stand in our unique national dialogue with the State of Israel, we transcend common nation-alism even as we affirm our ethnic bonds with the Israelis.

THE UNIVERSAL PERSPECTIVE

Were it possible to make this a reality in world Jewry, the *Centenary Perspective* suggests, it might set a worthwhile example for all humanity. Nationalism has proven to be a live and dangerous phenomenon in our time. In Asia, Africa, and the Middle East, groups have come to new national self-consciousness and demanded the right of political self-determination. This has often led to rebellion and terrorism, the establishment of totalitarian governments and the repression of individual rights—all in the name of creating or preserving national states. The document has in mind this worldwide phenomenon and not merely the chauvinism of assorted American and European politicians when it speaks of a "humanity largely concerned with dangerously parochial goals." And the way the United Nations has regularly been used for selfish rather than global purposes must also be included in this condemnation.

In such a world, a Jewish nationalism which showed how a people can be true to its legitimate national aspirations, and yet see them within a context of being part of humanity as a whole, would have universal significance. Our *Centenary Perspective* does not often speak of what the Jews today can directly do for humanity. Mostly it concentrates on our immediate priority, what the Jews need to do for their survival, allowing the messianic implications of this service to arise from such particularism. Yet here the rabbis point to one aspect of Jewish life which might have an immediate effect on what the world is doing to itself. I see it as somewhat ironic that the very aspect of Jewish life which would seem to be the height of Jewish self-concern, the State of Israel, might at the same time be the medium by which contemporary Jews might most directly do something on a universal level. The dialectic nature of Jewish faith—faith in the universal God and faith in God's relation with this particular people—here powerfully reasserts itself and again produces compelling if paradoxical consequences.

PART IV

The People of Israel and All People

Early Reform Jews, newly admitted to general society and seeing in this the evidence of a growing universalism, regularly spoke of Jewish purpose in terms of Jewry's service to humanity. In recent years we have become freshly conscious of the virtues of pluralism and the values of particularism. The Jewish people in its unique way of life validates its own worth while working toward the fulfillment of its messianic expectations.

**VI.
Our
Obligations:
Survival
and Service**

Until the recent past our obligations to the Jewish people and to all humanity seemed congruent. At times now these two imperatives appear to conflict. We know of no simple way to resolve such tensions. We must, however, confront them without abandoning either of our commitments. A universal concern for humanity unaccompanied by a devotion to our particular people is self-destructive; a passion for our people without involvement in humankind contradicts what the prophets have meant to us. Judaism calls us simultaneously to universal and particular obligations.

From the Centenary Perspective

CHAPTER NINE

What Happened to "The Mission of Israel"?

JEWISH PURPOSE

When the *Centenary Perspective* says that "Early Reform Jews ... regularly spoke of Jewish purpose in terms of Jewry's service to humanity," its reference is to what was commonly called "the mission of Israel." Until recent years Reform Jews talked mainly about what Jewish life did for all humanity. Specifically, it was argued that the Jews had a unique role in human history, to teach the idea that there is but one God and that ethics is the chief means of serving God. The Jews existed for, and Jewish practice was directed toward, the dissemination of this concept: ethical monotheism.

That seems so presumptuous a claim to people today that it may help to elucidate something of the intellectual substance behind it. For most of the past century it has not been clear whence the life of the spirit would draw its strength. The modern mind seemed obsessed with science and the modern soul with materialism; neither then could be the source of man's highest human striving. The great religions of Asia had little concern for the world and history, hence one could charge them with being insufficiently ethical. By contrast to the society-shaping, messianic activism of liberal Judaism, they seemed almost indifferent to the this-worldly fate of humankind. The daughter religions of Judaism, Christianity and Islam, had learned too much from the Bible to be so easily dismissed. Yet Christianity with its doctrine of God as Trinity and Protestantism with its special emphasis on faith as against works, seemed far from the demanding purity of Judaism. Islam, though rigorously monotheistic, was indicted for the paucity of its ethical sense, as evident in its limited number of religious duties. Judaism, enabled by the experience of modernity to read and proclaim its message to all peoples, stood out in stark relief. No other religion or cultural force was so fully committed to ethical monotheism and therefore as useful to humanity.

LIBERALISM AS A JEWISH "PROGRAM"

The devotion Reform Jews brought to this belief derived much of its power from the experience of emancipation. Having lived in ghettoes and now being free of them, Jews knew from their own lives that society could radically change for the better. A segregation of some 1,500 years and a record of having been subjected to some of the worst persecution recorded in history seemed to have come to an end. They saw liberalism, that is, ethics defined as a program for positive political change, as revolutionary. If all people could be brought to understand and act on such a program, the messianic age would inevitably come. Because the Torah predisposed Jews to emphasize action and to live under law, because Jews personally experienced the benefits of moral activism, they felt Judaism uniquely equipped for, and thus divinely endowed with, the destiny of bringing this insight to all humanity. This was their modern version of the Torah's injunction, "Because you were slaves in the land of Egypt therefore ye shall . . ." and the prophet Isaiah's charge, "Behold, I have set you as a light to the nations."

One should not, however, overlook the negative motive to this enthusiasm. It was a defense against a major theme in Jewish defamation. In the struggle against the emancipation of the Jews, the anti-Semites had regularly argued that the Jews have no real interest in humanity but only in the Jewish people. When they were Christian polemicists, they contrasted the new, universal sense (the original meaning of "ecumenical") of religion brought by the Christ with that of the Torah, in which the world is divided into Jews and "the nations," with the latter decidedly inferior. When they were secularists, they pointed to the distinctions in Jewish law between Jew and gentile, as well as the evidences of Jewish clannishness and parochialism. If the Torah was essentially directed toward fellow Jews, and Judaism had no strong doctrine of humanity as a whole, how could Jews be given the rights of other citizens? If they could not be relied upon to work for the common good, why should they be given equal opportunity? Arguments such as these were heard during the early decades of the nineteenth century, when the fight for emancipation in Europe was most intense—and their echoes still resound. The idea of the mission of Israel must then also be seen as a response to these charges. The Jews insisted that, rather than being the enemies of humankind, they were the chief bearers of the vision of a humanity which redeemed itself, for they alone proclaimed the thesis that people had the spiritual and moral capacity to bring the messianic fulfillment.

Perhaps the giddiness which resulted from the breathtaking advancement of Jews, and the anxiety that Jews might lose their rights because they were thought to be interested only in themselves, explain what seems to us their overemphasis on existing to serve others. There is something ennobling about accomplishing something for humanity, but that should not be a substitute for finding worth and dignity in one's own life as well. Reform Jews of previous generations said so much about Israel's mission to humanity, one is left to wonder what they thought of Jewish life in its own terms. When the mission idea is not balanced by a sense of the intrinsic value of Jewish life, it seems more an over-compensation to emancipation and anti-Semitism than a balanced vision of Judaism.

SELF-HATRED: TRUTH AND UNTRUTH

Some critics have found a more unpleasant motive underlying this doctrine, namely, self-hatred. They argue that psychologically healthy people do not explain their worth in terms of other people. One has dignity naturally, simply by being a human being. (In religious language, because one is a child of God.) Of course, we are social beings and will not fully be ourselves unless we are involved in society. (Here, too, biblical teaching is quite evident.) Yet our fundamental value in existing comes not from what we have done for others but from our being a person in our own right. Think for a moment of what it is like to listen to people who always talk about how much they have meant to others and how important to other people their lives have been but who never talk about themselves, their goals, and their satisfactions. To hear them constantly justify their existence in terms of those they have served is to recognize that some pathology is at work. Are they so worthless as not to be worthy of their own concern and striving? Apparently many people have buried in their psyche a streak of dislike for themselves.

Before that was recognized as a personal

problem it was described as a social phenomenon. Minority peoples learn from the majority they have tried to join that their group is inferior. Thus, against their natural inclinations, they unconsciously begin to deprecate themselves for being Chicanos, Indians, or blacks. So, too, Jews secretly learn to hate the fact that they were born Jewish. This can, in rare cases, move them so deeply that they not only dissociate themselves from anything Jewish but begin to act like anti-Semites, for in their psychic depths, that partially is what they are. More normally, we see the phenomenon in Jews who don't want to be identified as Jews or who find open displays of Jewish loyalty distasteful and unbecoming. This syndrome, it is alleged, has produced the idea of Israel's mission, of the Jewish people's existing for someone else's benefit. Perhaps one can find some truth to this charge. I have known some Jews who spoke almost exclusively of service to humanity as a whole and shied away from identifying with any particular Jewish concerns. They might be accused of harboring this virus. Yet most Reform rabbis who were excited by the mission of Israel were also interested in keeping home and synagogue Jewish, in a modern way, to be sure. If in reading their works today one is struck by the preponderance of their concern with being Jews-for-others as against being Jews-for-ourselves, I am convinced we must see this as more a result of their social excitement than any inner loss of Jewish self-respect.

REDEFINING THE "MISSION OF ISRAEL"

Its old bases having eroded, and our experience in recent history having been so negative, the doctrine of the mission of Israel has as good as disappeared from Reform Jewish thinking. The excitement of emancipation has been replaced by a stark realism about the persistence of anti-Semitism and the depth of the human propensity to do evil. We know that the charges of anti-Semites that we are interested only in other Jews will yield neither to reason nor protestations of our universalism. If anything the continuing virility of Jew-hatred despite what we do has prompted us to a healthy assertion of self-interest as our first moral concern. We are not ashamed to be Jews but are proud of our people and its way of life. Considering the values and concerns of other groups, Jewish life needs no special defense. We stand up very well. If the mission of Israel was largely meant to justify Jewish existence, it does not speak to our situation. Perhaps our people still serves a purpose which is more than ethnic. The *Centenary Perspective* continually links Jewish ethnicity to the messianic time and the fulfillment of human history. Giving up the mission of Israel does not mean giving up Jewish universal hopes. It only means that we reject the notion that we should speak of "Jewish purpose [essentially] in terms of Jewry's service to humanity."

We have intellectual and social reasons for speaking of our people in less grandiose terms. As we have come to know other religions better we have come to see that, while great differences remain, there is more overlap of concern between us than our predecessors had thought. Most Jews in free countries do not find their ideas about human life and destiny markedly different from those of their neighbors. They do not see themselves living radically different lives. Rather as immersion in general culture has continued and contact with others at home and abroad has increased, most Jews find themselves to be very much like most other people. True, we have a strong sense of particular Jewish identity and even a feeling that Jews are somehow special. Nonetheless, only some tiny majority among us can still confidently proclaim that our group has a special message for all peoples, a unique idea they have not truly heard of, or a teaching that would solve the basic spiritual problems of humankind if it would only listen. The mission of Israel seems too great a claim for us, too little an appreciation of others, for us to rally behind it.

HORACE KALLEN AND CULTURAL PLURALISM

We have what we consider a much better way

of thinking about the differences of peoples and the unity of humanity. The *Centenary Perspective* says, "We have become freshly conscious of the virtues of pluralism and the values of particularism." This is true of all Americans, Reform Jews among them. We take it for granted these days that all of us need not look alike, dress alike, live alike, or believe alike. People are not only reasonably free to do "their own thing," we even consider it something of an enrichment when ethnic or religious groups bring their customs and celebrations into our civilization. That was certainly not the social climate in which I grew up in Columbus, Ohio in the 1930s. Attending elementary school I was taught by content, rule, expectation and, above all, by the fact that the true authority was unwritten, that immigrants were expected to conform; and Jews, whose millennial stubbornness set certain limits to their adjustment, should make special efforts to make themselves inconspicuous. To the best of my knowledge nobody ever told my parents or me that Columbus, Ohio was a melting pot, but it was clear that the town had little tolerance for deviation from the Protestant, middle-class norms that then passed for true Americanism.

I do not know if anyone in middle America in those days had ever heard of Horace Kallen. He was a philosopher of democracy who, if he did not coin the phrase *cultural pluralism,* is the person who gave the idea its most sophisti-

cated articulation in the period between the
two World Wars. Of course Kallen was a big
city dweller—New York, no less—and was,
therefore, accustomed to the persistence of immigrant enclaves and cultures. We midwest-
erners looked askance at big cities in general
and at New York in antipathetic particularity.
We knew it would take them longer to arrive at
the American ideal; New York would probably
never become America at all. It took the civil
rights movement, the counterculture, the anti-
Vietnam War agitation, the college student
rebellion, the new distrust of our central social
institutions, for an appreciation of ethnic pluralism to arise in America. Today when I visit
Columbus, I am struck by the many things I
see which testify to the acceptance of diversity.
I can still feel something of old pressures not to
deviate too much from accepted norms, but
these now seem to me to be rather broadly
construed where their range used to be rigorously narrow.

In such a pluralistic climate one hardly has
to justify group existence at all, much less do
so in terms of what the group does for humanity. I am certain that Kallen's being a Jew gave
him a special openness to the idea that a democracy might mean a collection of diverse
groups—he liked the symphony simile—though
I doubt that his ideas had much to do with the
change in our social reality. He was a secular
humanist. Democracy being Kallen's religion,

he would have been somewhat surprised that we wanted any other. Nonetheless, he would have gotten great satisfaction from our *Centenary Perspective*'s endorsement of pluralism, especially its interplay between the particular and the universal. Our statement, "The Jewish people in its unique way of life validates its own worth," expresses our feeling for ethnic identity with simple dignity. The following phrase, "While working toward the fulfillment of its messianic expectations," reminds us that our people still hopes that its life and historic career will effect all humanity. That says something like the older idea of the mission of Israel but puts it in a way we find truer to ourselves and our neighbors on this shrinking planet.

CHAPTER TEN

The Joy of Jewish Living

A TERM WITHOUT DEFINITION

Whenever someone begins to talk about "the Jewish way of life" we begin to hope that we may finally be able to get the solution to a number of problems. It would be nice to know just what a Jewish way of life is. Is there one mixture of tradition and innovation which would give us an authentic Jewish existence? Besides since we prefer to avoid challenges about what Jews ought to believe, we would be happy to concentrate on what actions are expected of us. The *Centenary Perspective* is even more enticing, for it speaks of "the unique" Jewish way of life. Since we see our many similarities with those among whom we live, we are particularly anxious to know just what Jews do that others do not do, or what constitutes the peculiar Jewish mix of things that many other people do in their ways.

But though the *Centenary Perspective* asserts that Jews live differently from other people, it never explains what it means or substantiates its assertion. I think that is because delineating what are admittedly often subtle shades of difference is impractical for a document of this sort. Even with greater space, the intellectual problems in trying to identify something as elusive as a distinctive American ethnic way of life are quite great. I shall make some comments below about our American Jewish style, but I wanted first to indicate that the *Centenary Perspective* does not fulfill the expectations it may arouse by its phrase on the "unique" Jewish way of life. Most of the committee was satisfied to have the phrase taken in descriptive fashion as referring to the way Jews live which, though it is like other groups, is different and in that sense "unique." No special claims would be attached to such a statement of uniqueness/difference. Yet even on this minimal level of significance, the committee could say in the spirit of cultural pluralism, that "The Jewish people in its unique way of life validates its own worth . . . ."

I want to go beyond this and say some positive things about our Jewish life-style. As a matter of balance, let me first briefly indicate that I think that for all its high human quality there are many problems in Jewish life. If anything I feel that because Jewish life is so promising, its failures and foolishness are especially troublesome. I think we should foster a high level of healthy self-criticism among us as a practical expression of every caring Jew's effort to be a person of more than common standards. But while I believe in the Jewish virtue of moral complaint, this is the place to say something positive about the special quality of Jewish life.

POSITIVE ASPECTS OF "UNIQUENESS"

When I try to point toward our uniqueness, I find I can get closest to it, though still not very precisely so, by talking about our values and how they skew the way we live in this culture. Where tradition identified a Jew in terms of Torah and commandments, and the early Reformers talked of ethics, where more humanistic contemporaries are content to say we have our ethnic way as each people has its own, I think we are best seen when what we consider most important is clarified. Without trying to be exhaustive or to analyze the sociological data, Jews attach an uncommonly high importance to a number of activities many people would associate with humanity at its best. For example, Jews value very highly marriage and marital fidelity, having children and rearing them to personal and social productivity, education and learning, culture, community betterment, political participation, moral government, the promotion of mental and physical health, concern for the oppressed, and other such matters.

As soon as one articulates such a list, one sets off a series of rebuttals—which is another Jewish value, thinking for oneself and arguing with those who think differently. The first rejoinder is that these items are not uniquely "Jewish" for other people care about them as well. That is both true and irrelevant. If everything that the Jews share with other people can no longer be called Jewish then almost nothing will be left that is "Jewish" except a few ethnic eccentricities. Thus the Ten Commandments—except perhaps number four on the Sabbath, though Sabbatarian Christians practice it—would no longer be considered "Jewish," obviously an absurd idea. The word Jewish cannot reasonably be limited to things believed or done exclusively by Jews. The values described above are, in themselves, general. If they were uniquely Jewish we would have no English terms but the language would have to borrow the original, as it does when it utilizes the words *Torah, savoir faire, weltanschauung, bel canto, mana* or other terms that have become the common property of intellectuals. Thus, one cannot hope to identify "Jewish values" in any exclusivist sense since values are, by definition, universal.

A JEWISH CONFIGURATION

Our difficulty is eased somewhat if we argue that what is unique about the Jews is which values they have chosen and the relative weight they have given them. Yet if one suggests, for example, that the Jews give unusually great prominence to family life and education, the usual retort is that the Italians do the one and the Chinese do the other. The odd statistics of the Jews in one or another area can be matched by other ethnic groups, but when very many values are studied, a distinct Jewish configuration emerges and it has uniquely humane features. This judgment cannot be defended against the charge of subjectivity, for I am a Jew and it is not clear what measures of group existence may objectively be called significant. I think many people would agree that cigarette consumption seems less important than whisky consumption as an index of human quality but this is difficult to argue. I would then want to contend that the unusual statistics of Jewish action reflect our sense of what a member of the Covenant people ought to do. Jewish ethnicity involves a nagging sense that living properly requires a high sense of personal and communal duty. The way Jews live, as their eccentric statistics indicate, has a good deal to do with their carrying over into their secular lives some effective vestige of their old sense that they are commanded.

My argument is not basically affected by the way Jewish life keeps changing. I think by now we have had enough experience in America, with all its dynamism, to see that though patterns shift somewhat over a period of time, a Jewish sense of values continues to manifest itself. The result is that many Jews affirm their

Jewishness not merely as a fact of their ethnic identity, but because of the special quality of Jewish life. When they say it "validates its own worth" they mean not only because every people does so but because what this people affirms and rejects, lives and avoids, and stubbornly transmits from generation to generation, is exceptionally appealing. This people has produced, not in every case or equally, but in astonishing statistical disproportion, unusually worthy individuals; loving families; concerned communities; a noble teaching; a folk that, given the opportunity, rushed to serve humanity and, for its paltry numbers, has had an extraordinary influence on humankind. I do not see how one can avoid making comparisons to other groups, as odious as that practice may seem. When we see what various classes, peoples, nations, even religions have made of their adherents, the Jewish people, for all its faults and failures, is most admirable. Despite our insistence on individual choice, we cannot avoid such social influences on our life. Much of what we are stems from the environmental factors we allow to shape our lives. Perhaps I can say this because I am writing in a time when there is grave doubt about culture and society, at least insofar as its affirming and transmitting a high sense of human value is concerned. Today when the threats to our integrity are all about us and we have great skepticism about our general culture's providing us values, the

Jewish way of living stands out as unusually positive and commendable. Indeed, taking one's personal stance within the Jewish people has now become a way of meeting the awesome challenges our civilization poses to us as individuals.

OUR SENSE OF "BEING COMMANDED"

Yet all of this depends on one's sense of values. Should one not share the sense of true humanity being appealed to here, Jewish life will not seem qualitatively significant. This leads some rigorous thinkers one step further, from arguing about values to asserting their religious basis. One is entitled to ask, particularly in a skeptical age, why just these values and why not some others. At this point contemporary moral philosophy deserts us. Mostly its practitioners then begin to stammer about intuition or metaethical premises. Yet it is just here, because one so often senses the depth of the Jewish response to the struggle to remain human in our time, that I think we brush up against the faith implicit in Jewish lives. Though we know about Freud and Marx, social relativism and conditioning, we believe that what a person and society ought to be are not radically open. There are things we must try to do and others we must bend every effort to avoid. Our values are not accidents; rather, our deepest sense of reality tells us that this is what people are and what we must be and try to become. Our tradition would have said it more simply: this is what God wants of us. Not being Orthodox, we do not identify this simply with Jewish law. But being Jews, we know that to be human is to be responsible for our actions in some cosmically important way. We may find it easiest to talk of living by our values, but when we must explain why our people chooses to emphasize just the ones it does, we must acknowledge that even we live out of a sense of being commanded. What finally makes Jewish life unique for people such as me, is that for all our modernization of the tradition—often even in our disregard for it—we remain involved with God as individuals and as a people. Were we consciously to face up to our relationship to God and live by it, the uniqueness of our way of life would become far more manifest. Yet even in our current state of relative disbelief and faithlessness, I am suggesting that the source from which the special quality of our people's life comes is its lasting attachment to God.

CHAPTER ELEVEN

When the Jews Were the Test of Democracy

THE HUMANIZING ROLE
OF JEWISH EMANCIPATION

Much of the *Centenary Perspective* has been devoted to the interplay of our concern for our people and for humankind. In section VI, "Our Obligations: Survival and Service," attention is focused on the practical working out of these two beliefs in our lives. To see the special difficulties which now confront us, a word must first be said about the happy days when they appeared to be almost completely congruent with one another.

In response to the Emancipation, Jewish thinkers developed the teachings in our tradition which mandated an elevated standard of conduct to non-Jews, to one's nation, and to humanity as a whole. As Jews in the various free countries put these ideas into effect, they accomplished much in actualizing democracy for all the citizens of their lands and in creating a climate which would lead to a rational international order. Thus the struggle for Jewish voting rights or office-holding in Europe was regularly defended in the name of humanity.

122

Jews might be the immediate exemplars of the disenfranchised, but their case involved the rights of all citizens. When Jews fought for their rights they could thus see themselves carrying the banner for the advance of all minority and marginal groups. Since they had almost always been the favorite target of European oppressors, to enfranchise them meant a major step in the humanization of history. Thus, in the early decades of Reform Judaism there seemed a happy confluence of Jewish social responsibilities to one's people and to humanity.

LIBERALISM AND JEWISH RIGHTS IN AMERICA

The same pattern quickly developed in the United States, though here the Jews were free of a long history of discrimination which now needed to be corrected and overcome. Though some states had special disabilities for non-Christians, there was no major constitutional question of gaining rights for the Jews. What happened as American Jewry fought to overcome such barriers as remained was an extension of the European experience. American Jews were not merely concerned about the rights of others while fighting for their own gains. They developed the strategy of fighting for the rights of all groups even when there was no immediate Jewish issue involved. In securing the democratic status of others, they felt that they would make their own more enduring as well. Let us consider the rise of American Jewish liberalism, for it forms the political background of our present problem. During Franklin Roosevelt's presidency the Jews, though still essentially an immigrant community, had relatively few new recruits arriving and were well into the process of acculturation. The overwhelming majority of them saw their ethnic needs closely linked to the liberal, reformist attitudes of the Democratic Party. This was not because of any specific Jewish cause, for Hitler did not become an issue in American politics until shortly before World War II. On a universal social basis, Jews were taken by the then-radical notion that the government should become directly involved in providing jobs, stimulating the economy, caring for the needy, and promoting human equality—as limited as all the Roosevelt steps in these areas seem to us today. All this seemed important for the country as a whole and thus for the Jews who identified with the many other suffering communities. They apparently found in the social welfare programs of the Democrats a fusion of what was good for the Jews and, at the same time, for all people. This trust in the Democrats seemed vindicated in the bold action of this country in declaring war against Hitler, even though we had been attacked only by the Japanese, and in the prosecution of the European War with what seemed like the higher priority.

This conviction, that liberal, socially oriented politics was a mandate of Jewish ethics and the best safeguard of Jewish security, carried on through much of the 1960s and was seen in every major political movement of that turbulent decade. Thus, the number of Jews involved in the struggle for civil rights was disproportionately large. Freedom rides, demonstrations, protest marches, fund-raising that involved whites almost always had more than a three percent Jewish representation, though Jews were not being mistreated. Yet Jews responded to the call for volunteers because they believed it to be their duty and because securing the rights of blacks meant establishing Jewish rights more substantially. The Jews involved in these activities were often unconscious of or actively denied that they acted from any Jewish motive. Yet most studies of the participants in these movements showed that the single most significant factor involved in predisposing whites to be so involved was to have been born into a liberal Jewish family. No other social or economic or psychological factor came even close. The suggestion has been offered, with much to commend it, that the young people involved were repeating in more bourgeois fashion what Jewish idealists of a previous generation had sought to accomplish in socialist or communist endeavors or at least in the "radicalism" of liberal Democratic social reconstruction.

PARTICULAR AND UNIVERSAL IN ACTION

The dynamics of the mutual reinforcement of Jewish particularism and universalism are easily explained. As long as the drive for personal survival was the highest priority of the Jewish people, its first concern was adjustment to the new host culture. Then, every effort at universalization was equally an advance for the Jewish people. Every Jew who became a professor, or concert artist, or government official, or prominent in business—no matter that they were required by the system to hide their Jewishness or were coopted to keep other Jews in their place—was a triumph for the Jewish folk and for humanity at once. Democracy was working and the Jews were its test case. What benefitted the Jews, that long despised minority, was good for all Americans. And, as the Jews no longer occupied that role and the struggles of other minorities, particularly of black people, became critical, the Jews joined their ranks for on the deepest level they knew it to be their own.

In those years it seemed inconceivable that there could ever be any serious conflict between Jewish particularism and universalism. Surely in the United States one was free to practice one's religion even if it differed greatly from that of the majority, and this was the only area where Jews might have substantially different concerns from most other Americans. Thus, when some American Jews worried lest

Zionism be the basis of their being accused of having two, divergent loyalties, most Jews paid no attention to them. American immigrants had always remained attached to their homelands without their American loyalties being impugned. Yet part of our easy assurance on this score came from our blissful certainty in the harmony of what was good for the Jews, for America, and for global humanity. The events of the past ten years have broken this confidence and, instead, raised disturbing possibilities of numerous conflicts between our universal and particular commitments.

CHAPTER TWELVE

Tension Between Jewish and Human Obligations

CONFLICTS BETWEEN JEWS AND OTHER MINORITIES

A changed social situation, national and international, has disrupted the smooth rhythm in which Jewish duties to self and to others once functioned. In the United States, the interests of Jews and other minorities have, on occasion, come into direct conflict. One major focus of difficulty has been in the area of housing and neighborhood change. Jews, having benefitted greatly from American economic growth and eager to rise in social status, have chosen not to stay in their old neighborhoods as, for example, Italians and Poles tend to do, but have moved on to "better" areas as they were able to do so. When the economic advance was slow, such moves were few and the empty places created by upward mobility were easily accommodated. But as the process accelerated and as the minorities who had long been restricted to undesirable housing now gained the rights, money, and social power to break out of their "ghettoes," once-Jewish neighborhoods became a prime target for their settlement.

With the minorities having for so long been desperately in need of decent housing, the possibility of providing for the orderly transition of neighborhoods or the establishment of biracial, or multiethnic areas was impractical. In many an old Jewish neighborhood in a large city, a battleground developed between the remaining Jews and the new settlers. With the poor, the aged, and the socially limited unwilling or unable to move, the problem of Jews in these situations became—and in some cases still is—particularly disturbing. Suddenly, what was good for other minorities was not good for the Jews, particularly since Jewish life depends on having a community within which to function. Many other examples of the new pattern of confrontation between Jews and other minorities might be adduced. Each big city—the major areas of Jewish population—can offer its own version of the new difficulties. Worse, the old patterns of decorum in civil disputes were now shown to be a major tool to control groups out of power. The disenfranchised refused to be polite and servile. Confrontation became the accepted method for redressing persistent wrongs. The Jews who had put such effort into making gains by learning to behave well saw the rules of the game altered and, often, themselves the objects of the attacks, a doubly ironic situation.

A NEW SOURCE OF TENSION

These conflicts between Jewish and other

minority interests have received much attention in the Jewish press and in our community.
What has not as frequently been acknowledged
is the different content of Jewish self-interest.
Once Jews were outsiders to American society
and they were obsessed with making their way
into it and up its ladder of success. In surpris-
ing measure that has been achieved. Not every
Jew is rich and well-connected but the Jews
rank as high if not higher than any other religious or ethnic group in terms of income. They
managed this neither by revolution nor by a
government-induced social change which especially benefitted them, but by working through
the existing socioeconomic system whose openness to Jews, I think it fair to add, increased
somewhat during the middle decades of the
century. Thus, the Jews of the 1970s are,
essentially, insiders of the American social
system and at a rather high level within it. If
they are to remain at that desirable status and
benefit from it, they must support the system.

But for all its greatness, the American socioeconomic order has many unjust and discriminatory practices built into it. The major
American pariah groups—blacks, Chicanos,
Asians, Hispanics, Indians, and other powerless
communities—suffer from our failings, but the
Jews, in any proportionate way, do not. To
fulfill our society's democratic ideals better,
now means to alter the system in some regard.
That can be as simple as asking more tax

money from the well-to-do to help the needy, or as demanding as suggesting special benefits be given minorities to compensate them for what our society has done to degrade them. Were the Jews still largely underprivileged, they would immediately see such calls for social change as in their interest, and Jewish particularism and universalism would again be in harmony. But Jews are among the privileged class. Their continued gains are dependent upon the system's operating largely as it has. Thus, efforts to restructure our society so as to remedy its faults, though good for other people, may easily work to the harm of the Jews. Not infrequently now we perceive a tension between our duty to ourselves and to others.

A NEW MOOD OF CONSERVATISM

This description is more theory than practice. For the moment most Jews still seem to follow the old ethical-political strategy: making democracy more effective for everyone is in the long-range self-interest of Jews. I do not know how long that will last. We have entered a time when "working through the system" has replaced demands for rapid innovation. With activism passé, being a liberal is not very difficult. How long this conservative mood will continue we cannot know. Once it passes or intensifies, the majority of Jews may face much harder choices than they now know. A minority of Jews, however, has consciously committed itself to the relative dissociation of Jewish and general interests. They are not so much against other people's rights as they are determined that Jewish concerns will have undivided priority in their lives, that Jews should not make any special sacrifice for the supposed general good.

Some have identified the largest number of Jews involved with this trend, particularly in their voting records, as being at the extreme ends of the social scale, the richest and the poorest Jews. The former want to preserve their wealth and status; the latter, for all their problems, prefer making special deals with a known structure, despite its inequities, to backing an unknown system which one might not be able to manipulate nearly as well. My limited experience with the latter group suggests that many of its members are post-World War II immigrants, scarred by their experience and essentially untrusting of all government. They are quite willing to abide by the "czarist" system where one can learn how to get benefits even from a corrupt government, rather than become involved in what they see as the discredited idealism of trying to change things for the better.

THE NEEDS OF ISRAEL

More important and practical, however, has been the impact upon us of the needs of the State of Israel. It appeals to us positively and is increasingly isolated internationally. Requiring zealous American Jewish support here, it tends to turn what is good for the Jews into what is good for the State of Israel. Fortunately for American Jews, the interests of our country in the Middle East and the concerns of the State of Israel have largely been identical. Yet the Arab oil embargo of 1973 raised the possibility, demonstrated in a number of European countries, that local national needs could contradict Israeli interests. Jews already must begin to decide about certain political issues whether they still follow their old political strategy or subordinate it to the needs of the State of Israel.

One living issue among us concerns our attitude toward defense spending in the United States. The use and loss of arms in the Yom Kippur War of 1973 exceeded anything anyone had anticipated. Supplying the Israelis depleted some forty percent of key American armaments, leaving the country, in the opinion of some experts, woefully short of its own needs. Since the Israelis must have arms to survive and the United States is its major source of supply, any cut in the United States' arms budget means a smaller stockpile from which the Israelis can draw in time of need. Furthermore any diminution in the United States' development of new weapons means that the Russians may equip the enemies of the Israelis with sophisticated new equipment which will, unless there are counterdevices, ultimately cause the defeat of the Israelis. Thus it is argued that for the sake of the State of Israel, American Jews ought to become avid supporters of the United States military budget. The tension arises from the opposing view that defense spending is the only source where additional funds can come from either to reduce our inflationary budget deficit or, more positively, for restoring funds to social welfare programs. Other issues might well be raised—the inherent wastefulness of military spending and the operation of the arms program so as to keep suppliers profitable—but the issue was raised here not for proper analysis but only to indicate how a clash between Jewish responsibilities now arises.

THE JEWISH VOTE FOR NIXON

This danger surfaced dramatically in the United States' Presidential election of 1972. Israeli officials let it be known—apparently Ambassador Yitzhak Rabin himself made some unfortunate statements in this regard—that it would be good for the State of Israel if American Jews voted for Richard Nixon. Not quite ninety percent of them had voted against him and for Hubert Humphrey in the election of 1968. Some Jews who normally vote Democratic were undoubtedly put off by Nixon's 1972 opponent, Senator George McGovern, despite his appeal as an anti-Vietnam War candidate, and either voted for Richard Nixon or did not vote at all. Yet that does not explain the large shift toward Nixon in the 1972 Jewish balloting. He received an additional twenty-odd percent of the Jewish vote, just about what Zionist leaders in the United States had publicly said they would deliver. Pundits have discounted this shift in political loyalties, attributing it to the specific choice involved or pointing out that Jews remained the single largest group of supporters for McGovern. The statistics in the election of Jimmy Carter in 1976 partially bear them out. Again, the long-range effect of the election figures is not significant but only the illustration of the new possibilities of conflict in Jewish ethical obligations.

It may help to exaggerate the sort of contradiction the average Democratic Jew faced in 1972. By the old strategy, McGovern appeared to be better (or at least less bad) for the United States; Nixon, for the State of Israel. How, then, does a loyal Jew make a choice? In 1976, no such dilemma developed. Both candidates were publicly embraced by leading Jewish figures, and privately the word was out that both were acceptable to the State of Israel. I cannot prophesy whether the tensions in Jewish social obligation created by a changing America and the needs of the State of Israel will increase or diminish. They surely will not go away altogether. All Jews must now, therefore, learn to live with unpleasant possibilities of choice they once thought they would easily be able to avoid. Since Reform Jews have a continuing special devotion to the ethical aspects of Jewish obligation, despite our positive concern for the State of Israel, this problem is particularly troublesome to us.

CHAPTER THIRTEEN

On Living with
a Conflict of Duties

There are only a few things one can do to dissolve the sort of dilemma in which sensitive Jews now occasionally find themselves. One can ignore the reality which produces it; or, rarely, change that reality; or, more likely, give up one or both of the conflicting values one holds. None of these alternatives seems reasonable for us. With American Jews among the haves, and most other Americans, particularly those with problems, have-nots; with the State of Israel making demands that do not seem easily to coincide with the United States' domestic needs or global strategy of detente— reality will foster, not diminish, our sense of Jewish ethical conflict. One can, of course, insist there is no problem. In one discussion of the *Centenary Perspective*, I recall a colleague's insisting that there can be no conflict between Jewish particularism and universalism. The citation of one instance after another did nothing to shake his dogma. He was so enamored of the old Jewish experience in this area that he refused to see that anything had changed between the mid-1960s and the 1970s.

ETHNIC SUICIDE IS NOT AN ETHICAL DUTY

More realistically, there is a strong temptation to give up one of our clashing values. The *Centenary Perspective* specifically rejects this option. "We must . . . confront them without abandoning either of our commitments." The older temptation was a flight into humanity. It was powered by the glories of emancipation and still attracts many Jews who see themselves as uncompromising idealists. They, therefore, have "A universal concern for humanity unaccompanied by a devotion to our particular people." For such elevated souls self-interest seems sinful, even shameful. For Jews to spend much time worrying about other Jews seems selfish and narrow, the sort of parochialism a truly ethical person will avoid. No matter that they can have sympathy for every struggling people but their own, or that an unusually high proportion of people allied with them in their universal causes are from a common ethnic source, the Jewish people. They are often so repressive of their Jewish identity that it must stem from an unconscious source, most likely self-hate. The document rejects such inauthentic universalism by pointing out the self-evident truth that not to care for one's own is "self-destructive." Surely suicide is not an ethical duty even for ethnic groups. The command to love one's neighbor as oneself implies that one begins with loving oneself. Altruism not balanced by self-regard is morbid. We have no reason, even no right to give up our Jewish particularity for the sake of serving humankind.

CHAUVINISM IS NOT AN ETHICAL POSSIBILITY

Self-hate being a recurring possibility for Diaspora Jews, I do not think we shall see the end of Jews who feel superior to the concerns of their folk. However, at this moment, identification with the State of Israel is so great, and the general paranoia intensifies Jewish suspicion so greatly, that I am more troubled by that minority of Jews who have "a passion for our people without involvement in humankind." Our moral duty to our people must not be identified with making all other concerns subsidiary to the needs of our ethnic group. Thus, few Jews would disagree that operating old age homes with fraud and perhaps with medical negligence, so as to yield great profits to subsidize Jewish charities in America and the State of Israel, is ethically repugnant and Jewishly intolerable. Chauvinism declares one's group independent of moral judgment. The patriotism of "my country right or wrong" becomes the tribalism of "what is good for my country is good." The glory of Jewish prophecy was its unstinting judgment of the Jews by universal standards of decency and in terms of the special Jewish responsibility under the covenant.

In our time, when Jews are so often on the defensive and our alleged friends seem to disappear, it is easy to forget what we owe the world and sink into chauvinistic self-pity.

THE LURE OF NATIONALISM

Nationalism being so seductive, I see this as a greater danger facing us in the immediate future than is naive universalism. The *Centenary Perspective* makes no such judgment. It merely rejects directing Jewish duty only toward Jews, saying it "contradicts what the prophets have meant to us." The circumlocution was unavoidable. We could not say simply "what the prophets said" for much contemporary Jewish scholarship argues that the prophetic message is directed essentially to the people of Israel and concerns only their duties within a Jewish society. Yet "what the prophets have meant" to a free Jewry in the modern world goes far beyond this antiquarian concern for what they meant in their own day. (Would Jews have read the Bible all these years if they did not think it had something special to say to them in their own time?) The prophets have appealed so strongly to us because they refuse to be intimidated by all the centers of power and glory in a civilization. Rather, they know that all human pretensions, not excluding those of king and priest, of nation and people, must stand in judgment before a transcendent standard. Many of the divine imperatives by which they arraign the people of Israel apply not only within the Covenant community but to the proper relations of all humanity. Pre-Emancipation Jews could hardly conceive of Jews and gentiles living in intimate social relationship with one another, but it is the daily reality of our lives. And so the prophets speak to us not only of what Jews owe one another, but of what they owe all human beings. Reform Jews, having been the first to explicate our universal teaching, are particularly indebted to this understanding of the prophets; but I think very many Jews, out of their everyday experience, share this humanitarian commitment. Though self-concern precedes universalism in the sentence on our clashing commitments, it, too, is part of our Judaism.

CONFRONTING OUR DILEMMAS

If we do not hide our eyes or alter our faith, we cannot dissolve our dilemma. We will from time to time be thrown into situations where the things we hold most dear will prompt us to conflicting actions. How can one give a rational solution for living with a contradiction? The *Centenary Perspective* accepts that troublesome reality unflinchingly. "We know of no simple way to resolve such tensions." It only says that "We must, however, confront them." That mandate comes from our faith. For Jews, to believe is to live. If God involves us with humankind as with our folk, then we must live

with both responsibilities. Often they comple-
ment each other, and our humanity is enriched
by our Jewish specificity, while our Jewish life
has its effect not only upon us but upon humankind generally. When, then, in occasional
instances one belief clashes with another, we
must not be surprised or evade the difficulties
which Jewish faith then causes us.

Facing our dilemmas is not solving them, but
it is the only way a responsible approach to
them may be possible for us. The *Centenary
Perspective* says no more. It calls us to be true
to our beliefs though they lead us into difficulty. What is not articulated is the prayer for
God's nearness and mercy for all who must
face such disturbing situations.

THE EXISTENTIALIST STANCE

I should, however, like to add some personal
comments about learning to live in such a situation. Here, I think, we are usefully instructed
by modern personalist philosophy, what often
comes to us under the catchall term existentialism. It has taught us to recognize that
much of human life consists of situations in
which we find we cannot fulfill the several
goods to which we are committed. We want to
be true to ourselves yet we want to do things
for spouse or children, a dilemma we thought
we understood but one which the feminist
movement has opened up for us in dizzying
perspective. We want our businesses to be prof-

itable but we want to advance the welfare of society. We are loyal to our friends but need the best possible person for a given cause. Again and again the demand to do the good exceeds our ability to fulfill it. Doing the right to self or business or friend we will often also have done something bad to spouse or society or our cause. No rules can tell us how morally to choose between two goods or decide between evils. In life's most significant moments, our every choice involves a risk of self. We cannot live in any truly human way without taking such risks. Even refusing to respond to our challenges is to make a certain choice.

When it comes to choosing despite a lack of certainty, being Jewish is no different from being human. Generally one benefits from knowing what others have done in similar situations and, more importantly, from trying to be honest with oneself about one's values and goals. Jewish tradition brings to the individual the resources of an exalted faith applied to life in an extraordinary variety of circumstances over centuries. Insisting on the social dimension of being a person, it sets our individual choice within the framework of a community. How can my fellow Jews help me clarify my choices, support me in my stands, and how will my choice affect my relationship with them? How are they, with whom I share so much, trying to meet such problems? How did Jews face similar conflicts in the past? Our tradition, for all its need of reinterpretation, remains our teacher.

But mostly Judaism helps us to face the paradoxes of life by strengthening our relationship with God. The religious life sensitizes us to what is expected of us and gives us a personal appreciation of the steady cycle of command, judgment, and forgiveness in which a Jew lives. So much has been said in these pages about ethnicity and peoplehood that it is important, even for a few sentences, to remind ourselves that Judaism begins in the individual heart that, as Bahya ibn Pakuda put it in the eleventh century, Jews have compelling "duties of the heart." Particularly as we are caught in conundrums which have no right answer, we need to go beyond teaching and rule to stand in the presence of God from which we may be sent with a sense of what we now must do.

I am not suggesting that being a pious Jew dissolves our dilemmas or gives us the right way of choosing between evils. I cannot say it will give us the assurance we have done the right thing in each case. I am only saying that when in a moment of choice we are ultimately thrown back upon ourselves alone, our feel for what is right is the one resource that can still help us. To have a living relationship with God in such a moment is to know as much as a human being can know then. Knowing the God of Israel as well as the tradition and people of Israel, a Jew is not spared human dilemmas but now has rich resources with which to meet them.

OUR OBLIGATIONS AND OUR DILEMMAS

A further word must now be said, linking this topic retrospectively with the two which preceded it. Each of these sections on religious obligations, the three primary problems the committee felt we must confront in this *Centenary Perspective*, involves facing a dilemma. Religious obligation found us caught between the demands of individual conscience and Jewish tradition. Our relationship to the State of Israel and to our communities in the Diaspora pits our ethnic loyalty against our existential experience. And here our conflicting duties to our people and to all humanity has been our topic. I suggest that the two additional problems which became part of this document—Reform diversity, and hope in our time—similarly arise from trying to hold onto contrary views simultaneously. Thus, Reform Jews wish to be a unified movement yet insist upon ultimately giving authority only to the individual conscience. And while we do not see how we can live without hope, our recent historic experience has taught us that quick hope is mostly an illusion, for people are deeply brutish.

If what troubles us Reform Jews is that our beliefs inevitably lead us into dilemmas, we should at least ease our anxiety by giving up the false expectation that Reform Judaism is a rational religion. Thinkers of a previous generation, particularly philosophers, insisted that the content of Reform Judaism followed a normal logical pattern. The idea of one God grounded the notions of scientific order and universal ethical responsibility. All religious activities were transformed into intellectual practices; loving God meant appreciating how nice it was to have a proper concept of God functioning in one's world view. Jewish ethnic practices were understood as pedagogic aids and psychological supports for the masses. With everything subordinated to one theme, an idea at that, Reform could claim to be a religion of reason. This is, of course, a caricature of what was an eminently admirable creation for its time and a feat of sophisticated thinking which still excites my intellectual admiration. I present it in so gross a form only to heighten the contrast with our sense that Jewish existence today is beset by a number of dilemmas, that, therefore, Jewish faith involves us in a nonrational stance toward life.

A TWOFOLD FAITH

From a centenary perspective, one can see not only a social distance between us and our predecessors, but a difference in outlook as well. Their Judaism was, in effect, based on one premise, the idea of God. Their religion was rational because everything flowed from that thesis. Because of what we have learned in recent years, we take the people of Israel and its relationship to God far more seriously. They are not secondary to our faith in God but part of its very essence. We believe in God not as isolated individuals but as part of a people covenanted to God. Hence we begin with a twofold fundamental faith, in God and in the people of Israel linked to God in Covenant. Our *Centenary Perspective* reflects this view. We speak of God in an ethnic content and of our people in relation to God. We see Torah arising from their relationship with one another. When one begins one's thinking with two premises, it is possible for the consequences of the one faith to conflict with those of the other. I think I could demonstrate that each of the five dilemmas treated in the *Centenary Perspective* results from a clash between something we believe flows from our faith in God, as against something which comes from our belief about the people of Israel or its universal equivalent, humanity. Contemporary Reform Judaism, then, cannot be called rational in any accepted sense, though I believe we need to explore the consequences of this sort of two-premised faith in a systematic and orderly, therefore, a rational way. It produces a pattern of thought all its own, what I have elsewhere called the Covenantal dialectic, though the *Centenary Perspective*, speaking for an organization, expresses this in ways rather different than I personally would.

PART V

The Conclusion:
Hope in a Time of Despair

Previous generations of Reform Jews had unbounded confidence in humanity's potential for good. We have

Hope: Our Jewish Obligation

lived through terrible tragedy and been compelled to reappropriate our tradition's realism about the human capacity for evil. Yet our people has always refused to despair. The survivors of the Holocaust, on being granted life, seized it, nurtured it, and, rising above catastrophe, showed humankind that the human spirit is indomitable. The State of Israel, established and maintained by the Jewish will to live, demonstrates what a united people can accomplish in history. The existence of the Jew is an argument against despair; Jewish survival is warrant for human hope.

We remain God's witness that history is not meaningless. We affirm that with God's help people are not powerless to affect their destiny. We dedicate ourselves, as did the generations of Jews who went before us, to work and wait for that day when "They shall not hurt or destroy in all My holy mountain for the earth shall be full of the knowledge of the Lord as the waters cover the sea."

From the Centenary Perspective

CHAPTER FOURTEEN

Rethinking Our Estimate of Human Beings

A MOOD OF RESIGNATION

Much of humanity, certainly much of the Western world, faces the last quarter of the twentieth century in a mood of resignation, if not despair. So much of what we believed has turned out to be illusion. So much of what seemed to fulfill our hopes has turned out to be the source of our new problems. The economy is unstable, freedom is threatened, culture is empty, morality is unsure, love is scarce, and fulfillment is spasmodic and fleeting. The past decade or so has profoundly disrupted the hopes which bloomed so luxuriantly in the decades of growth and development following World War II. Had we not come to expect so much, we would not now be so depressed.

Worse, we feel betrayed, for the institutions and ideas we had counted on to transform society and alter the human condition have often become the means of freshly degrading us. Government agencies and officials have subverted justice and denied us our rights. Business has corrupted governments, despoiled the environment, and bilked the consumer. The university trains instead of educating, the media dramatize instead of informing, our artists express themselves instead of sensitizing us, our families traumatize as much as they nurture.

We ourselves turn out to be unstable just when we most need to be resolute. Once we were full of hope because no matter what the ill, we had a treatment with which to remedy it. Many still put their hopes in plans, quick therapies, and instant religions, but they are more a sign of our desperation than of our confidence in the programs or their protagonists. The times have changed. From a day when we thought we could do anything, we have come to one when, being realistic about our problems and experienced in frustration, we are not certain that very much will work very well. And the greater the solution promised, the more cynical we become. We have known too many failed gods. People are more resistive to the benefits of drugs, therapy, recreation, proper nutrition, the joys of sex, and the gains of self-help than we had ever imagined. And society is far more recalcitrant with regard to moral improvement than democratic experiments, economic management, social planning, mass education, and our faith in the common urge of all people for a better life ever prepared us for. We believed in ourselves, and it turns out that we are not as much the masters of our destiny as we had thought.

JEWISH OPTIMISM

The Jewish community, having so long dedicated itself to becoming an integral part of Western society, could not now be unaffected by its malaise. The Jews who first knew the joys of Emancipation had special reason to believe that democracy and social change could eliminate most of the problems humanity faced. Seeing the segregation and persecution of Jews coming to an end, no wonder "Previous generations of Reform Jews had unbounded confidence in humanity's potential for good." The nineteenth century was a golden age of hope for Jews. They not only participated in the benefits which the end of monarchy and the rise of industrialization brought to all the Western countries, but they saw the removal of many of the indignities their forebears had suffered for centuries. This came about, they knew, not from religious motives but from the rise of liberal secularism. Human beings now recognized the power they had to shape their societies, dramatically in the American and French Revolutions, and their personal lives. Increasingly they were able to throw off customs that were harmful but had seemed necessary or God-given, and to substitute for them positive patterns of their own devising. Revelation, by contrast, still spoke in static terms. The church defended the *status quo*. Jewish freedom came from the conscious exercise of human power correcting old wrongs in the name of a new, human ideal. Reform Judaism, founded in response to this act of humanization, was, therefore, an early and enthusiastic advocate of building our lives on a high estimate of what people could do for themselves and for one another.

MODERN DISILLUSION

Today we are so disillusioned we automatically call such notions naive. Perhaps that may have to be our ultimate judgment about this understanding of human nature. Yet the early reformers were not so simpleminded as to think that merely with the dawn of democracy, people could be counted upon to do the right. They not only had profound faith in education and culture, taken in the broadest possible sense, but they worked hard at them for themselves and for all people. They knew the average citizen was fairly brutish, but they felt the gap between reality and their ideal could be bridged by awakening and developing the human reason now slumbering in each of us. For this was how the Jews transformed their lives. Through opportunity and industry, the ghetto dwellers became useful citizens. Seeing what Jews had accomplished over several generations, feeling that such limits as there were to their progress were socially imposed, not personally given, the Reform Jews had great confidence in what people were in essence and what they might become in practice. In this emphasis on human initiative, Reform Jews led the way for our people and were later joined in it by almost all the Jews who became modern.

Starting with greater belief, we have suffered deeper disappointment. The lessons that humankind at large has learned so painfully in recent years hit us with double force as we became able to face the Holocaust and then the reality that anti-Semitism threatened the State of Israel, Soviet Jewry, and American Jews as well. No further description of this change of mood need be given here. But we have spoken of it above in corporate terms, as leading to our fuller appropriation of our Jewish ethnicity. What has not been mentioned is the negative effect our Jewish experience has had on our faith in the goodness of people generally. Reform Jews of a previous generation had such confidence in the good people might do that they were largely unconcerned about the human capacity for evil.

THE CONCEPT OF SIN

Let us analyze, for example, the classic Reform reinterpretation of sin, its rejection of the traditional Jewish view and the modern version it put in its place. In the Bible and rabbinic literature, sin is most easily understood as breaking God's law; one sins, essentially, against God. Even taking "law" in the proper Jewish sense of values as well as rules, this concept seemed too restricted and theological for most modern Jews. In this view, any failure to observe a ritual law, say a blunder in performance or, less seriously, an omission due to forgetfulness, was a sin. And sin being a defiance of God, it carried heavy, fearsome overtones. This sense of foreboding had greatly intensified among Jews in the several centuries preceding the Emancipation. Jews moving into the modern world made ethical behavior the crux of their religious obligations. Emphasizing what humanity might achieve if it would only utilize its power to improve life, they found the traditional Jewish attitude toward sin too negative and undiscriminating. Believing that God's will was most clearly felt in the sphere of morality, they felt that it was wrong to equate other transgressions with those against human beings. And dwelling on our guilt inhibited our action, keeping us from the personal and social betterment we had within our reach. By contrast to liberalism's appeal to human initiative, traditional religion seemed almost morbid. Though Freud's characterization of religion as a "neurosis" now seems as foolish as it is false, he was reacting to the way much traditional religion in his day exercised power by engendering guilt, thus encouraging compulsive performance as a means of avoiding dire punishment.

By contrast to this attitude, Reform teachers understood sin—a term they said they preferred to avoid, because of its heavy Christian connotations—as essentially a matter of error. The favorite liberal exposition of this interpretation was developed from an analysis of the Hebrew word for sin, *het*. Since Hebrew is essentially verbal, one can get a sense of the essential meaning of a noun by taking a look at its verbal antecedent. The root *ht'* does not commonly refer to some abstract evil act, but often has a quite concrete, everyday usage. Thus, when one shoots an arrow at a target, to use the favorite case, and misses, that is described by the root *ht'*. One might then argue, with some scholarly basis, that the root meaning of sin in Jewish tradition is "to miss the mark." This notion appealed mightily to the Reform Jews. It immediately sundered the connection of sin with acts one must not do and linked it instead with not reaching one's proper goal. Rather than give meticulous attention to all the minutiae of tradition and incur a heavy sense of guilt by one's forgetfulness or faulty performance, the new view could focus on how people were doing what they should be doing. Sin now was essentially against one's own ideals and, thus, against oneself. As in shooting an arrow, we spend our lives choosing goals and seeking to reach them. We autonomously determine what we should be doing and to what end we direct our energies. If we utilize our opportunities to gain education and culture, we shall know the goals rational people desire and learn how to reach them. True, it may happen that even the wisest and most sensitive of us will fail in our efforts, but this is most certainly due to not having defined the goal properly or having gone about it in the wrong way. Failure does not mean people cannot do better or that we must rely on some supernatural agency to do the good for us. It only means we "missed the mark." Since we did so, it is now up to us to do a better job of reaching it. Perhaps, as in archery, we need to be able to see better what we are aiming at, or improve our technique, or work at it harder. Surely guilt will be of no help to us, and what we need is greater understanding and practice, not incantation or ritual.

This view of humankind and its failings is essentially rationalistic. People are thought of primarily in intellectual terms: doing wrong means one had not thought the problem through correctly or had not yet learned enough about it. So one responded to one's "sin" by making up the wrong one had done, and then thinking more clearly and acting more intelligently the next time. God retreats very far into the distance here in such a view. Since God is thought of as an idea, at best as cosmic intelligence, one does not talk very much about the effect of our having done evil on our relationship with God. We are concerned with whether we have been true to ourselves as rational beings or to the people with whom we live and to whom we have responsibilities.

CHANGING THE CONTENT OF "ENLIGHTENMENT"

Because this view stresses our responsibility, I think it has much to commend it. By contrast to the largely negative sense of sin it replaced, I consider it indispensable to any modern Jewish notion of relationship with God. But its emphasis on the ethical came at a high theological cost, for it taught us to be optimistic about humanity. It assumed that people were basically good and that all that kept them from acting on it was ignorance, superstition, social pressure, or a lack of self-confidence. More recent liberals have been somewhat less rationalistic and assumed that we also needed psychological health and economic stability. Still, the basic image of humankind must be called optimistic—only the content of the "enlightenment" needed had changed, not the view that we could save ourselves.

The past few decades were so tragic because they shattered our messianic faith in humankind. We could not believe human beings were capable of the horror institutionalized by the Nazis. We did not believe that educated, cultured, rational beings, fully conscious of what they were doing, could commit such bestial acts—and do them as part of an ongoing, considered routine of existence. Our optimism might have survived if we could believe that what the Nazis had done was an utter exception to what the rest of humanity was capable of. The events of ensuing years revealed that, to a considerable extent, many people could do something quite similar. In America it has not been Mafia brutality that shattered our optimism but our discovery, in event after event, that "the best and the brightest" of our culture are quickly corrupted and prone to do evil. We had hoped that reading books and magazines, participating in local politics, working for better housing and nutrition, creating jobs, and establishing mental health centers, would answer our personal and social problems. They still help somewhat—but that is far from what we once thought, that they would redeem humanity. So to speak, we liberals took the control of history out of God's hands and put it firmly in our own. We have done much good, but we have also done very much more evil than we had ever anticipated. I believe that there is much in the history of the past century to be proud of, but looking back on our record, I cannot say that we have merely "missed the mark," that our insight or technique was a bit off. There is far more will to evil in us than we have been willing to admit, and our ultimate self-reliance, therefore, seems ludicrous. I find it far more appropriate, partly because of the traditional connotations, to look at much of what we have done and say, "God, we have sinned. We have transgressed. We have done perversely."

All this, I think, lies behind the *Centenary Perspective*'s sentence, "We have lived through terrible tragedy and been compelled to reappropriate our tradition's realism about the human capacity for evil." The rabbis talked a good deal about the *Yetzer Hara*, the evil urge, in people. They took this image quite seriously and thought of our life as an unending struggle with this itch to do evil which continually surfaces in us. They considered it powerful, relentless, cunning, and not finally conquerable (until the messianic time). It seeks to overcome us until the minute we die. The rabbis were so realistic that they thought people, even the most learned and pious, were always capable of great evil and often committed it, with sin capable of overcoming the best of us in an instant. Where Reform Jews talked of humankind as being perfectible, the rabbis reminded us that no one is without sin, not Moses or King David, the begetter of the Messiah. All were more in need of God's forgiveness than able to claim merit for their accomplishments. For the rabbis, sin was no mere error or miscalculation, "missing the mark," but the result of something deep and mysterious in people which fought God and, therefore, was a major barrier to any proper relationship with God.

REALISM AND PESSIMISM

What makes the rabbis especially appealing to us in our reassessment of our view of humanity is that, while they were realists, they were not pessimists. We moderns do not want to surrender the values which come from our activism, even though we are now painfully conscious that not every ingenious plan of ours will bring more good than evil. The rabbis do not consider people incapable of righteousness because they are prone to do iniquity. Here we come across a fundamental difference between Judaism and Christianity, one which can be traced back to the earliest days of the division between these faiths. The rabbis, as against Paul and other early Christian teachers, do not consider sin, for all its offense against God, as disabling people in relationship to God. The rabbis say that after we have sinned, we restore our acceptability to God by sincere *teshuvah,* repentance, and God, in love, welcomes our return. People, though sinners, are not helpless. They can still, they can always, repent—and God accepts them. In Judaism, sinners need not wait for God to restore their relationship by some supernatural act of which they are utterly incapable. Jews see the need of a Messiah, but not of an atoning Christ. And Jews, therefore, have also felt that people, for all their sinfulness, can do the good in God's sight by fulfilling the commandments. Some rabbis even went so far as to say that the evil urge itself can be the basis for our doing good, for marrying, engaging in commerce, establishing a family, if only it is properly harnessed. (This was the liberals' favorite passage about the evil urge, and they cited it as proof of humanity's ability to perfect even its deviant impulses, and not as it was probably meant, that though we are normally victimized by our evil urge, it is not altogether valueless.)

Some people have been so shattered by the revelations of human viciousness in our time that they have concluded we can do nothing to change our social situation, and the best thing we can do for ourselves is to flee into the Infinite. The flowering of exotic religious cults in America in recent years seems to Jewish eyes an overreaction to our loss of faith in human perfectibility. A number of the Asian religions teach, in various ways, that the self is fundamentally an illusion, and that salvation comes in breaking free of it. Zen teaches the fundamental emptiness of existence, while most Hinduism considers the self valuable only as a means of reaching the Infinite, the only reality. Such faiths give one serenity, but do so by denying the human a role as cocreator with God. In this estimation of our world and our responsibility in it, we may see the fundamental distinction between much Asian and Jewish belief. A similar surrender of self goes on in the contemporary rush to various orthodoxies, Eastern or Western. In such groups one is active and this worldly in orientation, but one must follow the teaching of one's leader, generally as part of a tightly disciplined community. These religions believe in human responsibility but have little or no sense of human autonomy. One does what one is told and little or no room is left for independent thinking. In fact, in a permissive age this seems to be their appeal. Here orthodoxy rids one of the burden of freedom, of the responsibility for making up one's own mind as to what ought to be done and then doing it.

A NEW SENSE OF RELIGION

These religious groups, and the interest in mysticism which is their corollary—so soon after God was supposed to be dead!—point to a major religious shift in our time. Now that we have less than absolute faith in people, we are once again open to God's role in our lives and in human destiny generally. I believe that is true in the Jewish community, though most Jews are still so uncomfortable speaking about God in any personal way that they continue using the language of faith in humanity though they no longer believe it. Unrepentant liberals are likely to see in the "reappropriation" of the notion of the evil urge no more than a deepened consciousness of how much must be done educationally, psychologically, and politically, to alter the human condition. Many of the rest of us, I suggest, are postliberals, for we think sin is more serious than an error and something more than enlightenment and psychotherapy are needed to deal with it. Our evil urge is no fancy of the rabbinic imagination, but the reality of our lives and the problem we confront daily in trying to stay human. Though we do not believe people are depraved in some Christian sense, there is something fundamental in us which moves us to do evil. Though there is much we can do to sublimate and thus momen-

tarily overcome it, our lives are one long intimate struggle against its wiles. Despite that, we
are convinced we are free of its control. We are
grateful that God, too, has a part in working
out our lives. For us, God has become a very
present, personal reality. We have not surrendered our autonomy, but we now exercise it in
partnership.

DISCOVERING GENUINE PARTNERSHIP

May I suggest that this is one point where the
Centenary Perspective opens a critical issue for
the future of Reform Jewish belief. Much has
already been said of our new appreciation of
Jewish peoplehood. I believe there is a parallel
shift underway with regard to the recognition
of God's role in our lives. The numbers involved may be smaller, and it is not easy for
the many who for so long quietly prided themselves on the open-mindedness of their agnosticism to admit that they find, in the face of
contemporary nihilism, that they believe something. Mostly they have no words with which
to express their sense that orthodoxies gave too
little credit to human power while liberalism, it
is now clear, gave it too much. In my own
work over the years, I have utilized the term
Covenant to indicate what seems to me the
appropriate balance between God and humanity, or, more specifically, between God and the
people of Israel. While the term is not a new
one, it has taken on special usefulness in our

time from our contemporary understanding of relationships.

Mostly it was Martin Buber who taught us that in a genuine relationship, the partners remain themselves. If one dominates, if the other is required to be fully subservient, then that is servitude not love, the highest form of relationship. By analogy, if God forms relationships with people—covenants—then that ought to allow for us to be ourselves and not merely God's puppets. To some extent, Jewish teaching saw that and created its remarkable picture of the almighty Ruler of the universe fashioning creatures, people, who not only stood in relationship with God, but did so precisely because they also were free to ignore or flout God's will. Yet covenant in the Bible describes more a contractual than an interpersonal relationship. Buber reinterpreted the term so that what the partners mean to one another, rather than any specific duties they impose on each other, becomes critical.

I find speaking about this sort of relationship between God and people the best way of describing our postliberal faith. We wish to be less passive than the tradition made us, and cannot be as optimistically self-reliant as the early successes of liberalism seemed to warrant our being. Covenant means we are partners with God, able to accomplish something but not abandoned to our own devices. Being God's partners, we have great power and we should exercise it. Yet we live not as isolated selves or merely as a special sort of animal, but as people linked to God, thereby having personal access to the final standard for all human action. Covenant thus means that our concern with ourselves is balanced by our concern with God, that our sensitivity to the Divine is balanced by a recognition of our own capacities, both together, not one without the other.

I find that even those Reform Jews who now begin to use such terms to describe their belief still regularly prefer to stress the human side of the relationship. I assume that is because humanism has been the modern style for so long now that even in the reassertion of God's meaning to them they prefer to dwell on that about which they feel most secure, themselves. But I do not see how the language of Covenant can mean very much if the God who participates in it does not become a present reality in the lives of those who use it. All theological niceties aside, I suggest that if we are to continue to esteem humankind, God needs to be much more real to us personally than we have been accustomed to in much Reform Judaism. If we could admit how much our faith in humanity was a substitute for faith in God we might now recognize, seeing people more realistically as we now do, that we still believe in humanity because we believe in the God who, despite all their failings, keeps them in Covenant.

CHAPTER FIFTEEN

Hope As a Jewish Tradition

A RELIGION OF HOPE

The word "hope" does not occur with great frequency in traditional Jewish texts, yet Judaism can easily be seen as a religion of hope. The religions of Asia do promise surcease from human suffering and, in some cases, the bliss of unity with the Infinite or entry into Nirvana. By contrast to the day-to-day realities of much human life, these faiths are hopeful indeed. Judaism is far bolder in its teaching about the future. Traditionally, it calls for no sacrifice of self, or this world, or history. It envisions reward and punishment being meted out to us individually in a messianic kingdom established on this earth as the just consummation of human striving. Yet the connection of Judaism with hope is not for most Jews primarily a matter of doctrine but of history.

Time and again the Jewish people has had its existence threatened, and it has faced its successive tragedies without losing confidence in itself or its destiny. The enslavement in Egypt, so central to the Torah and its traditions, became a model for later Jewish experience.

Under the worst of social circumstances, the
Jews became a mighty people. For all their suffering, they did not abandon their corporate
identity and, in due course, they were saved.
The later biblical records are even more distressing. Though the Jews established themselves on the land promised to them and established the commanded form of worship in the
Temple, their kingdom was eventually conquered, their sanctuary destroyed, and they
themselves exiled. Most peoples in history do
not recover from such a catastrophe. The Jews
not only recovered, but made this experience a
further basis for their understanding of history.
They became fully conscious of their intimate
involvement with the God of all creation who
demands righteousness from human beings, and
particularly from the people who share a special Covenant with God. When they sin, their
intimacy with God will not spare them the
affect of the Divine justice, even if that means
the razing of God's house and the dispersion of
God's people from its land—but God does not
end their relationship. God's purpose will yet
be done. God will eventually restore them to
the land, and through them bring all humankind to acknowledge God's rule. That is hope,
indeed, and it sustained the Jews through another destruction of the Temple and in the
trials they regularly faced in their dispersion
throughout the world. If the measury of one's
hope is one's willingness to continue in the face

of adversity, then it is clear why Judaism is the religion of hope *par excellence.*

THE HOPE OF THE SURVIVORS

To our astonishment and wonder, that is true today despite the Holocaust. Perhaps we might have guessed that the Jews of America, guilty and grieving over what happened in Europe, would now take it upon themselves to lead in the reestablishment of Jewish life wherever Jews now find themselves. No one could have anticipated before World War II, considering their relative ignorance, nonobservance, and devotion to assimilation, that they would also begin to devote themselves to enriching and intensifying the quality of their Jewish life. But what shall we say of the survivors? What might reasonably have been expected of them? They had experienced the worst that people have ever done to other people. They had seen rationality, education, culture, and the other signs of modernity become instruments of their degradation and murder. They knew personally how vile apparently decent people can be—and they knew that the word Jew attached to them, often by others, not themselves, made them the special targets of this demonic treatment. One of every three Jews alive in the world was killed by Hitler. In some European countries, ninety percent of the prewar Jewish population was exterminated. The war over, their saviors first treated them as enemy aliens and then were loathe to give them a new place to live. If ever a group had a right to abandon history, it was those Jews. And some did. Either by conversion, or by denying their Jewishness, or by refusing to have anything to do with other Jews, or by caring only for themselves and their needs, they gave up on the Jewish people. But they were a minority, apparently a tiny one. Of the overwhelming majority it may be said, as our *Centenary Perspective* does, that "on being granted life, (they) seized it, nurtured it, and, rising above catastrophe, showed humankind that the human spirit is indomitable."

The Bible speaks of "wonders" and means by this those rare events in which people catch a glimpse of the Transcendent Reality which moves through all that happens. On one level all is natural—a bush burns. On another, a truth normally hidden from us is disclosed—God speaks and says the God of the Patriarchs will now redeem the Covenant people. We moderns are so secularized, we probably could not sense a wonder should there be one before us. We close out the sacred by quickly analyzing events as scientific or psychological phenomena. Regaining the possibility of religious reality is one of our great contemporary needs. But even we react to the simple human record of the Jewish survivors of the concentration camps. People who endured far less never recovered. They not only lived through the worst but responded to it with human greatness. By contrast, we of the western world, who live in such relative affluence and comfort, find our lives suffused with discontent and unease. We tend to despair of life and humankind. Hitler's survivors hardly had their lives and they carried an almost unbearable burden of memory and trauma. In refusing to die or go mad, by rebuilding their lives, by joining in the establishment of the State of Israel, by taking their place in history, they gave telling testimony to the depth of Jewish hope.

THE STATE OF ISRAEL: A SIGN OF HOPE

The *Centenary Perspective* says one can also learn about being human in our time from the experience of the State of Israel. No theological considerations are involved here, only straightforward political history. The State of Israel refutes much of our contemporary disillusionment which comes from seeing what power does to its possessors. In an age when most recent governments have turned to dictatorship as the only means of dealing with internal dissension, the Israelis have remained steadfastly, passionately democratic. In a day when terrorism has become a way of life and the needs of the state have regularly been used as an excuse for oppressing minorities and hating enemies, the Israelis have shown themselves to be uncommonly humane and farsighted.

Despite intense military pressures, they have refused to become militaristic. Instead, they have developed a neglected land and raised to dignity a citizenry largely composed of refugees and outcasts.

Above all, in the face of international prejudice and internal disagreement, despite a lack of natural resources and a threatening demography, with the world's heaviest burden of taxation and a raging inflation, against all odds and without any clear vision of how they might settle their problems, the citizens of the State of Israel have refused to give up hope. They say, darkly, *"Ein Breirah:* There is no alternative," and they remind one that their national anthem is *Hatikvah,* "the Hope." In the face of what this tiny, troubled people has accomplished, one cannot give up all hope for human politics. Our recent history has been almost unbearable, yet looking back upon our people's response to it, we can take great pride in what we have done. We remain undefeated and with us, therefore, humankind.

RELIGION IN AN AGE OF DOUBT

Personally I do not see how our reaction to the Holocaust and our accomplishments in the State of Israel can satisfactorily be explained in secular terms alone. On the one level, of course, it is a simple human, natural event. But why should this people continue to take so positive an attitude toward life? Why should it still want to continue as a people, considering what others do to it? If Jews of another age carried on despite everything, then we may say that they did it because they were so certain of God and the promised rewards, they could ignore the momentary convulsions which seized them. But modern Jews are not believers, and few of those who have some faith have certainty that an independent God guides history, despite human freedom, and that the Messiah and the resurrection are our sure destiny. Ostensibly, we are fully secularized and have only ourselves and other human beings to believe in, a poor basis to call for Jewish hope after the Holocaust. If God is dead as we were widely told a few years back and we are now, finally and fully, rid of belief and its illusions, why should survivors care for anything other than themselves? Why should they devote themselves to the tedious business of building a life and the idealism of making it moral? Can such a thing be biological impulse, the will to survive?

The drifters in our cities and the people broken by a flood or fire show how often we lose the courage to continue. Surely we will not argue that the survivors and the Israelis could see that humanity, having learned from the Nazi era, is now worthy of trust. We need hope to be human, yet secularity now gives us no grounds for hope. To be a Jew in any rich, historical sense of the term is even less explicable in simple natural terms. For to accept the high standards of this people, its modern sense of what constitutes a person, of what a decent society should be, of what humanity should become, means implicitly to stake one's life on the fundamental goodness of creation, a truth we cannot simply see before us. Secularity at its best can teach us that the world is neutral to our efforts. History has made plain that humanity is at least as evil as it is good. If, then, despite our new realism we insist that our faith in ourselves and our hopes for humankind are not illusion, it must be that we base them on the intuition of a reality which transcends what we see around us. I reiterate, seeing people more realistically opens us to the relationship we still have, have probably always secretly had, with God. We thought we had outgrown that old faith, but we had merely transferred our sense of the absolute from God to humanity. Now that we realize that we have made an idol of humankind and its power, we have lost our pseudoreligion but not our genuine trust in the Absolute.

The survivors and the Israelis often call themselves unbelievers. No one has the right to tell them what they "truly" believe. Yet their acts contradict their theories. In their extraordinary affirmation of human value, they testify that there is a standard of goodness which transcends us and our immediate experience. It lays a command upon us to live beyond our animal drives, and it says that the reality of this ideal will one day be manifest in all human lives. In this wonder we come to recognize that the God of Israel lives, though we do not understand or condone the horrors God has allowed us to endure.

JEWISH SURVIVAL — A WARRANT FOR HOPE

I take the summary sentences of this section quite literally. "The existence of the Jew is an argument against despair; Jewish survival is warrant for human hope." I do not think one needs to be a believer or a Jew to see that. We believers, however, will also take the next sentences as fact and not as rhetoric. "We remain God's witness that history is not meaningless. We affirm that with God's help people are not powerless to affect their destiny." God has not made divinity easily visible to us in our time but the Jewish people, by its affirmation of life despite everything, has testified to God's reality. We know we cannot trust ourselves alone to solve our basic human problems, but we have also learned from our people's triumphs over tragedy that human beings can yet accomplish great good in history if God somehow lends us help. The concept of Covenant here shows its effect. Faithful to our Partner, we Jews by our very existence proclaim the Divine reality before humankind.

THE SEARCH FOR
A NEW SYMBOLISM

I must carry this one abstract step further. In *Reform Judaism Today: Reform in the Process of Change*, I discussed the difficulties our committee had in trying to make our messianic visions more explicit. What I was saying there dealt largely with our difficulties in finding a proper symbol for our hope, in depicting what fulfilled existence might be like for us. Now we can note that the problem is further complicated by our not yet being able to think through how our messianism is affected by our reduced confidence in humanity and our greater trust in God. When we believed that education, culture, and social welfare politics would transform human life, it was relatively easy to create a new image of messianism. Many of us cannot quite admit that the old liberal messianism is behind us, and I am sure there remain many Reform Jews who still sincerely believe in a humanistic Messianic Age. But going beyond it to admit that we are limited but not alone in our efforts and that our activism makes sense only in the context of our Covenant with God, has thus far yielded no new symbolism in which to express our belief. Despite this difficulty, I think now we must move on to say not we but God is the ultimate ground of our messianism. We have our role to play, but our confidence in it comes not from what we have seen ourselves accomplish but from our knowledge that God, in continuing the Covenant, still has hope for us and for our relationship. This understanding, which is too activist to be traditional and too realistic to be liberal, still seeks an appropriate image.

CHAPTER SIXTEEN

The Mission of Israel Recast

If the *Centenary Perspective* is characterized by the reassertion of our sense of peoplehood and the working out of its balance with Reform's continuing universalism, then we may say that this tension comes to a climax in this final section. The committee did not consciously plan a dramatic conclusion. Early in our deliberations we had agreed that our affirmation of hope should be our final word. But we did not make a conscious effort to have this last section carry forward and fulfill what was said before. Yet rereading this section months after its composition and after this intensive study of the entire text, it seems to me that unconsciously, we not only continued but climaxed our balancing of Reform particularism and universalism in our discussion of hope.

The issue itself is not simply one which faces the Jewish people, and in this respect this section is different from the three which immediately precede it. That is why it was not assigned a Roman numeral but given a rubric which would indicate it to be a summary to all that went before. (This made the printer's insertion of a VII here in the CCAR's first "of-ficial" printing of the *Centenary Perspective* somewhat annoying.) Yet the problem is posed in terms of the Jewish people's experience as is the answer it gives. One might infer, then, that what is said is again concerned with the Jews alone. But a broader claim is implicit in the three operative terms "argument," "warrant," and "witness." What the Jews represent in history speaks not only to them but to all humanity. While the document usually speaks essentially to Reform Jews and to the Jewish people, in this case something of a universal significance is being asserted. The committee had in mind the widespread feeling of human despair in our day, and declared in these sentences that this ethnic group had something to teach humanity con-cerning it.

A MESSAGE FOR HUMANITY

There is nothing new about this sort of argu-ment. Ever since the Jews became involved in explaining their people and its tradition to cul-tures which claimed universal horizons, the stan-dard Jewish argument has been that at the heart of what seem the folk concerns of this tradition, there lies a message for all humankind. Though the content of their teachings varied widely, a similar case was made by Philo in Alexandria, Maimonides in Egypt and Hermann Cohen in Germany. What is fresh about the presentation here is its reworking of the older Reform Jewish version of this contention. It said that the Jewish people had a special role in history, the Mission of Israel, which they defined as teaching ethical monotheism to humanity. The Jews, by virtue of being the first people to stake its corporate existence on the unity of God and recognizing God's insistence on righteousness (ethics being the essence of the Torah in this view), were now inseparably linked with the universal, rationally valid idea of ethical monotheism. The Asian religions and Islam seemed to have little of this sense of activist ethics. To the extent that Christianity did—which some thinkers like Cohen and Baeck doubted—it was compromised by a trinitarian notion of God which inevitably affected its ethical sensitivity. So the Jewish people was needed in history to serve as the bearer of this unique idea. A generation or so back, Reform leaders would have reminded a despondent humanity that human beings have an unparalleled capacity to do the ethical and to give it rational structure. Difficulties should not engender despair, for life is fundamentally an ethical challenge, and without problems we would not be able to utilize our ethical and rational talents.

There is still much to the idea that human beings have great ethical capacity; and thus resignation, refusing to act, is a self-negation approaching suicide. Yet the ethicist Mission of Israel hardly seems tenable in our time. Surely there are other ethical monotheists beside ourselves—the Unitarians, for example, and, considering how little was made of God by some Reform teachers, we might as well include the Ethical Culture movement and that broad stream of ethical humanists found at most universities and large cities. Besides, ideas hardly seem that important. The notion that humanity is in trouble largely because it does not have a proper concept of ethics and God ludicrously underestimates the gap between thought and performance. Then, too, few of us can confidently assert the inferiority of other people's religion and make great claims for our own. Considering how little most Jews believe and observe, our primary mission would seem more reasonably directed to the spiritual education of our own people rather than to converting the whole world to our universal teaching. Jewish survival is now "of highest priority" to us; the Mission of Israel seems an anachronism.

THE JEWISH PEOPLE AS WITNESS

This does not imply that Reform Jews no longer believe our people has something to say to humanity. To the contrary, the *Centenary Perspective* makes some grand claims for us. We are "an argument against despair . . . , [a] warrant for human hope . . . , [a] witness that history is not meaningless." In any time, that would be a glorious contribution to make to humanity. In our time, when low-level despair is our common mood precisely because there are so few indications that existence need not be frustrating, to give such testimony is redemptive. The *Centenary Perspective* does not argue that no one else can perform this task, or that without the Jewish people humankind has no grounds for hope. That would be spiritual arrogance. Yet, by implication, I see this passage claiming that the positive feeling which may be gained from the Jews is difficult to match, particularly because of its social scope. Private and personal experience of the worthwhileness of life may not be so difficult to come by, but evidences of hope in the history and politics of our time are rare to the point of nonexistence.

In this reinterpretation, a radical shift of emphasis has taken place. What the Jews now offer humankind is not an "idea," but their "existence . . . survival . . . witness." The emphasis on peoplehood has become the ground of a new universalism. That the Jews continue to be Jews, refuse not to be Jews, want to be Jews, is not important only to them but says something about the human spirit. One need not be Jewish to perceive the human greatness involved in such ethnic determination. In a world cynical about words and ideologies, preaching a doctrine is not likely to have more than a passing effect. But example may still count for something. We do not need much talk from someone whose life is rich with value. The Jews do not have to speak of hope. They exemplify it. And they do so best when they are true to their Jewishness. The

"Mission of Israel" today is to be the best Jewish people before God that we can be. That will give the world whatever lesson we have to teach them, in what is presently the most effective way of doing so. In an earlier time, Reform Jews subordinated their particularism to their universalism. Today we must reverse that balance, but we need not, thereby, lose the universal in the particular, as the *Centenary Perspective* has consistently demonstrated.

WITNESS FOR OURSELVES

Like all humanity, we Jews, too, take hope from the wondrous record of our people's survival. This does not mitigate our anguish at our past suffering or help us understand why we must suffer such trials as we have had. Yet for all that still pains us we cannot deny what we know to be true. The people of Israel lives. Despite ignorance, apathy, and disbelief, it still manages to live in identifiable Jewishness, sanctifying lives and communities in recognizable continuation with our tradition in a modern though often flawed fashion. Despite the Holocaust, the Jews have not died out. In the State of Israel, with incredible vigor and determination; in the Soviet Union, despite generations of areligion and Russification; in America, though everyone thought it would by now be completely assimilated, the people of Israel lives. We have much to worry about, we modern Jews, and like our ancestors in the wilderness, we complain a lot.

But we also have reason to hope. If, after all we have been through, we can survive—with all the spiritual dimensions that the term takes on in our vocabulary—then there is hope for all humanity. If, despite all we have had to endure, the Covenant-promise still operates and we continue on through history, then we have good reason for reasserting our messianism; "We dedicate ourselves . . . to work and wait for that day . . . . " I cannot help but think that another generation of Reform Jews would have been too activist ever to want to "wait," an attitude they would have seen as too passive and traditional. They would have insisted that we talk only of our "work." Yet that demands too much of us, it leaves too little to God. I suppose our Reform Jewish diversity will result in different interpretations of the balance of "work and wait" appropriate to our situation. Yet that the one needs to be balanced by the other, the faith in humanity so central to moderns by the faith in God so central to our tradition, seems exactly the sort of Reform Jewish dialectic which I see as central to the *Centenary Perspective*.

OUR NEW MESSIANISM

The last words of the *Centenary Perspective* are a biblical quotation, the only one in the text. None was used previously in an effort to speak to the reader as directly as possible. The committee agreed to deviate from that policy here and chose this passage as most representative of the meaning it wished to convey. One reason it turned to the Bible in this instance was its own inability to provide a compelling image for our revised messianic hope. An equally compelling reason was the special power which, it was hoped, the unexpected introduction of a familiar and beloved biblical passage—part of the *Union Prayer Book* Friday evening Torah service—might bring to the conclusion of the *Centenary Perspective*. Since no personal Messiah is mentioned here, it preserves the understanding of most Reform Jews while not excluding the minority who take the doctrine in a personal sense. What greatly appealed to the committee, if I remember correctly, were the contrasts mentioned in the verse. "They shall not hurt or destroy" seemed particularly meaningful to us whose days are filled with reports of violence, much of it simply senseless. "All my holy mountain" was taken as a figure for the whole world, as if in the messianic time the entire globe would be as sacred as the Temple mount. There is some hint of that in the positive conclusion, "for the earth shall be full of the knowledge of the Lord as the waters cover the sea." (While "earth" might conceivably mean here the land of Israel, we read that broadly, too, as the Hebrew permits, taking it to mean all places.) The messianic image of the earth's being full of the knowledge of the Lord in as full and natural a way as the waters cover the sea, touched us deeply. By contrast to the violence with which the passage began, it seemed as rich an indication of what fulfilled existence might be like as we could think of.

This brought the *Centenary Perspective* to an end on a poetic, imagistic note. We felt the change in tone was right for what we were now talking about. The earlier sections of the statement had been written in simple descriptive prose. If the *Centenary Perspective* was to reach people, we thought it should have a spare and direct style.

But our section on hope required something different. We knew that now we were appealing especially to the reader's intuition. In this case, we needed to reach far beyond the readily accessible sentiments that make up Jewish belief to as deep a level of faith as we could summon. And we wanted, against much of the experience of our day and our time, to project our sense of trust into the fullest future people could conceive. This section of the *Centenary Perspective* was, therefore, permitted a rhetorical tone. It seemed the best way we knew not only to speak to our readers but to summon them to faith, *emunah*, the Jewish "holding fast," through all the history that remains to humankind. For we did not write merely to provide intellectual guidance to our community, but to bring it to richer Jewish living.